D0195398

Science, Technology, and Public Policy

Science, Technology, and Public Policy

Richard Barke
University of Houston

A division of Congressional Quarterly Inc.
1414 22nd Street N.W., Washington, D.C. 20037

Printed in the United States of America

Library of Congress Cataloging in Publication Data

Barke, Richard, 1951-
    Science, technology, and public policy.

    Bibliography: p. 219
    Includes index.
    1. Science and state—United States.
2. Technology and state—United States. I. Title.
Q127.U6B275   1986   338.97306   86-17531
ISBN 0-87187-394-X

Preface

Science and technology have affected society and government for thousands of years, but that relationship has never been more important than it is today. Technological progress has become an expected way of life, yet at the same time technological disasters such as the loss of the space shuttle *Challenger* and the explosion of the Soviet nuclear power plant at Chernobyl are reminders of technological limitations. In spite of overall budgetary cutbacks, public support for research and development has continued to grow because of widespread recognition that scientific and technological progress is crucial for economic and military security. Furthermore, researchers are continually making advances that raise new questions about the fundamental rights of life, death, property, privacy, and so on—questions that increasingly dominate headlines and political agendas.

Some books on science and technology policy contribute to our understanding by offering detailed analyses of particular policies. Others examine the implications of science and technology for democratic government and a free society. In contrast, the premise of this book is that public policies are constrained and compelled by complex but comprehensible forces that can be studied, understood, and applied to particular types of policies. Many proposed reforms have no chance of occurring or succeeding because they ignore fundamental limitations in the policy process. Understanding science and technology policy and finding ways to improve the relationship between knowledge and government depend on recognizing these limitations and treating them as opportunities.

The range of policies that support, use, or regulate science and technology is too broad for a succinct general theory about how they are made; but through the use of a general framework of four types of constraints, this book explores several general characteristics of all science and technology policies. The framework and the definitions on which it is based are presented in the first chapter. Chapters 2 through 7 apply the framework to Congress, the president and the Executive Office, the bureaucracy, the courts, the public, and scientists as participants in the science and technology policy process. As each of these is examined, its power, limitations, and interactions with other participants are discussed. Proposed reforms are assessed in light of the tensions and forces that have created the policies and the climate for policy making that exists today.

Because a single case study would not be able to expose the full range of forces and issues that characterize science and technology policies, many particular examples are used in Chapters 2 through 7. After dissection of the policy process it is important to put it back together and see how the pieces fit. To this end, Chapters 8 and 9 offer two illustrations of how all of these institutions and constraints work in specific cases. The recent evolution of legislation on hazardous wastes shows how scientific and technological information is used in shaping controversial policies. The discussion of the Space Telescope, scheduled for launch in 1988, reveals tensions and cooperation among scientists and public officials as they developed and implemented a major "pure science" project.

The final chapter presents an overview of the science and technology policy process. The most common criticisms are discussed and evaluated in light of the fundamental characteristics described in the preceding chapters: the fragmentation of decision making, the inseparability of facts and values, and the need to balance many sorts of demands. The book closes with general observations about the prospects for improving the science and technology policy process.

Acknowledgments

Like a public policy, this book has drawn upon a variety of resources that have shaped its initial definition, its formulation, and its implementation. These include colleagues who have read portions of the manuscript, listened to ideas that may have found their way into these pages, or were instrumental in providing me with information. I am indebted to Jim Anderson, Malcolm Goggin, Hank Jenkins-Smith, Stephen Huber, James Lester, and Paul Sabatier. The University of Houston Center for Public Policy provided financial assistance, and I benefited from earlier support from the National Science Foundation. Barbara Lees was an able and cheerful research assistant. I owe special thanks to Susan Hadden of the LBJ School of Public Affairs at the University of Texas-Austin, who offered useful comments on the entire manuscript. Joanne Daniels at CQ Press provided the precisely correct combination of pressure and tolerance, and in editing the manuscript Margaret Seawell Benjaminson greatly improved the clarity of both the language and the ideas. I am grateful to both of them.

Because they provide daily reminders of what it is that we are all working for, I dedicate this book to my wife, Nancy, and to Kirk and Julia.

Contents

Preface   v

1 A Framework for Understanding Science
  and Technology Policy   1
    An Example: Nuclear Fusion Policy   4
    Defining the Terms   6
    Constraints on the Science and
      Technology Policy Process   13
    Summary   18
    Conclusion   18

2 Congress in the Policy Process   21
    Congressional Policy Tools   23
    Law and Congressional Policy Making   26
    Knowledge and Expertise in Congress   27
    Congress and Coordination   33
    Politics and Science in Congress   36
    Conclusion   40

3 The President and the Executive Office
  in the Policy Process   43
    Presidents and the Law   44
    Knowledge in the White House   48
    Coordination of Executive Branch Science
      and Technology Policy   54
    Politics and Presidential Science and
      Technology Policy   57
    Conclusion   59

4 The Federal Bureaucracy in the
  Policy Process   61
    The Science and Technology Bureaucracy   63
    Legal Constraints on the Bureaucracy   75
    Knowledge in the Bureaucracy   79

Coordination of Bureaucratic Science
and Technology Policy   87
Politics and Bureaucratic Science
and Technology Policy   90
Conclusion   92

5 The Courts and the Legal System
   in the Policy Process   95
The Expanding Role of Courts in Science
and Technology Policy   96
Legal Constraints on the Courts   98
Scientific and Technological Knowledge
in the Courts   102
The Courts and Coordination   107
Politics in the Courts   110
Conclusion: Responsibility and
Accountability of the Courts   111

6 The Public in the Policy Process   113
Scientific Disputes and Public Controversy   114
Law and Public Participation   117
The Public and Scientific and
Technological Knowledge   120
Coordination of the Public   125
Politics and the Public in Science
and Technology Policy   127
Conclusion: Virtues and Vices of
Public Politics   129

7 Scientists in the Policy Process   133
Law and Scientists in the Policy Process   136
The Constraints of Scientific Knowledge   141
Coordination of Scientists in the
Policy Process   144
Politics and the Scientist   148
Conclusion   152

8 Using Science and Technology in Policy:
   Hazardous Wastes   155
Law and the Policy Use of Science
and Technology   156
Obtaining and Using Knowledge about
Hazardous Wastes   164

Coordination of the Use of Technology in
   Hazardous Waste Policy   170
Politics in Hazardous Waste Policy Making   174
Conclusion   179

9   Policy for Science: The Space Telescope   181

Setting the Stage for the Space Telescope   182
The Design of the Space Telescope   184
Legal Constraints on the Space
   Telescope Project   186
The Constraints of Knowledge, Technology,
   and Funding   188
Coordination of the Space Telescope Program   195
Politics and the Space Telescope   202
Conclusion   205

10   Science, Technology, and Public Choices   209

What Is Wrong with Science and Technology
   Policy Making?   209
What Will Make Science and Technology
   Policy Better?   210
What Improvements Are Feasible?   213
Conclusion   216

References   219
Name Index   235
Subject Index   239

Science, Technology, and Public Policy

1

A Framework
for Understanding
Science and Technology Policy

It is common for people who discuss evolution or natural selection to speak of traits of animals in the following way: "The stegosaurus had plate-like fins on its back because they allowed this cold-blooded reptile to absorb or radiate heat more effectively." Of course the dinosaur did not intend to have a dorsal air conditioner, so the cause and effect relation suggested here is backwards. Causality worked in the opposite direction: the stegosaurus existed because it had fins that exchanged heat. Neither dinosaurs, fishes, birds, nor humans had a conscious intent to develop fins, gills, wings, or larger brains.

What was once loose language is about to become accurate, however. One day, almost certainly within our lifetimes, a researcher will purposefully create some new human characteristic that will allow a human to better adapt to the natural or social environment. Biotechnologists will be able to reshape humans by engineering genes that enable the body to resist disease, or perhaps even to grow stronger and more intelligent. Sooner or later the necessary combination of knowledge, ability, and motives will exist, and for the first time in the earth's history natural selection and random mutation will no longer explain changes in a species.

This is not science fiction or antiscience hyperbole. Human history does not reveal a long list of useful innovations being permanently shelved no matter how great their potential for mischief; people, and those who lead them, generally choose "more" and "better" over "we'd better not." Because of scientific uncertainty about the results of experiments and the implications of experiments for deeply held values, elected officials and judges will be asked to decide whether the promises of biotechnology outweigh the risks of stumbling into the same destiny as the dinosaurs. Their answer will be one of the most fateful political decisions ever made.

Even in the mid-1980s science and technology pervade almost all aspects of American life. Any issue of a daily newspaper or any evening television news broadcast will include information about problems and opportunities that flow from science and technology, such as high-technology industries, space weapons, artificial hearts, environmental pollution, and nuclear power. The *Challenger* and Chernobyl accidents in early 1986 were global news events, and for at least a short time many people became interested in O-ring seals on space shuttle booster rockets and the flaws of graphite-core nuclear reactors. "Research and development" (R & D) is used as a synonym for national security, investment, and jobs; yet as computers, lasers, and other innovations become more commonplace, our gaps in understanding seem to threaten our ability to deliberately shape the future.

Because the words "science" and "technology" often evoke images of sterile laboratories and complex machines, we may tend to think of them as relatively recent phenomena, products of the Industrial Revolution. Primitive humans, however, observed and recorded natural events such as lunar cycles and animal habits, and technology began with the first use of a tool. As long ago as 580 B.C. the philosopher Thales of Miletus taught that events could be explained by natural causes rather than by divine intervention. What *is* new in human history is the recognition of the scope and importance of science and technology, not only in commerce and warfare, but in nearly all aspects of society. Both government and private industry continue to spend increasing sums on research and development (see Table 1-1). The more we learn about the way the world works, the more complex it seems; scientific research often shows us how little we know.

Questions about the governance of science and technology have broad implications for government. Who is to govern? What did President Eisenhower mean when he warned in his Farewell Address that "public policy could itself become the captive of a scientific-technological elite" (*Public Papers* ..., 421)? In regulating the safety of foods, drugs, or the workplace, how do policy makers balance economic costs, social benefits, human values, and scientific uncertainty? Has technology itself become "a political phenomenon" that "now legislates the conditions of human existence"? (Winner 1977, 323-324). Science and technology are accused of no longer aiding the search for the good life, but instead depriving people of their natural rights. Nuclear arms and workplace chemicals threaten life; computers and restrictions on information threaten liberty; toxic wastes and mechanized farming techniques threaten property.

Moreover, the consequences of scientific and technological advances for the first time in human history transcend national or regional boundaries. Although not yet deliberate, "planetary engineering," for example, is nonetheless under way. That is, many effects of technological progress are global, such as acid rain, the dangers of nuclear war, "the greenhouse effect"—a rise in the earth's temperature due to an increase in carbon

Table 1-1 National R & D Expenditures by Source as a Percentage of
GNP, 1960-1985

Year	Current Dollars (billions)		Constant 1972 Dollars (billions)		Percentage of GNP	
	Federal	Other[a]	Federal	Other[a]	Federal	Other[a]
1960	8.7	4.8	12.7	6.9	1.72	0.95
1961	9.3	5.0	13.3	7.3	1.77	0.95
1962	9.9	5.5	14.0	7.7	1.75	0.97
1963	11.2	5.9	15.6	8.1	1.88	0.99
1964	12.5	6.3	17.2	8.7	1.96	1.00
1965	13.0	7.0	17.4	9.5	1.88	1.01
1966	14.0	7.9	18.2	10.2	1.85	1.03
1967	14.4	8.8	18.2	11.0	1.80	1.09
1968	14.9	9.7	18.1	11.7	1.71	1.11
1969	14.9	10.7	17.2	12.4	1.58	1.13
1970	14.9	11.2	16.3	12.3	1.50	1.13
1971	15.0	11.7	15.6	12.2	1.39	1.09
1972	15.8	12.7	15.8	12.7	1.33	1.07
1973	16.4	14.3	15.6	13.5	1.24	1.08
1974	16.9	16.0	14.8	14.0	1.18	1.12
1975	18.1	17.1	14.5	13.7	1.17	1.10
1976	19.9	19.1	15.1	14.4	1.16	1.11
1977	21.6	21.2	15.4	15.1	1.13	1.11
1978	23.9	24.2	15.9	16.1	1.10	1.12
1979	26.8	28.1	16.4	17.2	1.11	1.16
1980	29.5	33.1	16.5	18.6	1.12	1.26
1981	33.4	38.4	17.1	19.6	1.13	1.30
1982	36.5	42.8	17.5	20.7	1.19	1.39
1983	40.3	46.3	18.6	21.5	1.21	1.40
1984	44.7	51.2	19.9	22.9	1.22	1.40
1985	49.8	56.8	21.4	24.5	1.26	1.44

Source: National Science Board (1985, 217).

[a] All sources other than federal government.

dioxide in the atmosphere from the burning of coal and petroleum.
Mathematician and computer pioneer John von Neumann anticipated such
problems in 1955 when he asked whether technology was making the world's
fragmented political and geographic institutions obsolete (von Neumann
1955, 106-108). As genetic experiments alter the basic mechanisms of life,
science and technology have even the potential to change what it means to be
human.

What roles do science and technology play in politics and policy? David
Easton (1965) suggested thinking of a political system of "input" (demands,
support, and pressure for government action) working through a "process"

(institutional structures and procedures) to produce "output" (policy decisions), with "feedback" allowing output to affect subsequent input. On the one hand, science and technology can be input, as are economic data, political pressures, or threats from abroad. The phrase "science or technology *in* policy" means the input of researchers, for example, their warnings about the risks of nuclear power plants or food additives. On the other hand, science and technology can also be output, that is "policy *for* science or technology." This output may be any one of the many types of things that the government produces, such as funding for research into pesticide accumulation in the environment (Brooks 1968). The example in the following section illustrates the limitations of simple descriptions or explanations of the relationships among public policy, science, and technology.

An Example: Nuclear Fusion Policy

Since 1951 the U.S. government has spent more than $3 billion pursuing a technological goal that few now believe will be reached without additional decades of research and billions of additional dollars. Nuclear fusion has been promoted as the ultimate source of energy. It is fueled by a basic component of seawater, produces little or no radioactive waste, and is safe from meltdowns. Today's nuclear power plants produce energy through nuclear fission, the splitting of uranium atoms. Fusion, however, creates huge amounts of energy as the nuclei of hydrogen atoms collide and combine at temperatures of millions of degrees.

The technological challenge of nuclear fusion is enormous. Stripped of their electrons, the nuclei of atoms in a plasma are positively charged and repel one another, as would positive poles of magnets, so they must be forced into high-speed collisions. This can be accomplished only by extremely high temperatures, but any contact between the plasma and its container will lower the temperature. Hence the most advanced scheme for containment of a fusion reaction calls for a powerful and leakproof "magnetic bottle" to hold and shape the plasma. Other approaches include the use of a network of powerful lasers to blast simultaneously a tiny pellet of fuel. The variety of designs for fusion reactors proposed throughout the past thirty years is evidence of the technical challenge, yet the promise of fusion is large enough to have justified the search. In principle, a fusion reactor could supply the electrical needs of the entire United States with water supplied by a five-inch pipe.

During the 1950s fusion was pursued with great optimism. Congress willingly funded small experimental devices being developed at several laboratories, and the launch of the Soviet satellite *Sputnik* in 1957 accelerated the international competition in fusion research. Because panels of expert scientists were forecasting full-scale demonstration tests by 1975, even elected officials usually preoccupied by the short term could see fusion technology as a worthwhile long-term goal. The program has had an uneven course since the early 1960s, however. Members of Congress began to demand results, asking why money was being funneled into basic science rather than technological development. They became suspicious of fusion scientists, accusing them of "mere, unreflective, 'tin-bending' " and of wastefully pursuing many possible designs for fusion reactors rather than obeying Congress's instructions to focus on a few schemes (Bromberg 1982, 65). Congress tried to reduce the complexity of the technology to a few easily understood indicators of progress, forcing development teams to work as much on short-term milestones as on long-term breakthroughs. The legislators were unable to understand why the technologists could not make detailed project plans, or why they frequently turned to scientists for ways to overcome engineering problems. Thus, arcane knowledge and scientific uncertainty became tools manipulated both by program directors at research centers and by policy makers in government (Heppenheimer 1984).

At the same time, fusion researchers were jockeying for funding and institutional security, not only during times of budgetary cutbacks but also during more generous periods. Although the scientists were sharing their findings (both within the United States and with other nations, including the Soviet Union), they still raced against one another to show they were making progress. Coordination and competition were major factors as strategic decisions about new experimental directions were made by the project teams at Princeton University and the National Laboratories at Oak Ridge, Lawrence Livermore, and Los Alamos.

Not until environmental and energy issues became salient in the early 1970s did fusion develop a few political advocates outside the research and energy arenas. Touted as a clean alternative to fission reactors, fusion became a common topic in the mail of members of Congress. The varying levels of public interest were partially reflected in the willingness of presidents to support increased funding for fusion research. Political pressures joined congressional mandates, organizational factors, and the state of scientific and technological knowledge as a determinant of fusion energy policies.

In many ways fusion technology has been an unusual governmental program. In return for sizable current expenditures it offered benefits as much as a half-century away. It offered only a few members of Congress the electoral gratitude of constituents who would receive federal funds; fusion has never had many supporters beyond those involved in its development. The program has also entailed close cooperation with the Soviets in spite of changing foreign policy climates and the possibility of military spinoffs from fusion technologies. The president's Office of Management and Budget offered additional funding to the program ($30 million in 1979), which fusion project leaders turned down as unnecessary given the current state of progress.

Although fusion research was in some ways unique, it also illustrates common features of science and technology policies. It was characterized by decision making by expert panels, budgetary constraints, cycles of public attention and boredom, and competition among government organizations. Fusion policy was most significantly influenced by a triumvirate—a congressional committee (for many years, the Joint Committee on Atomic Energy), employees of federal agencies that implemented the research policies, and private firms with an interest in fusion. It acquired the characteristics of "big science," with huge investments that became a justification for further expenditures.

Finally, this example reveals both the difficulty and the importance of careful definitions of terms. Was fusion policy an energy policy, a technology policy, or a science policy? Congress had no trouble with the first two labels, but became quite upset when technological development became mixed with basic research. Unfortunately (for the goal of tidy labels), it was logical and inevitable that the demands of a frontier technology policy would intertwine with the curiosity of basic scientists. Throughout this book many cases will be mentioned where "science policy" and "technology policy" are inseparable. Similarly, fusion policy shows that there are cases where it is difficult to separate policy making to promote science and technology from the application of science and technology in policy making. The following section presents definitions of the key concepts used throughout this book.

Defining the Terms

Science

We can distill the many meanings of the word "science" to two. It is both a *method* by which knowledge is gained and the *knowledge* that results from that process: "the constellation of facts, theories, and methods collected in current texts" (Kuhn 1970, 1). Although it would be clearer to use different words for "scientific process" and "scientific knowledge," a sharp distinction cannot always be made between the process and its result.

In ideal form the scientific process, or method, entails observing a problem, forming a hypothesis, gathering data, testing a hypothesis, and forming general conclusions. It is based on constant challenges of assumptions, replications and validations of experiments, and a willingness to reject old explanations in favor of better ones. Scientific knowledge consists of the explanations, theories, and laws that have been produced by the scientific process. When science is done well, it provides not only "facts" for policy makers but also "a 'language' and reference point that allows for informed discourse" (Schmandt 1984, 26). Because the scientific method is not always scrupulously followed, however, and the label "scientific knowledge" is not always judiciously applied, the political institutions that make science and technology policy frequently must assess the quality of information. As discussed throughout this book, the political system was not designed for that task.

A distinction is also frequently made between *basic science* and *applied science*. Vannevar Bush, an important shaper of American science policy during the 1940s, once described basic science as having no "specific practical ends" but which intended to produce "general knowledge and understanding of nature and its laws"; applied science, by contrast, is undertaken with a particular objective (Penick 1972, 191-193). President Eisenhower's secretary of defense offered a more down-to-earth definition: "Basic research is when you don't know what you are doing" (Boehm 1958, 134). Confusion over this terminology has had important consequences. Attempts to draw a line between basic and applied research have shaped American science and technology policy and the institutions that affect it. Some laws define the tasks of government agencies in terms of "basic" or "applied" science. During the 1980s, for example, Congress held hearings on the need to create a National Technology Foundation (NTF), which would provide funds for "applied research" and engineering, in contrast with the focus of the National Science Foundation (NSF) on "basic research." Some congressional witnesses saw the NTF proposal as an attempt to pressure NSF to devote more funds to engineering than to "fundamental knowledge" (U.S. House of Representatives 1981a).

Such moves have been prompted in part by doubts about the social benefits of spending public funds for basic research. Findings that "basic research in biology has yet to have a major impact on the prevention and treatment of human disease" and that improved health is more attributable to improved sanitation and other public health measures raise questions about the value of public investment in basic biomedical research (Baltimore 1978). Proponents of continued emphasis on basic research can, however, point to such examples as the study of magnetism carried by atomic nuclei, which eventually led to nuclear magnetic resonance devices used in medical diagnosis (Lederman 1984; David 1985). Again, the distinction between "policy for science" and "science in policy" reflects the often futile attempt to separate basic and applied research precisely.

Technology

An historian of science has written that distinctions between science and technology are useful primarily when scientists want "to get money," "to get out of responsibility," or "to get status" for themselves (de Solla Price 1973). In general, technology can be defined as a body of knowledge about the production of goods and services (Rosenberg 1982, 143; Kuehn and Porter 1981, 11-12). Unlike science, which aims at understanding reality, technology is intended to put knowledge into practice to "alter and control the material conditions of life" or to "create a reality according to our design" (Grove 1980). Scientists study the chemical, geological, and health effects of hazardous waste; technologists are concerned with methods to increase the safety of landfills or other disposal practices. As discussed in later chapters, ambiguities between science and technology have occasionally had major effects on public policy.

Because technology is based on knowledge, it is common to assume that technological applications must follow scientific breakthroughs. But does a nation's technological and commercial development depend on financial support for pure scientific research? Should the public hold scientists accountable for producing useful payoffs in return for the public investment in science? In fact, *neither* science nor technology always precedes the other. Numerous historic scientific advances (for example, Joule and thermodynamics, Pasteur and bacteriology, Carnot and the law of conservation of energy) resulted from attempts to solve practical problems (power generation, wine fermentation, steam engines). Technology serves as "an enormous repository of empirical knowledge to be scrutinized and evaluated by the scientist," as well as a source of tools and techniques for scientific inquiry (Rosenberg 1982, 142, 144). In general, scientific methods and knowledge play a complex yet crucial role in the process of technological innovation, and demands for answers to practical problems often "pull" scientific advances.

Public Policy and the Policy Process

A public policy is not simply a government decision, since decisions may have unanticipated effects or no effects at all. In 1976 and 1978 Congress amended the National Aeronautics and Space Act to state that

> the general welfare of the United States requires that the unique competence in scientific and engineering systems of the National Aeronautics and Space Administration also be directed toward ... petroleum-conserving ground propulsion systems, ... advanced automobile propulsion systems, ... [and] bioengineering programs to alleviate and minimize the effects of disability.

It thereby *declared* a policy, but with no effect until money was appropriated and programs were implemented. Similarly, policy is not just a government action, since nonaction sometimes has deliberate consequences. A definition of public policy must be sufficiently general to cover both mistaken and inexplicit policies: "a goal-directed or purposive course of action followed by an actor or a set of actors in an attempt to deal with a public problem" (Anderson 1975, 3). Like "science," "policy" refers to both a process and a product.

The policy process is fluid and varied; it changes over time and from policy to policy. Many parts of the policy process cannot be observed directly, and very few can be measured. There is far more to the policy process than the constitutional structure of the executive, legislative, and judicial branches. Authority and responsibility are fragmented within the federal government and are divided as well among federal, state, and local governments.

Charles Jones (1984) outlined five stages through which public policies usually pass. First, citizens, interest groups, or policy makers must *perceive and define* a problem and thereby bring it to the public agenda. Studies of recombinant DNA regulation and nuclear reactor policy have shown that the definition of the problem (as short-range or long-range, economic or public health, national security or freedom of inquiry) can have a major effect on the remainder of the policy process (Goodell 1977; del Sesto 1983). Second, policy makers *formulate* and debate possible solutions in Congress or the executive branch. Third, they eventually *adopt* a set of solutions as a law, an executive decision, or a regulation. The executive and the legislative branches are the most active and visible participants at this stage of the process. In the fourth stage bureaucrats study the program and allocate resources to *implement* the policy. This task is usually complicated by uncertainty about the true intent of Congress, by bureaucratic second-guessing, or by political pressures to delay or alter a program. In the fifth stage, policy makers *evaluate* the outcome of the first four stages, but an assessment can be performed during any phase of the process and by any person, group, or institution. All of these tasks are subject to political maneuvering and bargaining, and they rarely follow a neat chronological order. Perceptions and the definitions of the problem, for example, continually change throughout the policy process.

Models of the Policy Process.   Several general models have provided useful perspectives of the policy process. One is the rational model, which assumes that policy makers have clear goals, the ability to assess many alternative courses of action, and the willingness to choose those policies that achieve their goals at the least cost. This model emphasizes neutrality, objectivity, thoroughness, consistency, and the use of quantitative measures whenever possible, so it bears a close resemblance to the ideal scientific method.

Because the real world is often much less logical and precise, other models emphasize the limitations on policy makers. Lindblom (1959) argued that policy makers take current policies as a starting point and make only incremental changes, thereby avoiding the need for clear definitions and searching analyses. Although goals such as consistency and objectivity are also included in this model, it assumes that policy proposals and analyses will be far from comprehensive. Policy makers lack the time, ability, and resources to be thorough; instead, they "muddle through," adjusting past policies only as necessary. The incremental policy model might sound familiar to practicing scientists because it blends the spirit of the perfect scientific method with the real obstacles of being thorough.

The incremental model cannot easily account for the sudden or dramatic changes that sometimes rearrange the policy agenda. In its place, a garbage can model has been proposed in which government is described as an "organized anarchy." Personal preferences are unclear, learning is by trial and error (and is therefore incomplete and not easily shared), and policy participants change frequently due to personnel turnover or the reassignment of tasks (Kingdon 1984). Policy choices are similar to a "garbage can into which various kinds of problems and solutions are dumped by participants as they are generated" (Cohen, March, and Olsen 1972, 2). Policy outcomes depend on the coincidence of three major process streams: problem recognition, policy formation, and politics. The garbage can model describes a messy policy process that is difficult to predict. Just as the sciences occasionally undergo unexpected changes ("paradigm shifts" or "scientific revolutions") due to inadequacies of earlier theories, delayed and limited responses to poorly understood problems characterize the policy process (Kuhn 1970).

The Scientific Approach and the Politics of Public Policy Making.   The formation of public policy is an inherently political activity that requires both the accumulation of facts and the weighing of personal values. In any area of policy making the fundamental task is to move from what *is* to what someone believes *should be*. Yet while the present state of things can be objectively known (at least in principle), public policies are formed from an aggregation of individual desires that may not be based on present reality. The general policy process is pervaded by tensions between careful—often scientific—procedures for gathering and analyzing knowledge and the amorphous give-and-take of political bargaining. Tensions also characterize science and technology policy: tensions between simplicity and reality, scientific understanding and social utility, public participation and professional competence, and short political time horizons and long scientific perspectives (Brooks 1982; Yellin 1984; Lakoff 1974).

If the process of policy making depended solely on political forces, the techniques and results of scientific inquiry would be either (1) ignored or squelched, since objectivity would be irrelevant or inconvenient, or (2) subverted to disguise subjectivity. In contrast, if policy making depended solely on rationality and logic, scientific knowledge would be embraced and encouraged. In practice, however, public policies usually fall somewhere between these extremes, combining political necessities with somewhat scientific hypotheses. Economic policies, for example, are based on a mixture of current economic data and theories about the flow of labor and capital, and agricultural policies require information about the relationships among soil conditions, biological growth, and meteorology. Yet these "objective" parts of the policy process are nearly always supplanted—or contaminated—by the subjective values of interest groups, public opinion, or even the decision makers themselves. The careful calculations of economists and agricultural specialists are also shaped by ideology, self-interest, and variable willingness to accept risk. Just as scientists find it difficult to adhere to the ideal model of the scientific process, policy makers usually are unable to follow either the purely scientific or the purely political model of the policy process.

Studies of public policy often focus on the role of political values in the policy process: for example, how policy makers respond to pressures from business and labor. But in the realm of science and technology policy, it is more pertinent to emphasize the role of purported *facts* and, consequently, the tension between facts and political values. Although scientists are not totally value-free, policy makers may treat them as such, particularly when the scientists' "facts" support a policy maker's position. In comparisons of the costs and benefits of policies, the conflict between scientific facts and political values becomes crucial. Many values, such as unpolluted vistas of the Grand Canyon or the promise of prolonged life, are difficult to measure in dollars or with scientific precision, compared with the ease of determining the economic costs of pollution abatement or worker safety programs. After all, "scientists seek to develop *general* laws—laws that hold, *other things being equal*"; but policy makers must know how things work "in the real world, where *other things are not equal and where nothing is constant*" (Breyer 1982, 155, emphasis in the original). The policy arena of science and technology provides a critical test of policy making in general, for if "correctness" (in the sense of logical connections between objective facts and public policies) is to be found anywhere, it should be there.

Of course, claiming that "logical" policy making is based on the use of scientific knowledge and methods is not the same as arguing that what passes in the policy arena as science is always infallible, benign, objective, or easily translatable into public policies. It is precisely because the scientific process never has all of these characteristics that science and technology have an uneasy relationship with the political process. It is in the nature of science that mistakes and shortcomings are treated as opportunities for progress. Those who make political decisions rarely have the time or the security to find positive benefits in failures. As Henry James wrote, "practical politics consists in ignoring facts" (Mensch 1975, 28).

Science and Technology Policy

As the earlier discussion of nuclear fusion policy illustrated, it is often impossible to separate "science policy" and "technology policy," so the phrase "science and technology policy" will be split in this book only when necessary to explain some aspects of the policy process. It will usually suffice to define science and technology policy as *a governmental course of action intended to support, apply, or regulate scientific knowledge or technological innovation.*

Support includes direct funding of basic research, subsidies such as tax credits for research and development, and other indirect programs such as financial assistance for education in science and technology. The government deliberately applies science and technology when it turns to scientists and technicians for their expertise in solving public problems ranging from agriculture to ballistic missile defense systems and when it procures equipment or services (thereby affecting the pace and direction of R & D). Government regulation of science and technology can be both positive (that is, promotional, as when environmental regulations require advances in antipollution technology) and negative (as when policies restrict the types of genetic research experiments that scientists can perform).

In practice, science and technology policies frequently include all three types of actions. After all, the formation of policies to support or regulate science and technology depend on the application of knowledge. The government supports science by, for example, funding research into plant and fish metabolism in high-acid environments; it applies the results of that research as it sets pollution emission standards; and it regulates some aspects of the research, such as field tests.

The use of knowledge in policy making frequently includes no explicit statement of intent to support or regulate research, but the application of science and technology in policy often has at least the indirect effect of making someone want to know more—often because knowledge was missing, uncertain, or misused. As in the five stages of the policy process, there may be no definite chronological starting point to the support, regulation, or application of science and technology in the policy process. Nevertheless, all policy making involves the application of knowledge; it follows, then, that this aspect of the science and technology policy process attracts the most attention.

Because a definition of science and technology policy could include the realms of energy, health, defense, transportation, housing, and education, one may ask whether the topic of this book is really a distinct type of public policy. As one writer has observed, "Technology is so much a part of society's missions that it becomes difficult to know where a technology policy ends and a military, environmental, or transportation policy begins" (Lambright 1976, 187). The Organization for Economic Cooperation and Development surveyed many developed nations and concluded that six factors distinguish science and technology from other public policy issues (Nichols 1979):

1. The rapidity of change in science and technology
2. The novelty of many issues in science and technology

3. The scale, complexity, and interdependence among technologies
4. The irreversibility of many scientific and technological effects (such as global warming due to the increase in atmospheric carbon dioxide from the burning of coal and petroleum)
5. Public worries about real or imagined threats to human health and safety
6. Challenges to deeply held social values (such as the definition of legal death and the control of genetics)

In addition, many science and technology policies are unusual (but not unique) in that they often are not essential. That is, many foreign, social, and economic policies result from an expressed need for government action on, for example, an international crisis, rising unemployment, or malnourished children; policies that support science and technology, by contrast, often result from opportunities rather than from problems. At most, only a few thousand astronomers would consider it to be a "problem" not to have a $1.1-billion telescope orbiting the earth.

There are specialized institutions in the science and technology policy process. Some agencies, such as the National Science Foundation, the Nuclear Regulatory Commission, and the National Aeronautics and Space Administration (NASA), were created to support, apply, or regulate science and technology. Don Price has described these agencies as forming an "establishment": "a set of institutions supported by tax funds, but largely on faith, and without direct responsibility to political control" (Price 1965, 12). The courts sometimes agree: in a dispute over the safety of nuclear power plants, for example, the Supreme Court ruled that in cases "at the frontiers of science . . . a reviewing court must generally be at its most deferential" (*Baltimore Gas & Electric Co. v. Natural Resources Defense Council, Inc.,* 103 S.Ct. at 2256 [1983]).

Constraints on the Science and Technology Policy Process

Like everyone, policy makers have limited time, resources, intelligence, and information. Organizations and institutions exist to divide labor and reduce information costs, but they also face limitations, as the incrementalism and garbage can models of policy making showed. Whether public officials are actually public-minded or greedy, both their virtues and their vices are constrained by factors beyond their immediate control—by what could be labeled "the real world" of laws, knowledge, organizations, and politics.

The concept of constraint fits into the behavioral tradition in the social sciences. A common assumption is that some form of rationality—a relationship between goals and actions—is at the root of human behavior and social choice. Strict "objective rationality" considers constraints imposed by the environment as part of the decision calculus of a person or organization insofar as these constraints restrict choices and impose costs. "Bounded rationality" includes a recognition of the constraints imposed by a decision maker's own limitations, particularly his or her capacities for knowledge and analysis (Simon 1985, 294). Similarly, theorists have described the limits on organizational goals as a set of constraints on what outcomes are acceptable (Cyert and March 1963; Simon 1964). Fenno (1973) found it useful to discuss the "environmental constraints" that affect the behavior of members of Congress, and Anderson (1981) pointed out the need for consistent justifications as a constraint on foreign policy. Kingdon has perceived policy constraints not as absolutes but as "conditions that make some events highly unlikely and other events more likely to occur" (1984, 218).

Although no brief scheme of categories can capture all the nuances of a policy realm, focusing on four major types of constraints reduces the complexity of science and technology policy making. These four constraints provide the framework that will be applied throughout this book.

Law

There are always statutory and constitutional mandates to which policy makers must respond. That is, some policy actions are prohibited by law and others are required or strongly encouraged. The Constitution forbids, for example, "cruel and unusual punishment," so medical experiments on unwilling or ignorant prisoners are not permissible.[1] The statutes that are produced by the legislative process are more likely to contain explicit provisions regarding policies than is the Constitution. The 1984 Hazardous and Solid Waste Amendments, for example, specified that the permeability of hazardous waste landfill liners must be no more than 0.0000001 centimeter per second (see Chapter 8). Yet statutes can also be quite vague. Section 4(f) of the Toxic Substances Control Act provides that, after being notified of a possible cancer risk posed by a chemical, the Environmental Protection Agency (EPA) has 180 days either to initiate regulatory action or to explain why the risk "is not unreasonable." The agency is not, however, required to explain what constitutes "reasonableness."

Through judicial review and oversight the courts and Congress try to ensure that the requirements of law are observed, often in spite of strong pressures from interested groups. The precise wording of laws can be crucial for the application of scientific knowledge. Did the Occupational Health and Safety Act, for example, require qualitative ("more" or "less") or quantitative (exact numerical) assessments of health and safety risks? Through legal mandates and attempts to interpret them, legal constraints provide incentives, requirements, and limitations on science and technology policy making.

Knowledge

Nature provides policy makers with an abundance of worries—like shortages and peculiar geographic distributions of resources—and often with an agenda as well, as when an earthquake or an epidemic warning forces public action. NASA must worry about radiation zones around the earth, solar flares, and intergalactic cosmic radiation when planning new space vehicles, missions, and budgets. When the Federal Communications Commission formulates a policy for the exploitation of new satellite technologies, its options are limited by the laws of gravity that determine satellite orbits and by the laws of electromagnetism that determine which radio frequencies are appropriate for particular uses.

Sometimes scientific and technological knowledge reveals clear logical connections between government policy and what nature demands and allows; for example, we *know* that asbestos is an extremely dangerous substance. More often, however, we do not have exact answers to scientific or technological questions. Just how likely is a major earthquake along California's San Andreas fault, and when? Has a laboratory definitely proven that a new strain of flu endangers the entire American public? Are saccharin and cyclamates really carcinogenic (cancer-causing) artificial sweeteners, and in what doses?

These are matters beyond the immediate and direct control of policy makers. They must take the natural world and its laws as "givens," so they must turn to nonelected experts from laboratories and universities for "theoretical or practical understanding of and information concerning" science and engineering (Greenwood 1984, 3). Statutes and judges cannot successfully require what is physically impossible, nor can the president or Congress habitually ignore the opportunities and limitations that scientific and technological knowledge supply. Kingdon found that policy specialists are fond of the word "actually" (as in, "will it actually accomplish what we want to accomplish?") because it allows them to imply victory over the constraint of feasibility (Kingdon 1984, 139). Nevertheless, the effect bureaucrats, the public, and scientists can have on the policy process depends on their understanding of what is known and what is uncertain.

Coordination

Coordination can mean direct control, voluntary cooperation, or careful organizational arrangement; it has been defined as "the conscious process of assembling and synchronizing differentiated activities so that they function harmoniously in the attainment of organization objectives" (Haimann and Scott 1974, 124).[2] Ideally, two public institutions (or two divisions of the same institution) should not work at cross-purposes.

Many examples of contradictory or inharmonious behavior between or within institutions can, however, be found. Sometimes the lack of coordination is deliberate, obvious, and easily attributable to such factors as political pressure. Congress, for example, has retained the Delaney Amendment to the Food, Drug, and Cosmetic Act, which forbids the use of food additives that cause cancer in humans or animals; but political pressure induced Congress to exempt the artificial sweetener saccharin in spite of evidence that its use causes cancer in laboratory animals. Laws usually are ambiguous about what is to be done and by whom. Thus, agencies can often set their own standards for accepting statistical data, for projecting trends, or for balancing the costs of long-term research projects against programs with faster payoffs.

In addition, many institutions of science and technology policy have fragmented or overlapping jurisdictions. Congress is divided into hundreds of committees and subcommittees, many of which have jurisdiction over aspects of science and technology policy. Health and safety risks are regulated by numerous executive and independent agencies. Authority to regulate the safety of genetic engineering, for example, has been distributed among the National Institutes of Health, EPA, the Department of Agriculture, and the Food and Drug Administration. Even an agency with as clear a mandate as NASA often shares its responsibilities with other parts of the government, such as those with interests in military or commercial applications. Furthermore, problems of coordination arise within policy-making institutions because of subdivisions of labor, competing perspectives, or poor communication.

As subsequent chapters will point out, lack of coordination is often a major cause of delay, confusion, or unanticipated consequences of science and technology policy; yet it occasionally helps to reduce the chances of overlooking important aspects of policy questions, and it provides multiple routes for the public and for interest groups to affect policy. Therefore, "the key concern now is not how science and technology can make more efficient the administration of our policies but how conflicts arising out of competing scientific specialties may be resolved under some system of constitutional accountability" (Price 1983, viii). Problems of coordination are largely an unavoidable consequence of the basic values that have shaped our political system.

Politics

Another constraint on policy makers is politics. Science and technology policies must accommodate certain facts of political life that, like the laws of nature, are not subject to the immediate and direct control of elected officials, judges, or bureaucrats. A proposed policy may be consistent with legal principles, based on sound scientific or technological evidence, and methodically implemented, and still fail if some group makes a concerted effort to block it. In the American political system, at least an effort at openness, accountability, and responsiveness is required of publicly funded research (except for classified defense projects).

The constituency that supports a policy such as nuclear power may have very different political resources (more money, better organization, and professional lobbyists) from those of a group that opposes it, which may rely instead on grass-roots activists. A group's political resources affect both the forum and form of policy debate. Politics in the policy-making process is not, however, synonymous with poorly informed troublemaking. Political opposition can reveal the weaknesses in a proposal's legal, factual, or organizational foundations.

> Knowledge does not and cannot govern. Even if we knew everything there would still be obstacles that would ensure the failure of knowledge. America would have to be quite different from what it is for knowledge, alone, to prevail. The diversity of our society and institutions set the conditions for conflicting values to be maintained (Meltsner 1976, 270).

Because of the need for policies to be congruent with political forces, the policy process sometimes violates the constraints of the legal system, organizational coherence, and logical connections with the physical world. There is no rigid hierarchy of constraints in which politics always wins over the laws of nature or the laws of the nation. Nor are these four constraints independent. For example, the groups that dominate the identification and definition of problems at the first stage of the policy process will shape the resulting laws or regulations, the amount of coordination in implementation, and the salience of different aspects of policy makers' "real world." Similarly, legal constraints may limit the time for researching a problem or the rules of evidence that may be used to justify a policy choice.

Both for observers of the policy process and for policy makers, understanding these four constraints—law, knowledge, coordination, and politics—is useful not only in reducing the complexity of the science and technology policy process but also in evaluating policy prescriptions or reforms. Identifying where particular problems of science and technology policy face the greatest institutional and procedural tensions should make it easier to predict which changes in the policy process would produce improvements. It is difficult, however, to know what would constitute improvements. Because the policy process does not think, it does not define its own goal; rather, its goal is what policy makers and the public expect of it. Policies should be consistent with the fundamental social and political values incorporated in the Constitution, but that is hardly a precise prescription.

Demands that laws never be contradictory or that government institutions always be efficiently organized and operated are impossible to meet in a complex pluralistic republic. Nor should scientific consistency be thought of as a goal, because political decisions require more certainty and stability (even if artificial) than scientific and technological knowledge provide. The framework of constraints used throughout this book is not a formula for finding answers, but it can help explain the weaknesses in current and proposed practices.

Summary

The major points about science and technology policy bear repeating at this stage.

1. The implications of science and technology for society and government have grown enormously since World War II and will continue to do so.

2. The policy process is complex; issues do not move through the process in a simple linear manner prescribed by carefully designed institutions or rules.

3. Although we can define science, technology, science policy, and technology policy, we cannot expect always to find sharp boundaries between them. Science and technology both refer to the process and the results of gathering knowledge—about how the world works, and about how to make it work better, respectively.

4. Science and technology policy includes the support, use, and regulation of science and technology. Although this policy area has several distinguishing characteristics, it is not always clearly separable from other policy areas, such as health, energy, and transportation.

5. There are inherent tensions between science and politics that are manifested in four types of constraints: law, knowledge, coordination, and politics.

Conclusion

Each public policy decision is analogous in some ways to a scientific experiment. Each begins with a set of knowns and unknowns and is intended to induce a change that will decrease the number of unknowns. The change may be a chemical reaction from which a researcher can discover properties of a polymer. It may be a new tax credit that makes it possible for industries to increase spending for R & D; from this sort of change policy makers can learn about incentives that have desirable effects on corporate behavior. Uncertainty and dissatisfaction are both the impetus and the major obstacle for scientific experiments and for public policies.

The analogy can be extended a bit farther. Public policies face legal and external constraints just as scientific experiments are limited by the laws of nature and physical constants. Decision makers may chafe at the restrictions of some laws or constitutional principles or at the inability of engineers to produce safe cars that consume fuel at only one gallon per hundred miles;

though these constraints fetter the options, they may also reduce the set of feasible alternatives to a manageable number. Similarly, physical constants, such as the speed of light or the amount of energy that subatomic particles can borrow from one another (Planck's constant), provide scientists with fixed reference points as well as barriers. And just as physical and biological systems reflect a tension between orderliness and disorder, political systems must balance fragmentation and coordination.

Similarities break down when we examine political constraints that affect, in complex and shifting ways, public policies based on strategic and deliberate decisions by cognizant individuals. It is as though volcanoes occasionally decided to outwit geologists by withholding their eruptions, or waves and cliffs reached a compromise on a mutually acceptable rate of erosion. Such behavior would introduce a new dimension to scientific study, and it goes a long way to explaining the difficulty in producing laws of the policy process comparable to the laws of the natural world. Nevertheless, science and politics both undergo a kind of testing: in science, when two theories compete for acceptance, and in politics, through lawsuits, oversight, public opinion, and elections.

Notes

1. Unfortunately, there have been violations of this constitutional protection, in part because the definitions of such words as "cruel" and "unwilling" are not always clear or easily applied; see Shapiro (1982) and Jones (1981).
2. See also *Interagency Coordination of Federal Scientific Research and Development: The Federal Council for Science and Technology,* a report prepared for the Subcommittee on Domestic and International Scientific Planning and Analysis, Committee on Science and Technology, U.S. House of Representatives, by the Science Policy Research Division, Congressional Research Service, Library of Congress, July 1976.

2

Congress in the Policy Process

Since its discovery in 1878, saccharin has caused headaches for policy makers—a political side effect of uncertainty about the artificial sweetener's toxic and carcinogenic properties. After passage of the Pure Food and Drug Act in 1906, chemists at the Department of Agriculture attempted to regulate saccharin as a dangerous food additive but were unsuccessful because of opposition from manufacturers, users of the sweetener, and even President Theodore Roosevelt (Priebe and Kauffman 1980). After the commercial use of artificial sweeteners increased greatly following World War II, the Food and Drug Administration (FDA) began to look closely at saccharin and cyclamates.

By the 1960s FDA was operating under a congressional mandate to prohibit the use of any food additive known to cause cancer in humans or laboratory animals. The Delaney Amendment, passed in 1958, was clear: any evidence of a substance's carcinogenicity required a complete ban. By 1969 FDA had become convinced that cyclamates fit that description and invoked the Delaney clause to prohibit their use. Three years later FDA cited studies finding bladder cancer in test animals and placed saccharin in regulatory purgatory by banning additional uses until its safety was firmly established. The producers of Coca-Cola, Pepsi, and diet foods joined the manufacturers of saccharin, such as Monsanto and Sherwin-Williams, in public protests that the benefits of saccharin to overweight Americans and diabetics far outweighed the merely speculative risks.

The accumulating scientific evidence offered tentative links between saccharin and uterine cancer, bladder stones, and other disorders. A lengthy study by the National Academy of Sciences (NAS) failed to conclude that saccharin was definitely a health problem, but by 1977 FDA had become convinced that the evidence—though not absolutely certain—was sufficient to justify a total ban on the sweetener. Members of Congress received enormous amounts of mail to protest FDA's action. Some ridiculed the conditions of the study on which FDA based its decision (rats were fed the equivalent of 800 12-ounce cans of diet soft drinks per day), but FDA insisted that under the congressional mandate of the Delaney clause, no amount of toxic or carcinogenic substances in food additives was legally permissible.

During long hearings in the Senate and House of Representatives legislators complained about "the present lack of consensus within the scientific and medical communities" and "the inconclusiveness of the scientific and medical data" (Congressional Quarterly 1977, 497). Members of Congress were able to pacify their saccharin-using voters by ordering a "temporary," two-year moratorium on the FDA ban and calling for further studies to be conducted by NAS. Attempts to require health warnings in broadcast advertisements succumbed to warnings of restrictions on commercial speech and, again, to scientific inconclusiveness. Congress also stipulated that no research on saccharin conducted before 1978 could be used by FDA to justify its prohibition.

In 1979 Congress extended the ban on FDA action for another two years and did so again in 1981, 1983, and 1985. The Delaney Amendment remains law, but no law requires Congress to pass legislation that is logically consistent or scientifically valid. The political arena remains the final judge of the validity and applicability of scientific evidence.

Congress is a dominant force in four of the five major stages of the policy process—perception/definition, formulation, adoption, and evaluation—and oversees the implementation of policies by bureaucrats. It is the central arena for public policy making and the continuous focus for national politics because it undergoes elections every two years, has mostly open procedures, and offers the media, interest groups, and voters access to decision makers. The legislature is where policy and politics converge most dramatically.

Congress has always been active in science and technology policy making, and it has assertively taken the lead from the president on some types of issues. On atomic energy, health policy, and creation of the National Science Foundation (NSF) legislators have been reluctant to yield to the discretion of the president or bureaucrats (Lakoff 1974). Similarly, science and technology have a long history of affecting congressional decision making. As long ago as the early 1800s, Congress was worrying about the reasons steamboats on the Mississippi River were exploding. The debate over constitutional authority for congressional regulation of the design and operation of steamboat boilers lasted from 1816 to 1852 and produced the nation's first technological research grant (to the Franklin Institute) and several laws requiring increasing federal control (Burke 1966). Since then members of Congress have confronted scientific and technological issues as components of health, defense, and other types of policies. Especially since the growth of social regulation in the 1970s, Congress has paid much more explicit attention to environmental, health, and safety consequences of science and technology (Coates 1982). For example, the word "risk" appeared in the abstracts of 177 bills submitted to the 96th Congress (1979-1980), and more than 200 bills were introduced during the first three months of 1983 with the aim of improving technological innovation in the United States (U.S. House of Representatives 1981g; Dickson 1984).

Congressional Policy Tools

Congress is a complex organization with complex political and policy tasks. Its members respond to a wide range of goals, incentives, and constraints as they attempt to promote both the public interest and their own. Congress has several tools at its disposal to influence science and technology policy.

Legislation

Congress often uses its grandest tool, the passage of laws, to shape science and technology policy. Some legislation is vague, couched in terms like "reasonably necessary," "best available technology," or "so far as possible." Other laws, such as the 1984 hazardous waste legislation discussed in Chapter 8, are extremely specific about required agency actions, technical standards, and deadlines.

Both approaches have problems. Before policies can be implemented vague mandates must be interpreted, thereby shifting much of the policy-making process to bureaucracies and courts. For this reason much of the public health and safety regulation passed by Congress since the late 1960s has found its way into the judicial system where courts have had to determine congressional intent (see Chapter 5). A precise and specific mandate may, however, be beyond Congress's resources (time, staff, or expertise), and it can quickly become obsolete as new knowledge is gained. When scientists became able to measure carcinogens in concentrations of parts per trillion rather than parts per million, questions were raised about total legislative bans on the presence of such substances in food additives.

Even a clear congressional mandate may be disputed or ignored. The Occupational Safety and Health Act required regulators to reduce worker exposure to hazardous substances to the lowest extent feasible regardless of the cost to employers, but extensive judicial resources were consumed over ten years before the Supreme Court ruled in 1981 that Congress meant what the law said. In other cases agencies have decided that a literal interpretation of a legislative mandate would produce results unacceptable to Congress. The Environmental Protection Agency (EPA) was instructed by the Clean Air Act to control air pollutants that "result in an increase in mortality or an increase in serious irreversible, or incapacitating, illness." Because doing exactly what the act required could entail shutting down major industries, EPA proposed instead an "ample margin of safety" standard.

Finally, regardless of the specificity of its mandates, Congress faces difficulty enforcing its will. When the National Aeronautics and Space Council was placed in the Executive Office against President Eisenhower's wishes, he simply refused to appoint a director or allow meetings to be scheduled (Price 1965, 253). More commonly, delays can arise because of deliberate bureaucratic stalling, the need for additional studies, discovery of new information, or legal procedures that allow challenges to a statute's interpretation and implementation (Barke 1984).

Publicity and Investigations

Congress can affect science and technology policy without going the full route to passage of a law. A statutory policy change must pass many tests in the legislative process. Sometimes exposure and discussion are sufficient either to alter the implementation of a policy or to quench proposals for new policies. Specific bills are rarely used to proclaim broad directions for science and technology policies, and very narrow matters, such as a case of misused federal funds, are not appropriate for full legislative action.

Congress occasionally undertakes a comprehensive examination of science and technology policy. In the 1880s, the Allison Commission, a joint commission of the House and Senate, investigated the federal science organization; this commission has had several modern incarnations. During the late 1960s the Subcommittee on Government Research, chaired by Sen. Fred Harris (D-Okla.), spent three years discussing the long-term implications of scientific research. In January 1985 the House Science and Technology Committee, under chair Don Fuqua (D-Fla.), established an eighteen-month Task Force on Science Policy to provide a comprehensive analysis of the relationship of science to government, education, industry, manpower, and foreign relations.

Congressional committees commonly investigate particular policy issues through staff studies and public hearings. Although new legislation may not emerge from such hearings, policy changes nevertheless can occur. Hearings can generate publicity that mobilizes voters or interest groups to apply pressure on an agency, and oversight "by raised eyebrow" (where displeasure is suggested but changes are not explicitly ordered) can relay warnings of future budget trouble if congressional concerns are not respected. The Oak Ridge National Laboratory, looking for ways to diversify its functions after fulfilling its initial tasks in nuclear energy, was warned against "empire building" by the congressional committee with jurisdiction over its budget (Teich and Lambright 1976, 464). Even the failure of Congress to gather information can generate controversy that may affect policy. After a fire killed three Apollo astronauts in 1967, the National Aeronautics and Space Administration (NASA) was strongly criticized for refusing to release "intimate and confidential" information about the accident to a congressional committee (Roback 1968). NASA's administrator promised to keep committee members better informed, but soon after the space shuttle *Challenger* was destroyed in January 1986, several members of Congress became outspoken in their belief that NASA was covering up its mistakes.

Individual members of Congress can also attempt to embarrass funding agencies. Since 1975 Sen. William Proxmire (D-Wis.) has presented his well-publicized, monthly "Golden Fleece" awards, often to government-funded research projects that have easily ridiculed titles. To the delight of many scientists, in a 1979 case involving studies of aggression in animals (such as biting and jaw clenching by angry monkeys), the Supreme Court ruled that there are libelous limits to such publicity. Proxmire's mistake was to lampoon the research on television interview shows and in speeches away from the Senate floor (99 S.Ct. 2675, 2887 [1979]).

Appropriations

One of the most effective tools of Congress is its power of the purse. With the growth in federal R & D expenditures from $10 billion in 1955 to $48.7 billion in 1985, Congress has acquired more budgetary opportunities to shape science and technology policy. Because the process consists of two stages (program authorization and appropriation), performed in both the Senate and the House of Representatives by committees whose jurisdictions may overlap, the science and technology budget is subjected to numerous influences before the president has a chance to sign it into law. This complexity also means that congressional actions sometimes may be misleading. The Magnetic Fusion Energy Engineering Act of 1980 authorized—but did not appropriate—the expenditure of $20 billion on magnetic fusion R & D over the next two decades. Actual expenditures peaked at about $470 million in 1984 and dropped to $325 million in 1986.

The outcome of the appropriations process is neither the president's budget nor Congress's budget. Since the president begins the budget process and Congress has limited time and resources to review it, only controversial items are likely to be subjected to significant changes by Congress. Nevertheless, the president's budget submissions are shaped by anticipation of congressional acceptability, and Congress has demonstrated its ability to direct the science budget. In 1971 Congress passed the amendment of Sen. Mike Mansfield (D-Mont.) to a military authorization bill, prohibiting the Defense Department from funding research "unless such a project or study has a direct and apparent relationship to a specific military function or operation." The amendment had little immediate direct effect, but it warned the military of increased congressional scrutiny of the Defense Department's R & D budgets and had a long-term, chilling effect on some types of military research. Similarly, in 1975, in reaction to Man: A Course of Study, an NSF-sponsored elementary school curriculum for behavioral science (deemed "godless" by some), the House—but not the Senate—accepted a measure by Rep. Robert Bauman (R-Md.) that would have required the NSF to submit all research grants for congressional approval.

Congress's control of the budget is limited by its ability to determine exactly how money should be spent. Sometimes Congress finds that funds intended for technological research are spent instead on science because researchers realize that further basic study is needed (Bromberg 1982, 117). Or Congress may find that the estimates of costs, risks, or benefits on which it based an appropriation were exaggerated or mistaken.[1] These problems are reduced somewhat when members of Congress work closely on budgets with science and technology agencies, but the budget often remains a rather blunt tool for shaping science and technology policy.

Confirmations

Congress also influences science and technology policy through the nomination process. The heads of the executive departments, executive agencies, and independent regulatory commissions are nominated by the president for Senate confirmation. Presidential nominees are rarely turned down, but members of Congress can use confirmation hearings to express congressional dissatisfaction with current policies. Nominees to the National Science Board (the governing body of the NSF), for example, never faced full hearings until 1974, when two senators used hearings to urge the board's new members to be more active in policy making and to work more closely with Congress than had their predecessors (Shapley 1974).

Law and Congressional Policy Making

In the hierarchy of laws, statutory law ranks just below constitutional law. As the source of federal statutes Congress is not formally constrained by any laws except the Constitution. The absence of any explicit constitutional reference to congressional powers affecting science and technology other than patents, weights, and measures has been important in shaping science and technology policies. In the early days of the nation Congress was reluctant to underwrite research with no immediate economic payoffs or to regulate scientific and technological activities because of narrow interpretations of constitutional powers. The congressional role in science and technology policy changed only incrementally until the 1930s when the Supreme Court expanded the powers of Congress with a more liberal reading of the Founders' intentions. During the past fifty years judicial decisions and presidential acquiescence have allowed Congress increased influence.

Congress also imposes statutory constraints upon itself. Many policies affecting science and technology were delegated by law to the executive branch and independent regulatory agencies, which are beyond the direct or routine control of Congress. These delegations of authority have been justified by Congress's limited time, human resources, expertise, and information to make many specific policy decisions. Delegation also allows lawmakers to insulate themselves politically from those unhappy with agency policies. Although they may be revoked or altered by new statutes, delegated powers, as a practical matter, are quite stable because of organizational inertia and objections from interest groups that are well adjusted to existing practices.

In addition, because "the statutes defining a modern agency's mission no longer map the boundaries of real institutional authority," those laws make it difficult for Congress to oversee and evaluate the implementation of its policies (Yellin 1983, 1303). As late as the mid-1980s, no specific laws on the regulation of genetic engineering existed, so congressional committees coped with a vague policy spread among EPA, the Food and Drug Administration, the National Institutes of Health, and the Department of Agriculture. In an attempt to retain some control over the delegation of policy-making authority to agencies, Congress tried during the 1970s to expand its use of the legislative veto to allow either chamber, or even a committee of the House or Senate, to overturn a presidential or agency decision. In 1983 the Supreme Court imposed the ultimate legal constraint on Congress when it ruled that the legislative veto violates the constitutional separation of the executive and legislative branches by circumventing the prescribed procedure for making and changing laws.

Knowledge and Expertise in Congress

Efforts by generalist legislators to cope with scientific and technological progress have ranged from a nineteenth-century attempt by the New Jersey legislature to ban "the use of X rays in opera glasses" (to protect ladies' privacy) to modern debates about whether X-ray lasers could destroy Soviet missiles (Kevles 1978, 75). Like all policy makers, members of Congress must obey certain rules as immutable laws of nature. Some things they may wish to do—quickly find a cure for cancer, for example, by means of a huge increase in research funds—are impossible even in the absence of budgetary constraints. Although limitations in scientific or technological knowledge sometimes undercut policy goals, legislators need to recognize when scientific or technological advances present new opportunities or new problems requiring public action.

In recent years Congress has tried two general strategies to improve health, safety, and environmental quality: (1) outright prohibition of dangerous or unhealthy products and practices, and (2) "technological transformation," which requires regulators to force technological improvements in products and processes by setting progressively stricter standards in such areas as control of toxic substances and automobile emissions. There has been extensive debate whether members of Congress have produced seriously flawed policies by inflexibly basing them on existing technologies (see, for example, Stewart 1981). Congress has not always avoided (or tried to avoid) the constraints and opportunities of changing science and technology. Is it possible for members of Congress to know enough to make science and technology policy? Do they respect the advice they receive from agencies, their staff, or scientists?

Elected Experts

Few members of Congress have been well trained in science or technology.[2] Former representative Mike McCormack (D-Wash.), a nuclear chemist, explained that "there seems to be a natural selection process in politics so that it is mutually exclusive of being a professional in an outside field. You've got to be schizoid to try both—both careers suffer" (*Congressional Quarterly Weekly Report,* April 7, 1973, 773). Nevertheless, two astronauts, John Glenn (D-Ohio) and Harrison Schmitt (D-N.M.) have been elected to the Senate, and several other members of Congress have had college or occupational experience that made it easier for them to understand scientific and technological issues. (Not all of that experience was beneficial; a Georgia representative and physician, Larry McDonald, was sued for prescribing laetrile to a cancer patient.) In the 99th Congress (1985-1986) only a handful of House members could claim a strong background in science or technology: George Brown (D-Calif.), physics; Ed Zschau (R-Calif.), philosophy of science and statistics; Don Ritter (R-Pa.), metallurgy; Joe Barton (R-Texas), industrial engineering; and William Cobey, Jr. (R-N.C.), chemistry. John Glenn was the only remaining senator with an advanced scientific or technological background. Another four were physicians.

Members of Congress with a strong interest in science and technology policy have occasionally been very critical of their colleagues' level of knowledge. Former representative Charles Mosher (D-Ohio) complained of a "profound, historic strain of Know Nothingism," reflected in Congress's distrust of experts. John Dingell (D-Mich.), chair of the House Energy and Commerce Committee, has suggested that Congress, "with its vast ignorance of scientific matters," should allow EPA to decide which air pollutants to regulate (Carter 1975b, 1276; Taylor 1985). Yet attempts to alleviate such problems have had limited success. A two-day educational seminar at the National Academy of Sciences for newly elected legislators in 1985 drew fewer than a dozen of the forty new members (Sun 1985a).

Apart from their lack of specific training, members are hard pressed by the nature of their job to develop special skills in science and technology policy. A survey by the Library of Congress estimated that the average representative reads for about eleven minutes per day. After all, elected officials are "high achievers; people who have been rewarded for action, and they seek to distinguish themselves in an institution with few rewards for thoughtful reflection or the admission of complexity" (Naismith and Procter 1985, 2).

Congressional Staff

Although members of Congress are unlikely to be scientists or engineers, it is still possible for them to hire well-trained legislative staff to help them formulate and analyze policies with scientific or technological content. A small but increasing number of congressional staff are trained in science and technology.[3] Members of Congress have commented on the role of their staff in investigating science and technology policy issues, drafting legislation, and providing links with outside experts. By applying their training they not only save members large amounts of time but also make it possible for Congress to compete with the expertise found in agencies and the executive branch.

To assist legislators with scientific and technological issues, several scientific associations, such as the American Association for the Advancement of Science, the American Physical Society, the American Chemical Society, and the Institute of Electrical and Electronics Engineers, appoint professional scientists or engineers as Congressional Science Fellows. After working on a staff, usually for one year, many remain as permanent congressional employees when their fellowships end. Their effectiveness is limited, however, by several factors. Former fellows have reported an initial disorientation as they quickly try to adapt to the political environment of Capitol Hill, and members of Congress tend to be less interested in technical arguments than in finding support from authoritative sources for their own positions (Casper 1977).

Congressional staff appear in two major guises. First, they may be employed by individual members of Congress as personal staff. In this role a staff member provides policy analyses and new ideas to a legislator who usually sits on several committees. The staffer then must bear the burden of much of the fragmentation of the legislator's duties, including the obligations of campaigning for reelection. Sen. Jeff Bingaman (D-N.M.), for example, used his American Physical Society fellow (an expert on elementary particle physics) for advice on matters such as Central American policy, arms control, economic development, and polygraph tests (*Congressional Record,* October 5, 1984, S 13769).

Second, scientists and technologists may serve on committee or subcommittee staff where they have somewhat different roles in the policy process. Although they may become involved in the political aspirations of the committee chairs, internal congressional rules limit the overt appropriation of committee staff for campaign work. More important, because committee jurisdictions are narrower than those of members, the staff often develop considerable influence over investigations, hearings, the drafting of bills, and the formulation of policy alternatives from which Congress will choose. They have held seminars, retreats, and specialized briefings for experts and committee members, and they may participate directly in policy formation. In early 1984, for example, congressional staff members met with NASA officials to examine the advantages of developing an Extended Duration Orbiter (a space shuttle able to remain in orbit for twenty days) rather than a space station (U.S. House of Representatives 1984b, 21). Chapter 9 examines a similar episode, staff investigations of problems with the Space Telescope.

Support Agencies

Congress has also provided itself with several organizations capable of supplying expert advice on science and technology. The General Accounting Office (GAO), created in 1921, is frequently asked by members to determine the effects of current or contemplated policies. It assesses the costs and benefits, for example, of operating the Energy Department's nuclear physics accelerator facilities and of converting government laboratories to privately owned facilities. Another support agency is the Science Policy Research Division (SPRD), formed in 1965 within what is now the Congressional Research Service of the Library of Congress. The SPRD studies policy issues and organizes seminars on a variety of scientific and technological topics for members of Congress and their staffs. Since 1974 the Congressional Budget Office (CBO) has analyzed the economic costs and benefits of many government programs, such as pricing policy for space shuttle payloads and tax incentives for R & D.

The most conspicuous congressional effort to improve its access to scientific and technological knowledge is the Office of Technology Assessment (OTA). Proposals for a congressional science and technology office emerged in the 1960s as the social, environmental, and economic effects of R & D rose on the political agenda and increasing billions of dollars were being appropriated for research. Technology assessment has been defined as "policy studies examining the fullest range of impact of the introduction of a new technology or the expansion of a present technology in new or different ways" (Coates 1981, 231). The NSF and executive agencies first used technology assessment during the late 1960s and early 1970s; Congress formally began its own technology assessment program in 1972 by establishing OTA, which was "to provide early indications of the probable beneficial and adverse impacts of the implications of technology." OTA, governed by the Technology Assessment Board (TAB) comprising six representatives and six senators, undertakes studies when requested by congressional committee chairs or by its director.

The tension between political and scientific approaches strongly affected OTA's early years as questions were raised about whether its enabling legislation allowed the office to develop an in-house study capability (entailing a large staff that could be used to some members' advantage). There were also allegations that the first chair of TAB, Sen. Edward Kennedy (D-Mass.), filled OTA positions with persons loyal primarily to him.

Many of OTA's early studies were criticized for their superficiality and tardiness. One of its biggest problems was that it was expected to serve multiple functions—defining the science and technology policy agenda, clarifying issues, providing support for advocates—which led to widely varying uses by members of Congress (Whiteman 1982). Because most of OTA's work comprises complex mixtures of social, political, economic, and technical issues, its directors have needed considerable acumen to avoid political trouble.

By the early 1980s OTA seemed to have found a niche in the congressional system. Its staff of about ninety organizes advisory panels of expert volunteers who oversee OTA's studies. They produce book-length reports, thirty-page summaries, very short, oral briefings (of several minutes) for members, and even one-page memoranda for legislators too busy to delve into details. It published more than 100 reports in its first decade on such diverse topics as drug bioequivalence, rural communications, coal-slurry pipelines, and the effects of nuclear war. More recently it has studied surface mine reclamation, ocean waste disposal, retraining for workers displaced by technology, and the use of agricultural technology to provide food aid for Africa. One indicator of its role appeared in December 1985, when Congress chose OTA over the National Academy of Sciences for a study of the Strategic Defense Initiative and transferred $700,000 for that purpose from defense agencies' budgets.

In the mid-1980s the most common criticism of OTA—as of GAO and SPRD—was that it does not always find the perfect balance between the goals of its political masters in Congress and the goals of objectivity and neutrality that are more common to the scientists and engineers who perform its tasks. It "has to live with the House-Senate conflict, the Republican-Democratic split, liberal-conservative polarization; so that on almost every issue there tends to be disagreement and the director has to walk a tightrope in ten-dimensional space" (Wiesner 1980, 40).

Late in 1985 Congress voted to create another congressional agency, the Biomedical Ethics Board, to assist it on questions with serious ethical implications. Roughly patterned after OTA, it was to begin as a small agency ($150,000 in first year start-up funds) but was asked to examine some very large questions. First on its agenda were to be studies of guidelines for fetal research, treatment of research animals, a definition of death, and the ethical issues in genetic engineering.

Outside Advisers

Congress's search for scientific and technical information extends beyond its staff, its support agencies, or even officials from executive branch agencies. At committee hearings legislators listen to the prepared statements of scientists and engineers from universities, industry, and federal laboratories. They ask questions, discuss issues, and often deliver pointed opinions about the absence or overabundance of detailed information. The committee staff play a major role in selecting the witnesses and may brief the committee members or suggest questions, but much of a hearing on a technical subject consists of outsiders educating members of Congress.

Some legislators also develop personal ties with scientists. Sen. Paul Tsongas (D-Mass.) regularly met for four hours on Sunday mornings with scientists from his home state. He urged scientists to develop such relationships with other legislators since meetings convey not just information, but also concern, watchfulness, and political influence: "If all the pressure is coming one way, even if it is irrational we tend to go that way" (U.S. House of Representatives 1979, 86). It is also important for the experts to appear unanimous since dissent among scientists can be exploited. Sen. Charles Percy (R-Ill.) cited the lack of consensus among nutrition scientists as a serious weakness in a Senate report on nutrition and dietary goals (Orlans 1980, 522). Scientific consensus can also become a tool for forming political agreements. A study of the scientific advice to Congress on the Nuclear Test Ban Treaty of 1963 concluded, "The major importance of scientific advice lay not so much in that it provided the basis of decision as that it helped create a political consensus in favor of the decision" (Uyehara 1966, 153).

The ease with which outside advice can be exploited politically makes such advice a mixed blessing for Congress. "There is a mismatch between what Congress needs and what science perceives that Congress needs" (Curlin 1975, 839). Legislators need information that is useful in creating policies, and that information need not be scientifically sound. Members of Congress also worry about delegating decisions to what a senator in the 1960s referred to as "faceless technocrats in long, white coats" (Price 1965, 57). These worries that experts be "on tap, not on top" symbolize the uneasy relationship between Congress and science. Science needs no external reinforcement because it assesses itself by its own standards. But Congress relies on an unmethodical set of constraints—some self-imposed, but most dictated by political values, the difficulty of governing, the personal costs of being wrong, and also the costs of being right. Even their time frames differ: Congress moves in increments called fiscal years, while science and technology need long, unspecified periods of time to evolve tested truths.[4]

Members of Congress have faith, based on hope, that scientists can provide them with simple answers. Scientists have hope, based on faith and training, that much remains for them to discover. What they share is a particular type of ignorance. Most legislators have a poor understanding of how science works, and many scientists fail to comprehend political complexity.

Congress and Coordination

"Congress in session is Congress on public exhibition, whilst Congress in its committee-rooms is Congress at work," wrote Woodrow Wilson in 1885 (Wilson 1956, 71). The same is true today. The committee system divides the labor of members of Congress, allowing them to specialize and develop expertise in a few of the many substantive policy areas that Congress addresses. The advantages of committee fragmentation are important in the realm of science and technology policy since few members of Congress have relevant skills or experience. The committee system also reflects the varied constituencies of the legislators. It makes sense for Rep. Michael A. Andrews (D-Texas), whose district includes the 10,000 federal and contract employees at the Johnson Space Center in Houston, to serve on the House Science and Technology Committee where legislation affecting the space program is considered. It is efficient also for the congressional process to allow members with particular experience or interest in science and technology policy to act as entrepreneurs for that type of policy.

With the benefits of fragmentation come problems of coordination. If congressional committees and their members are centrifugal forces, pulling in an infinite number of directions, then the House and Senate leadership must act as the centripetal force that pulls the efforts of committees and individual members back to a center. Broad issues of policy can be lost as narrow scientific or technological questions are discussed. A rigid allocation of particular subjects to committees causes not only jurisdictional gaps that allow some issues to be overlooked, but also overlaps that can result in turf battles between committees.

Science and Technology Committees

The 99th Congress included 22 standing committees in the House of Representatives and 16 standing committees in the Senate, along with more than 200 subcommittees, 7 select committees, and 4 joint committees. The dominant committees in science and technology policy are the House Science and Technology Committee and the Senate Commerce, Science and Transportation Committee, each of which is divided into numerous specialized subcommittees (see Table 2-1). Nearly all congressional committees, however, can influence various aspects of science and technology policy as they authorize new programs and expenditures. The House and Senate Judiciary committees consider antitrust exemptions for joint R & D ventures by corporations; the agriculture committees investigate the implications of

Table 2-1 Science Committees and Subcommittees of the 99th Congress
(1985-1986)

Committee		Number of Members[a]
Senate Committee on Commerce, Science and Transportation		17
Subcommittees	Aviation	7
	Business, Trade, and Tourism	3
	Communications	9
	Consumer	3
	Merchant Marine	7
	Science, Technology, and Space	7
	Surface Transportation	9
	National Ocean Policy Study[b]	9
House Committee on Science and Technology		41
Subcommittees	Energy Development and Applications	19
	Energy Research and Production	10
	Investigations and Oversight	8
	Natural Resources, Agriculture Research and Environment	12
	Science, Research and Technology	11
	Space Science and Applications	15
	Transportation, Aviation and Materials	8

Source: Congressional Quarterly Inc., *99th Congress Committees 1985-86* (Washington, D.C.: Congressional Quarterly Inc., 1985), 32-33, 70-72.

[a] Data show the number of senators or representatives on each committee. A committee member may serve on more than one subcommittee.
[b] Not a subcommittee to which legislation is referred.

biotechnology for crop production; military R & D is within the jurisdiction of the Armed Services committees, and so on. The Appropriations committees of both chambers (and especially their relevant subcommittees) have jurisdiction over all federal spending for science and technology.

The efficiency gained by dividing the labor for science and technology policy among many committees is partially offset by a profound problem. Division of labor in large organizations succeeds best when it occurs within a hierarchy with clear lines of authority. It is difficult to coordinate science and technology policies when disparate and loosely joined committees have jurisdiction over its many aspects.

A vivid example of divided jurisdiction is nuclear energy policy. In the House of Representatives nuclear energy falls within the jurisdiction of the Interior Committee (budget authorization for the Nuclear Regulatory Commission), the Energy and Commerce Committee (regulation of nuclear facilities), and the Science and Technology Committee (nuclear research). In the Senate nuclear policy is most relevant to the committees on Energy and Natural Resources (energy development), Environment and Public Works (nuclear safety), and Governmental Affairs (nuclear waste storage). Nuclear issues are also partially within the jurisdiction of the armed services, government operations, and foreign relations committees of the House and Senate. Within each chamber, conflicting bills have been reported by these committees (Woodhouse 1983). In addition to contradictions, jurisdictional problems lead to delays. Largely because four congressional committees had jurisdiction over NSF, for example, its 1986 reauthorization—the first in five years—was preceded by confusion about congressional intent and doubts about the legitimacy of some NSF programs. In the absence of central congressional authority, influence over science and technology policy gravitates toward the executive branch where a hierarchy of authority is clear (Price 1965, chap. 7).

In spite of such problems attempts to rationalize congressional organization for science and technology also face obstacles. A lengthy experiment in centralized jurisdiction was the Joint Committee on Atomic Energy (JCAE). Created in 1946, it comprised nine members from each the House and the Senate and virtually dictated policy for both military and civilian atomic energy. By combining the tasks of promoting and regulating atomic energy in the JCAE, however, Congress jeopardized both tasks. Having nearly a monopoly over atomic energy policy, the joint committee was able, for example, to push harder for the development of civilian nuclear power reactors than was economically justified; and in its desire to share the benefits of nuclear power worldwide, it supported an Atoms for Peace program that led to a proliferation of the number of reactors in underdeveloped countries (Price 1965, 225). Congress abolished the JCAE in 1976 and spread its duties among several other committees.

Trade-offs are inherent in any attempts to improve the coordination of congressional policy making. Just as centralization reduces the scope of input into policy formulation, fragmentation and duplication help to reduce the possibility of overlooking or misinterpreting some vital aspects of science and technology policy. If a bill is obstructed in one committee, it may be possible for another to act independently on the same subject.

A corresponding problem might be called "underlapping" jurisdiction. Even with rather loose definitions of the purview of each committee, a chance remains that some topics will not fit into any committee's jurisdiction because of their novelty, breadth, or complexity. For a topic such as genetic engineering, which cuts across many traditional areas of concern, "problems have become more interrelated and it has become increasingly difficult to isolate particular issues without spilling over into other policy areas. As a result new, more complex issues are less amenable to congressional action" (Blank 1981, 133).

Entrepreneurs and Ad Hoc Groups

Because the committee structure can impede the coordination of science and technology policy making in Congress, other mechanisms are important. First, individual members of Congress, even freshmen serving their first terms, can investigate topics, initiate legislation, and publicize issues. These opportunities are especially useful in policy areas where few members have the interest or expertise to devote much time to new complex issues. In 1981, for example, a junior representative, Albert Gore (D-Tenn.), became a congressional authority on many science issues by holding hearings on topics such as genetic screening in the workplace. Later, as a senator, he asked the American Society for Microbiology to organize a national symposium titled Engineered Organisms in the Environment.

Similarly, programs need defenders, particularly if they include policies that legislators are more likely to perceive as pork-barrel issues than as complex scientific or technological questions. Rep. Marilyn Lloyd (D-Tenn.) explained that budget cuts in the magnetic fusion energy program were primarily due to the absence of "champions" on the House and Senate Appropriations committees (Lloyd 1985). "In the U.S. Congress, the path to success (and to reelection) seems more and more to lie in becoming a 'lay expert' in a certain policy area and then appearing to be in good communication with a certain cadre of experts from the private sector" (Brooks 1984, 48).

Members of Congress also attempt to organize their interests in ad hoc groups or caucuses, which circulate information and study legislative proposals on specific issues. Among the more than sixty informal groups in the early 1980s were several directly relevant to science and technology policy. The Congressional Space Caucus, for example, with a bipartisan membership of 143 in 1985, sponsored a three-day conference, The Future of Space Science, to give scientists an opportunity to educate members and their staffs about priorities in astronomical research. Similarly, the Congressional Caucus for Science and Technology sponsored white papers and organized symposia. Although the effect of these groups is indirect and limited (primarily to providing information and contacts), they show that the structure and coordination of the committee system leaves some large gaps.

Politics and Science in Congress

Political pressures affect science and technology policy not only because of its fundamental relevance to other politically charged policy areas such as energy and defense, but also because of the importance of tens of billions of R & D dollars for researchers and their communities. A policy that is in accord with law and the Constitution, that is well planned and coordinated, and that violates no natural laws can still fail if it conflicts with political realities. In fact, the most important aspect for the success of a policy may simply be that it does not conflict with political realities. Because Congress is a political institution, it "is under no obligation to analyze the factual predicate for its legislation" (Bruff 1984, 240).

Pork-barrel Pressures

Some things never change. In science, that perception leads to theories and laws; in political life, it is the basis for common sense and, frequently, cynicism. One of the most obvious of the constant forces in Congress is "pork-barrel" politics: providing publicly financed largess to grateful constituents and voters. When the wealthy English chemist James Smithson bequeathed his entire estate in 1829 "to the United States of America, to found at Washington, under the name of Smithsonian Institution, an establishment for the increase and diffusion of knowledge among men," a debate raged in Congress for a decade over whether Smithson's institute would be a university, a museum, a library, or a source of research funds. Educators and academics "made haste to proffer their pet educational projects for the munificent aid of the windfall request" (Dupree 1957, 66, 68).

One hundred and fifty years later a scientific advisory panel recommended that the Department of Energy stop construction of the Colliding Beam Accelerator (or "Isabelle") facility at the Brookhaven National Laboratory on Long Island, New York (though hundreds of millions of dollars had already been spent on it) partly because of technical problems and partly because a European research institute had already surpassed Isabelle's atom-smashing capabilities. Although physicists were warned that legislators from New York would be reluctant to vote for new experiments in other states after the cancellation, they wanted the high-energy physics budget to be reallocated to more promising projects. The forces that had delayed the Smithsonian Institution were not manifestations of Andrew Jackson's era alone.

Sometimes members of Congress propose methods of allocating research funds that defy logic. In 1965 a representative from Michigan proposed that NASA's budget authorization require that half the funds for the *Voyager* project (an unmanned spacecraft to explore the outer solar system) be awarded to companies in states then receiving small percentages of NASA R & D funds; at the time, California was receiving about half of NASA's contract dollars. The head of NASA responded that such geographical distribution was simply impossible, prompting a member of Congress to dispute the idea that contracts should be placed "where the competence is" (Jachim 1971, 91).

Lobbying over particular scientific and technological projects can be intense. After a bitter fight in Congress from 1963 to 1967 about the location

of the billion-dollar Fermilab particle accelerator, President Lyndon Johnson claimed that he "devoted more personal time to this problem than to
any nondefense question that came up during the budget process" (Greenberg 1967, 263). Members of Congress were joined by governors, mayors,
newspapers, and others in their efforts to have the facility built in
their community. It was eventually built just outside Chicago but only
after intense lobbying from legislators who wanted the economic benefits
for their constituents and after protests from civil rights groups because
of segregated housing patterns in the county where the facility was to be
built (Lowi and Ginsberg 1976; Jachim 1971). Similar lobbying occurred in
the 1980s for the Superconducting Supercollider (SSC), a far more powerful
atom-smasher costing billions of dollars. Texas, Illinois, California, and
many other states spent millions of dollars in their efforts to attract the
SSC, whose future had become clouded by budget-cutting moves in the mid-
1980s.

Most science and technology projects are smaller, of course. In these
cases scientists can be more influential; it has been said that "scientific
research is the only pork barrel for which the pigs determine who gets the
pork" (Greenberg 1967, 151). Yet when it comes to support for their
projects, researchers and their institutions cannot claim total objectivity. For
example, a proposal by the Pentagon (which spent more than $5 billion in
1985 on computer software) to create a $100-million, university-based
Software Engineering Institute caused competing schools to hire professional
lobbyists to plead their cases, and there were suspicions that the Defense
Department encouraged the pork-barrel lobbying as a way to convince
Congress that the institute deserved funding (Beazley and Wynter 1984, 35;
Pattie 1984).[5]

A major worry in the 1980s is the impetus to such pork-barrel lobbying
caused by the aging research infrastructure of American universities.
Obsolete and decrepit laboratories and instruments, a result of budget
cutbacks and the rapidly increasing costs of scientific equipment, increased
the competition for funds.[6] Some universities consequently bypassed the
traditional peer review decision-making procedures of NSF, NIH, and the
Department of Energy. (This issue is discussed further in Chapter 4). In
1983, rather than subjecting their budget requests to the usual merit-based
evaluations of funding agencies, Catholic University and Columbia University, among other schools, hired a Washington lobbying firm to appeal directly
to members of Congress. Their representatives in Congress were glad to
respond by promoting the requested appropriations, and between 1982 and
1985 fifteen universities received more than $130 million in special appropri-
ations. According to Frank Press, president of the National Academy of
Sciences, the problem was that many of his colleagues could not "resist
special-interest political favoritism that can only hurt the overall scientific
endeavor" (*Congressional Record*, January 3, 1985, E108).

One proposed cure for the problem of science and technology pork-barreling is stronger, more centralized congressional or White House leadership on priorities for R & D funding. Greater cooperation by the scientific community—through a "science budget," for example, that ranks research needs—would make special appeals more difficult to justify. Still, the basic causes of political competition for research funds will not disappear. One fundamental law of both science and politics is that there is never enough money to go around. Another basic principle is that there is no entirely objective way to assign priorities to budget requests. Like Congress, the scientific community has no algorithm for determining whether an investigation of molecular biology is more "valuable" than a study of subatomic quarks.

Insofar as the pork-barrel aspects of "policy for science" (that is, policies to support R & D) are unavoidable, scientific research itself becomes a tool for politics. Even when the scientific community is the only significant group pressuring Congress, the policy process is not, and cannot be, free of political values.

Coalition-Building

As a collective body Congress can act only when a majority agrees or acquiesces. When science and technology policy entail the expenditure of federal funds, the formation of coalitions is crucial. The formation of coalitions for the *application* of knowledge can, however, cause just as much trouble. The manner in which knowledge is interpreted and applied to policy decisions is rarely obvious. If it were, voting coalitions would fall apart more frequently since there would be less of the ambiguity necessary for bargaining. Therefore, coalitions are often stymied or broken apart because of disputes, such as which data are to be considered relevant and how much uncertainty is allowable. In short, congressional decisions can be based on expertise or ignorance and motivated by strategic voting or straightforward pork barreling.

The practical implications of this indeterminacy are everywhere in the legislative process. It is not, for example, a tautology to point out that the more controversial a proposal, the more difficult it is to form a successful co-alition, for the reverse may be true. The multibillion-dollar Clinch River Breeder Reactor program was supported by a strange coalition including the nuclear industry, eighteen labor unions, the National Association for the Advancement of Colored People, the U.S. Chamber of Commerce, and the National Association of Manufacturers. The project's opponents included the League of Women Voters, liberal groups such as the Sierra Club, and conservative groups such as the National Taxpayers Union (Katz 1984, 53). Some based their positions on technical data about the safety of breeder reactors and the proliferation of nuclear weapons using the plutonium that breeders produce; others focused on jobs and economic opportunities. No consensus on scientific or technological questions was required. Other science and technology policy issues have also been elevated above controversy by their larger ramifications. The Apollo program was justified as much by foreign and military policy as on scientific grounds (Logsdon 1970, chap. 5).

For some science and technology policy issues, no compromise seems possible, especially those with strong moral or religious implications. Controversies about issues such as the educational curriculum Man: A Course of Study and the teaching of evolution in public schools have no middle ground because they raise deep questions about the implications of anthropology and natural history for cultural and religious values. Some of the broader questions raised about life manufactured by genetic engineering face a similar problem (Blank 1981). In some cases, the strong views of one group can unwittingly forge a coalition of opponents. An attempt by Sen. Jesse Helms (R-N.C.) in 1981 to legislate a scientific definition of the beginning of human life aroused intense opposition not only from scientists but also from fellow Senate Republicans (Cole 1983, chap. 6).

One more vital participant in the congressional science and technology process is another political institution: the White House. Congress has always been partially constrained by the political ideology and policy preferences of the president. As chapter 3 will show, the executive branch dominates much of the flow of information about science and technology policy to Congress, along with the budget process and agenda setting. Their contests over science and technology policy have become even more important as the costs and ever-widening implications of R & D have increased, and as the number of government institutions with jurisdiction over science and technology has grown.

Conclusion

How well does Congress make science and technology policy? It is slightly easier to assess the quality of the process than the quality of the output. Each of the major types of constraints on the science and technology policy-making process in Congress has varied over time and from one specific issue to another. Nevertheless, some broad generalizations can be made. Uncoordinated fragmentation is a chronic problem, and because science and technology issues are rarely Republican or Democratic issues, party leadership can be counted on only as a weak cohesive force. It is also safe to assume that science and technology expertise in Congress, whether from staff, support agencies, or outside experts, will be politicized.

The core of Congress's problems with science and technology policy making is the issue of expertise. It explains much of such key congressional characteristics as division of labor, vague or quickly obsolescent mandates, reliance on agencies and the executive branch, and staffs growing in size and influence. Because science and technology policy requires the application of knowledge that is alien to most legislators, it is fair to ask whether it is really very different in this regard from say, tax policy or defense policy—which certainly can be complex and unfamiliar to most people. In fact, the distinction of science and technology policy is not its complexity, but its breadth and obscurity. Businessmen and lawyers may have the temperament or training to disentangle the tax laws or the nuances of antitrust regulations, but they will probably lack any reference points for understanding supercomputer architecture or molecular biology. On defense matters much of the complexity and foreignness is absorbed by deference to the commander in chief, generals, and admirals; and the ramifications of losing an ally, because of a frugal defense policy, are far clearer to legislators than the ramifications of losing a Nobel Prize. Although the mystique of white-coated laboratory researchers may have faded, their work has probably become even more incomprehensible to most legislators.

Several approaches to the expertise problem have been offered, but all have weaknesses. One suggestion has been to appoint or hire science advisers for congressional committees. They could filter the enormous amounts of scientific information that are potentially relevant to policy issues within their committees' jurisdiction and assess the reliability and applicability of outside expertise. Because Congress is fragmented into so many committees and subcommittees that deal with science and technology issues, a small army of advisers would be needed, and no mechanism has been suggested for coordinating them into a coherent source of consistent advice. In addition, it is unlikely that legislators would delegate a significant portion of the investigating task (given its importance as a political and a policy tool) to a new hierarchy of staff. In any case, the essential problem is not the absence of in-house expertise. The unavoidable problem for Congress is the balancing of interests.

Another cure might be greater centralization, to combine all relevant policy issues in House and Senate committees that would coordinate science and technology policies; but this solution also poses major problems. First, centralization conflicts with many of the basic characteristics of Congress, including division of labor, overlapping jurisdiction, and the dispersion of political power. It would concentrate jurisdiction over a vast range of congressional policies to a degree currently held by only the Appropriations and Budget committees. Members would not willingly relinquish so much influence.

Proposals for reform of science and technology policy making in Congress must start with an explicit statement of what needs to be fixed. If legislators must be scientists and engineers to be able to make such policies, there is no hope, since only a few will be trained this way. Nor is the problem a lack of information or an unavailability of expertise; to the contrary, there is a surplus of assistance. Similarly, some fragmentation is desirable, and politics cannot be exorcised. Just as the constraints that shape congressional policy making are not fixed, neither can the process be "correct."

The safest prescription for improving congressional policy procedures is unsatisfying to anyone who hopes for a straightforward, parsimonious policy process. What Congress needs is not a restructuring or a lecture on responsibility and public interest, but an electorate that understands the nature of governing. Appeals for a public more informed about science, technology, and their effects on public policy actually miss half of the picture: public stereotypes and misconceptions about politics are as rampant, and easily as damaging, as ignorance of the scientific method. "Special interest group" carries the tone of condemnation, "compromise" is presented as defeat, and "politics" suggests shady dealings. The essence of congressional policy making for science and technology is *balancing:* of vague mandates and specific requirements, of pluralist disintegration and reasoned consistency, of scientific rationalization and scientific uncertainty, and of diverse political values. Specific reforms could help the process, but only if they are consistent with the fundamental genetic and environmentally reinforced nature of the institution.

Notes

1. For this reason Aaron Wildavsky has suggested that "risk-benefit analysis and risk assessment are not appropriate" approaches for congressional decision making (U.S. House of Representatives 1979, 17).
2. A study in the mid-1960s found that only 2 percent of members of Congress had science or engineering backgrounds, compared with 19 percent of higher civil servants (Ripley and Franklin 1976, 25).
3. About 1 percent of congressional professional employees in 1977 were scientists, but that was double the proportion in 1970 (U.S. Senate 1976, 37).
4. Philip Handler, former president of the National Academy of Sciences, commented: "There is no relation between the useful life of a laboratory or scientific project and the time required for the Earth to complete one orbit around the Sun" (Lakoff 1974, 598).
5. Carnegie-Mellon University received the contract, leading Pittsburgh officials to describe their city as "the next Silicon Valley."
6. It was estimated that the cost of starting a synthetic organic chemistry laboratory increased from $116,500 in 1970 to $741,000 in 1979 (Association of American Universities 1980, 15).

3

The President and the Executive Office in the Policy Process

In his 1950 State of the Union message to Congress, Harry Truman called for the peaceful development of atomic energy and asked Congress to pass legislation creating a National Science Foundation (NSF). In 1958 Dwight Eisenhower spoke of the importance of exchanging scientific and technological information with "friendly countries" and announced that he would seek a doubling of NSF's budget. Four years later John Kennedy promoted the nascent space program as "a new frontier of science, commerce, and cooperation." Richard Nixon used his 1972 State of the Union address to call for "a new program of Federal partnership in technological research and development," and in 1979 Jimmy Carter promised to continue the nation's support for health, energy, defense, environmental, and astronomical R & D. In his State of the Union addresses Ronald Reagan spoke of his support for America's high-technology industries, the development of a space station as the Next Frontier, the wonders of subatomic physics, the promise of the Space Telescope, and even the reduced price of transistors.

It has become common for presidents to tell members of Congress that science and technology are vital to economic growth and national security, and therefore high on their administrations' agendas. But what do they know about such matters, and how do they obtain information about complex scientific and technological issues? Off-the-record accounts of President Reagan's decision to advocate the Strategic Defense Initiative (SDI, or "Star Wars") suggest that it was preceded by consultations with only a few scientists. The top experts in his own administration learned of the largest weapons-research program in history only a short time before SDI's televised unveiling: the White House science adviser was informed five days before the speech; the secretary of state and the Joint Chiefs of Staff, two days before; and the chief Pentagon scientist, nine hours before. This case vividly illustrates a common concern about science and technology policy making in presidential administrations. Given the structure of the presidency, along with the incentives and limitations facing the president and his top advisers, how are such decisions made?

Presidents have always been important figures in shaping science and technology policy, but the burgeoning of the federal research establishment after World War II has caused that influence to grow. Their control of information from the domestic and foreign policy bureaucracies, coupled with their political prominence, give them a special ability to shape the political agenda. Congress often waits for a sign of presidential agreement before acting on a legislative proposal. Similarly, a mere hint of White House support can be parlayed into legislative influence. A representative who solicited a letter from Jimmy Carter promising a review of magnetic fusion technology was able to use the letter to get both Congress and the bureaucracy moving on the program (Heppenheimer 1984). The president's domination of the policy process is hardly complete, however. Congress ignored Carter when he indicated his strong opposition to the Clinch River Breeder Reactor project. To understand the president's influence in science and technology policy, it is necessary to consider the relevant powers and limitations of the office.

Presidents and the Law

Like Congress, the president can do only what the Constitution either requires or does not forbid. Article II does not mention science or technology among presidential responsibilities, but the executive powers included in the Constitution have allowed presidents to develop an active role in science and technology policy making. Although Congress, the bureaucracy, and the courts may impede him through statutory and other devices, the president can usually find ways of skirting those obstacles.

Constitutional Powers

Foreign Policy.   As commander in chief of American armed forces, the president can take a wide range of actions in the name of protecting the national security with Congress acting as only a partial constraint. Although presidents must have the cooperation of Congress in authorizing and funding the development of new weapons systems, they usually get most of what they request. In addition, much of the R & D budget is invisible to the public and even to most members of Congress. Of about $40 billion in defense R & D in fiscal year 1987, nearly one-fourth of the funds were for classified programs that could not be discussed or debated outside the Pentagon.

The president's authority to restrict the flow of scientific and technological information affecting national security has become more controversial as the dependence of the military on sophisticated technology has grown.

Presidents Carter and Reagan have made it easier for the government to classify basic scientific research as secret, and recent changes in export control legislation have tightened restrictions on the export of technical information about weapons, armaments, or "militarily critical" technologies. In the absence of clear boundaries between national security and free speech, conflicts are inevitable (Ferguson 1985). The Reagan administration has been criticized for contending that scientific conferences, student exchanges, and the open publication of technical literature play into the hands of the Soviet Union, yet there can be little doubt that the export of sophisticated American technology poses commercial and military problems (Dickson 1984; Carey 1982).

As the constitutional head of state the president oversees negotiations leading to international treaties affecting, or affected by, science and technology. These have included topics as disparate as technical standards for communications satellites, cooperation in the seismic detection of underground nuclear tests, and understandings with the Soviets on tracking the migration of snow geese. That science can play a special role in international relations was demonstrated by the Antarctic Treaty, negotiated in 1959 by twelve nations (including the United States and the Soviet Union) at the height of the Cold War. The treaty outlawed military bases and weapons testing in areas south of sixty degrees south latitude and stipulated the exchange of scientific information and personnel among signatory nations. Although not completely sovereign, an international scientific committee has successfully governed the continent for nearly thirty years.

Domestic Policy.   The president also has an important constitutional function in the legislative process: he may recommend legislation to Congress, and he may choose whether to sign bills into law or to veto them. The process of recommending policies usually entails far more than a brief mention during a State of the Union speech. A science or technology policy may be formally introduced in Congress by a member of the House or Senate as an Executive Request (such as Gerald Ford's proposal that led to the National Science and Technology Policy, Organization, and Priorities Act of 1976), but it is more common for members of the president's administration to press Congress for new or changed policies through informal channels or testimony at hearings. In pursuit of these legislative goals the White House can usually recruit allies from the public, industry, interest groups, and sometimes even foreign nations. European technology companies, for example, not wanting to be left out of the R & D windfall flowing from Reagan's Strategic Defense Initiative, urged their governments to endorse the American defensive weapon proposal, which had the effect of putting pressure on Congress to fund Reagan's requests.

The president's constitutional veto power has been used to shape both general and specific science and technology policies. Harry Truman vetoed the first congressional attempt to create the National Science Foundation in 1947 because its directors, though ostensibly executive officers, were too insulated from the president: the foundation "would be divorced from control by the people to an extent that implies a distinct lack of faith in dem-ocratic processes" (Penick 1972, 135). Three years later Congress offered Truman an NSF whose organization and structure he approved. It is more common for presidents to use the veto on specific matters. In 1984, for example, Ronald Reagan vetoed legislation that would have established new arthritis and nursing institutes within the National Institutes of Health (NIH), arguing (with NIH's agreement) that Congress had tried to create "unnecessary, expensive new organizational entities" and that the bill would have usurped the president's authority to set policy for NIH (Norman 1984, 811). The veto is blunt, however, and because many acts of Congress include provisions that presidents would rather keep (for political or policy reasons, or because Congress may be likely to override the veto), this legislative tool is not frequently used.

Presidents have two additional functions that allow them to affect science and technology policy. First, they have the power to appoint the top administrators of most federal offices, or, if required, to nominate them for Senate confirmation, which is usually forthcoming. By this device presidents not only can select men and women of compatible ideology to manage government programs, but also can send a message to Congress and civil servants about policy changes to expect. For example, when Jimmy Carter (who had taken a strong position against nuclear energy) had the opportunity to name a director of the Energy Department's energy research program, his choice was a man with experience in nuclear fusion:

> To pick a man with a strong nuclear background would raise controversy and would send the wrong signal to Carter's antinuclear constituency. Also, it might well be seen as a softening of his position on nuclear energy. Fusion, by contrast, offered people who had appropriate backgrounds and expertise, but who would not pose these political problems (Heppenheimer 1984, 223).

In addition, as chief executive the president is responsible for carrying into execution the laws passed by Congress. Constitutional scholars have not completely resolved the debate over the precise meaning of "he shall take Care that the Laws be faithfully executed." Presidents judge the wording more loosely than members of Congress, of course, thereby giving themselves considerable latitude in how and when laws are implemented. Sometimes that flexibility is politically necessary. When the two-year congressional moratoria on prohibitions against saccharin expired before being renewed, the Food and Drug Administration (FDA) was bound only by the Delaney Amendment's mandate against carcinogenic food additives. Rather than faithfully execute the exact wording of the law, however, FDA chose (with Congress's clear consent) not to act—in accordance with the prevailing political mood.

Statutory Constraints

Although Congress cannot pass a law that infringes on the president's constitutional powers, it can forbid or require certain actions. The Foreign Relations Authorization Act of 1979, for example, instructed the executive branch to submit a yearly report to Congress on international science and technology activities, and the 1980 Energy Security Act required the president's Department of Energy to cooperate with the National Academy of Sciences on a study of the climatic effects of increased carbon dioxide in the atmosphere. Congress also influences the organization of the executive branch. Under the Reorganization Act of 1939 the president must submit proposed changes to Congress for its approval. President Reagan was not able to disband completely the Council on Environmental Quality—part of the Executive Office of the President—because of its statutory basis, though its professional staff was nearly eliminated.

Similarly, Congress can attempt to restrict the president's discretion over federal spending by appropriating funds for specific purposes, but for several major reasons statutes are not rigid constraints on presidential control over science and technology policy. First, because the president's budget and program requests to Congress often begin the legislative process, his initial proposals can shape whatever action Congress finally takes. If presidential budget requests include large cuts in funding for particular programs, members of Congress will have to fight merely to keep budgets at current levels. Another advantage for the executive branch is its role in administering programs and funding. At the end of 1984 the Office of Management and Budget (OMB), for example, ordered NIH to begin allocating all of the money for multi-year research grants in the first year of funding, which had the effect of cutting the 6,500 NIH grants for which Congress had provided to only 5,000; after an intense budget fight, 6,200 grants were finally authorized (Culliton 1985).

After congressional legislating and appropriating is completed, presidents can delay spending or simply refuse to spend the mandated funds. Deferrals and impoundments of expenditures have frequently angered members of Congress, especially when a president alters their legislated priorities. In 1972, for example, the White House announced that because the employment market did not justify $30 million in funds for NSF science education programs (more than half of congressional appropriations for these programs), it was impounding the legislated funds. The 1974 Budget and Impoundment Control Act imposed some rather weak limitations on the withholding of expenditures, but since Richard Nixon, presidents have used impoundments more delicately anyway. Finally, as discussed in Chapter 2, it is often difficult for Congress to make specific laws because of changing circumstances, inadequate knowledge, or poor congressional control over a recalcitrant bureaucracy or president. As a result, the executive branch bureaucracy has a large amount of maneuvering room within the constraints imposed by Congress.

The president can also control an enormous amount of science and technology policy making through Executive Orders, which usually have the force of law though they are not passed by Congress. Executive Order 12291, for example, signed by Ronald Reagan in February 1981, requires nearly all federal agencies to prepare cost-benefit analyses for "major" regulations. Most science and technology policies were affected by this order as agencies now faced the tasks of finding common metrics, quantifying, and measuring the economic costs and benefits of new technologies, health risks, and so on. Although the chief executive's centralized control over the executive branch gives the president an advantage in science and technology policy making through such devices as cost-benefit requirements, impoundments, and agenda control, it also creates problems as he attempts to use the huge quantities of complex information to shape his programs.

Knowledge in the White House

What can presidents possibly know about science and technology policy? George Washington was something of a civil engineer, Jefferson was a self-made expert on nearly everything, Herbert Hoover was a patent-holding mining engineer, and Jimmy Carter had training in nuclear engineering. No modern scientists, few engineers. Even worse, the men who have occupied the Oval Office sometimes have believed things that were not true. Theodore Roosevelt swore that saccharin was perfectly safe because his physician gave it to him daily as an elixir, and he referred to "biological laws" of genetics to justify calls for selective breeding of humans and tighter immigration laws (Priebe and Kauffman 1980, 558; Kevles 1985, 85). President Eisenhower, speaking at a press conference only days after the 1957 launch of *Sputnik,* predicted that "given time, satellites will be able to transmit to the earth some kind of information with respect to what they see on the earth . . . but I think that that period is a long ways off" (Penick 1972, 257). By mid-1963 the satellite Tiros had returned more than a quarter of a million photographs of weather patterns to earth. During the 1980 presidential campaign, candidate Ronald Reagan commented on evolution: "I think that recent discoveries down through the years have pointed up great flaws in it" (Holden 1980, 1214).

Although presidents may not know much about genetics or space technology, they do, however, have an idea of what policies they want and how to get them. They may not discuss the advancement of basic scientific knowledge as a major part of their political programs, but they are conscious of the importance of scientific and technological knowledge to their other political and policy aims. Thus, for the White House, science and technology have usually been instruments of policy, not policy goals. As a result, presidents' sources of knowledge about science and technology have traditionally been excluded from the inner circle of advisers.

Science Advisers

Every executive department except Treasury has a separate office for R & D. The departments' proposals for science and technology policies compete with social, economic, and other problems for the president's attention. Even within the area of science and technology policy the White House is subjected to conflicting pressures and demands from industry, the academic community, scientific and "public interest" associations (such as environmental groups), Congress, and the executive branch itself. The president not only needs translation of scientific and technological knowledge into terms he can understand; he also needs an information filter.

As secretary of state in 1790 Thomas Jefferson was responsible for administering the new patent law; when he was personally unable to assess the novelty and usefulness of inventions, he asked professors from the University of Pennsylvania for help. As president he created the Coast Survey and hired a Swiss scientist to provide research to aid navigation. Presidents since Jefferson also have turned to outside experts as needed, but as the interactions between science, technology, and the president's responsibilities grew, so did the need for a permanent presence of science advice in the White House.

The first personal science adviser to a president was Vannevar Bush, who informally assisted Franklin Roosevelt during World War II. Presidents Truman and Eisenhower had a Science Advisory Committee, which gradually became involved in matters of national defense. The launching of the Soviet satellite *Sputnik* in October 1957 prodded Eisenhower into forming the President's Science Advisory Committee (PSAC) and appointing the first full-time science adviser, James Killian, Jr. Since then all presidents have had science advisers, though their functions have varied according to the interests of their employers.

Presidential science advisers have an inherently difficult job, as they must perform a variety of functions. In its current incarnation the White House science advisory office is responsible for:

1. Advising the president and other parts of the Executive Office
2. Assisting the Office of Management and Budget with analyses of proposed R & D budgets for federal agencies
3. Coordinating federal R & D programs
4. Aiding in cooperation among federal, state, and local governments and with the scientific community
5. Communicating science and technology policies of the executive branch to Congress (Katz 1980, 229)

These multiple duties create tensions that complicate the advisory role. For example, science advisers have usually been prominent scientists (most commonly physicists) with strong academic records, which they are reluctant to jeopardize by engaging in blatantly one-sided political activity; yet their effectiveness in the White House rests on the president's reliance on their complete loyalty. They must be "a part of the president's mind-set" or they risk having their advice ignored, or even (as occurred under Richard Nixon) having their science advisory office abolished (Rabi 1980, 16). At the same time it has been equally important for them to be accountable to the scientific community. Science advisers' usefulness to presidents depends on their access to other scientists, which in turn depends on the respect of their peers—which derives more from the image of sympathetic, or at least informed, neutrality than from being a political hack.

The President's Science Advisory Committee.   From its creation in 1957 until its termination in 1973, PSAC had a significant role in the executive branch. It was deliberately and distinctly nonmilitary. Eisenhower made clear his desire to use PSAC to help him choose between the weapons development proposals of the competing armed services, and it demonstrated its civilian focus by urging that the new space program be organized under the civilian National Aeronautics and Space Administration (NASA) rather than under one of the military services, which already had rocket programs under way. Composed of eighteen scientists and engineers from outside the government (meeting two days a month for their four-year terms), PSAC was intended to inform and advise the science adviser, who was usually "able to adjust the final advice [to the president] to recommendations that were technically feasible and politically acceptable" (Averch 1985, 116).

PSAC usually operated through the appointment of a specialized panel after a significant science or technology problem was brought to its attention (as when the hazards of pesticides were publicized in Rachel Carson's *Silent Spring*). But even in its early years science advice in the White House had distinctly political functions as well. For example, Jerome Wiesner, science adviser and close friend to President Kennedy, "didn't offer PSAC an opportunity" to argue against the manned lunar program; he knew that the scientists opposed it (because it was not "good science") and that the president had decided in favor of it on political grounds (Wiesner 1980, 35). Under the direction of Wiesner, PSAC grew in influence.

The Office of Science and Technology.   As perceptions of the importance of science and technology grew during the early 1960s, Congress pressed for a statutory basis for PSAC, which would release it from the shield of executive privilege and allow access to the science adviser for confirmation and questioning. In response, and to deflect growing pressure to establish a separate Department of Science and Technology, in 1962 President Kennedy created the Office of Science and Technology (OST) within the Executive Office of the President. OST had its own staff of about two dozen professionals, a congressional budget, and a director to be confirmed by Congress. (The director was also the chair of PSAC.) The office was created not only to provide science and technology advice to the president but also to help coordinate the R & D activities of various federal agencies.

According to Donald Hornig, Lyndon Johnson's science adviser, OST was surprisingly effective at developing the personal contacts with White House staff that are so vital to being effective in presidential policy making. As the influence of OST staff grew, however, the office became fragmented and its power diluted, for "individual staff members frequently found greater satisfaction in personal impacts within their areas of expertise than in contributing to shaping major issues" (Hornig 1980, 50). Under Richard Nixon OST became insulated from the president, and the Executive Office began using political tests to screen appointments to advisory committees. The scientific community became increasingly cynical about Nixon's commitment to science and technology after he declared a "War on Cancer," called for energy independence by 1980, promoted a major coal gasification project, and advocated a modified antiballistic missile system—all either without expert advice or contrary to the advice of OST and his own science advisers.

Two examples illustrate the failure of science advice in the Nixon White House. In July 1971 John Ehrlichman, Nixon's assistant for domestic affairs, proposed the New Technology Opportunities (NTO) program as a way of addressing America's social and economic problems through "technological fixes."

> First, the government was to provide money for basic research under three circumstances: (1) if such research would lead to new industries, e.g., sea mining, desalinization processes, and energy conversion units; (2) if there were potentially high profits expected from the research, yet the profitability could not be recaptured by the particular firm paying for the R & D; (3) if research would lead to a new exportable product. Second, industry and government should be drawn to closer cooperation through mutual research ventures. Third, technology should be applied to solve social and institutional problems (Katz 1978, 205-206).

Management of the program was placed outside OST, and the programs that NTO envisioned (for example, weather modification, computerized traffic control, and crowd control drugs) were quickly gutted for budgetary reasons by the Office of Management and Budget.

The other example marked a major turning point in science and technology policy. Proposals for a supersonic transport aircraft (SST), debated on and off since 1959, were strongly promoted by the Nixon administration. The many analyses of the SST had produced inconclusive findings about its effect on noise and air pollution and conflicting estimates of its net economic cost. When a PSAC panel headed by IBM physicist Richard Garwin recommended in 1969 that the SST project be stopped, its report was buried, and a summary of only the favorable SST studies was sent to Congress. According to Garwin, "Administration spokesmen in formal testimony concealed relevant information and lied to Congressional committees," so in 1972 he offered his version to Congress without asking the permission of Nixon or PSAC (Garwin 1980, 127). Early in 1973, Nixon abolished PSAC and OST. Nixon's science adviser, Edward David, later recalled that "the White House advisers to Mr. Nixon thought that the scientists were using science as a sledgehammer to grind their political axes" (Hechler 1980, 614). The task of advising on civilian R & D fell, uncomfortably, to the director of the NSF; the task of advising on military R & D moved to the National Security Council. Science was formally out of the White House (see Beckler 1974).

The Return of Science Advisers.   Soon after assuming the presidency Gerald Ford began working to reestablish a science advisory office in the White House, this time with a firm statutory basis. His interest in science and technology policy was strengthened by his years on congressional committees with R & D jurisdiction, and as a representative he occasionally had been briefed by scientists from his congressional district. Ford assigned Vice-President Nelson Rockefeller to the task of working with Congress on suitable legislation, and Rockefeller became the first vice-president in history to testify (as a "guest," not as a precedent-setting "witness") before a congressional committee. In 1976 the National Science and Technology Policy, Organization, and Priorities Act created the Office of Science and Technology Policy (OSTP) with a director subject to Senate confirmation and a mandate to perform both short-term and long-term policy studies. The statute vested a responsibility for planning national science policy in OSTP, defined as "anticipating future concerns to which science and technology can contribute and devising strategies for the conduct of science and technology for such purposes ... [and] reviewing systematically Federal science policy and programs and recommending legislative amendment thereof when needed" (Public Law 94-282).

Within a few years, however, a study by the General Accounting Office (GAO) found that OSTP's efforts at strategic planning had been constrained by several factors, such as competition from planners within agencies, the lack of information and control over some policy areas, and the tendency to think in four-year cycles—the length of presidential terms (U.S. House of Representatives 1980, 230). As a consequence, under Presidents Ford and Carter, OSTP suffered a fate similar to that of its predecessors: some questioned its usefulness and called for its abolition, while others defended the idea—if not the record—of a science presence in the White House. Carter's science adviser, geophysicist Frank Press, successfully urged the president to increase defense R & D spending, but he objected in vain to Carter's plan to pump huge federal subsidies into the development of commercial technologies, such as solar energy demonstration projects.

In some respects there was a surprisingly small change in the direction of OSTP advice, particularly on technological development, with the advent of the Reagan administration. The Reagan White House openly espoused an ideology that found sharp boundaries between the R & D roles of the public and private sectors. Moreover, Ronald Reagan's science adviser, George Keyworth II, broke from the traditional behavior of his predecessors by playing an openly political function. He spoke out against "mediocre science" resulting from a lack of "hard-nosed discrimination about priorities" and acknowledged that his focus was more on telling the scientific community what the White House had in store than on telling the president what scientists wanted (Barfield 1982, 42-43; *National Journal* 1985).

In addition, the comparison of military and economic benefits against the financial costs of a federal role in R & D became a key element in the Reagan administration's approach to science and technology. Keyworth told Congress in 1983 that the Reagan administration "would look very hard at how science and technology could help advance national well-being" in contrast with "the traditional approach to S & T [Science and Technology] policy—which placed primary emphasis on ensuring the general health and vitality of science and its institutions." The policy of the Reagan administration was "decidedly not science for science's sake" (U.S. House of Representatives 1983a, 13, 9).

Keyworth's greatest visibility came from his very public role in promoting the president's Strategic Defense Initiative. Dissent within OSTP (including the doubts of John Bardeen, who had twice won the Nobel Prize in physics) about the antimissile plan was not passed on to the president, and staff members quit as a result. OSTP did, however, become actively involved in several major studies, such as coordinating an interagency policy on the risks of carcinogens, restricting the export of technical information, and investigating the flaws in agricultural research policies. By the end of Reagan's first term, some in the White House were calling for the abolition of OSTP, in large part because of Keyworth's outspokenness (R. Smith 1984). He resigned at the end of 1985. Six months after Keyworth's resignation in December 1985, Reagan nominated William R. Graham, deputy administrator of NASA, as his new science adviser and head of OSTP. An electrical engineer, Graham had experience in the design and testing of weapons systems and in analyzing supercomputer capabilities.

Given this array of experiences and expert policy advisers, has the presidency been sufficiently well-informed about science and technology to make policy that is consistent with what is known about the processes of the natural and engineered world? The record indicates that presidents have not been misled by their science advisers but that the White House has at times chosen to ignore its science advisers or to cut them out of the policy-making process. It is difficult to know whether Eisenhower was unique in his "exaggerated confidence in the unbiased judgment of the scientists whom he called upon to help him," or whether presidents are more likely to be skeptical of all advice. After all, information and advice easily translate into influence, and according to Edward David, "In a closed system such as the White House, influence is conserved" (Killian 1977, 228, 244). In other words, scientific knowledge must compete with other factors, and there are no guarantees that scientists and technologists will be in agreement.

Coordination of Executive Branch Science and Technology Policy

With about 4,000 government research facilities and many thousands of research contracts, all in pursuit of an enormous variety of knowledge, coordination of the federal science and technology establishment is an immense undertaking, for the individual character of each office and program is balanced with the need for an integrated government approach. Coordination requires much more than simply getting agencies to agree on their goals; it has many components, such as information exchange, sharing of research resources, relating program objectives to national needs, and budget planning (Staats 1980, 83). A member of Congress, despairing of the inability of NASA and the Department of Interior to reach an agreement on patent policy, lamented that he had "always thought Uncle Sam was one person" (U.S. Senate 1981, 43). One response of the executive branch to this challenge has been to establish new offices to oversee and coordinate federal R & D activities.

Councils and Task Forces

The first institutions created to coordinate science and technology policy in the executive branch were Roosevelt's very short-lived Science Advisory Board in the 1930s and Truman's Interdepartmental Committee on Scientific Research and Development. In 1959 President Eisenhower formed the Federal Council on Science and Technology, which enjoyed more cooperation from federal agencies but lacked the resources and the political clout to force agencies into agreement. With the creation of OSTP the coordinating function was brought into conjunction with the budgeting function, thereby increasing the potential for useful coordination. OSTP tended, however, to rely on ad hoc task forces rather than on permanent panels with the effect of fragmenting OSTP oversight. Nixon's science adviser summarized the problems of coordination when he observed that interagency "task forces inevitably are bound by the bureaucratic interests of their agencies. Their results tend to assume a bureaucratic least common denominator" (David 1980, 57).

Given such constraints, coordination of science and technology policy might be better performed by panels of outside experts, but external review tends to be too broad to be useful. Carter's Commission for a National Agenda for the Eighties included a panel called Science and Technology: Promises and Dangers, whose report issued vague recommendations such as "consider new mechanisms for establishing R & D priorities" and "improve relationships among the diverse performers of R & D." Similarly, the Grace Commission advised the Reagan administration to run R & D more like a private corporation with science agencies having more clearly defined goals and more careful strategic planning, but it offered few specific guidelines about how political agencies could define and plan in the same way as profit-seeking corporations. Like science advising, efforts at coordination depend on whether policy makers want to be coordinated (Burger 1980).

The Office of Management and Budget

One of the most important institutions for federal science and technology policy was created in 1921 as the Bureau of the Budget, then reorganized in 1969 with expanded duties as the Office of Management and Budget. As part of the Executive Office of the President, OMB is responsible for preparing the president's budget requests, coordinating the programs and legislative proposals of federal agencies with the president's goals ("legislative clearance"), and overseeing the management of the federal government. Given the inclination of agency officials to want more money and more programs, OMB's most important function is to act as a brake on the speed of government, and so it must be both an adversary and a partner to executive departments and agencies.

Some OMB staff are assigned to science and technology policy as "examiners," each responsible for a type of policy or a particular government office. Sophisticated training is not unusual for persons in these positions; in the OMB office that reviewed the programs of the Department of Energy in the late 1970s, five of the seven examiners had Ph.D's, including degrees in physics and astrophysics (Heppenheimer 1984, 226). Nevertheless, in part because the small teams of OMB analysts cannot match the breadth of expertise found in agencies such as FDA and NSF, there have been frequent criticisms of OMB interference with the scientific justifications of proposed agency actions. OMB staff evaluate the budget requests and policy proposals of the science and technology agencies, consulting with agency planners when necessary, and their analyses and recommendations are then passed up through OMB's managing directors to the director of OMB and eventually, if necessary to resolve a dispute, to the president.

Although OMB is a crucial part of the policy process, its deliberations are usually closed to outsiders, including the press, the public, and even members of Congress. Its decisions can have far-reaching implications for science and technology policies. For example, in 1963 its director ordered the head of NSF to stop making further financial commitments on the ill-fated Mohole project (designed to drill a hole through the earth's crust) because of enormous cost overruns (Greenberg 1967, chap. 9). In 1972 OMB demonstrated its role as the president's skeptic (what Sen. Albert Gore has termed "the Darth Vader of the Federal Government") when it forced NASA to decide whether it really wanted to spend billions of dollars developing a nuclear-powered rocket (Lambright 1976, 124-127). In Reagan's first term, OMB ordered the Alcohol, Drug Abuse, and Mental Health Administration to eliminate "social" research—"work with implications beyond the immediate purview of the agency, such as research on the mental health effects of bad housing"; and in 1984 it blocked an attempt by the Department of Commerce to transfer *Landsat,* the American remote-sensing satellite system, to a private company (Holden 1984).

Nevertheless, there are limits to OMB's ability to impose budgetary and programmatic constraints on science and technology policy. The most significant is the president. OMB suddenly reversed its strong opposition to NASA's plan for a shuttle when Richard Nixon publicly announced his full support of the project in 1972, and Jimmy Carter ignored OMB's recommendations about federal support for large-scale demonstration projects for commercial technologies, such as synthetic fuels and solar energy.

Congress can restrain OMB's influence through legislation. In late 1985 the Senate, for example, passed an amendment to an appropriations bill that stipulated "none of the funds appropriated by this Act or any other Act shall be available to the Office of Management and Budget for revising, curtailing or otherwise amending the administrative and/or regulatory methodology employed by the Bureau of Alcohol, Tobacco, and Firearms to assure compliance with" alcohol labeling requirements. Such specific mandates cannot possibly keep up with all of OMB's activities, however, so the idea of passing a general legislative chastisement of OMB interference has been gaining support in Congress. The courts can also constrain OMB, as when a federal judge ruled in January 1986 that the office lacked the authority to "encroach upon the independence and expertise of EPA" by delaying implementation of hazardous waste legislation.

Finally, OMB can also find itself under pressure from groups outside the White House. In 1979 OMB issued Circular A-21, which would have required researchers receiving federal funds to prepare frequent "activity reports" to substantiate their claims that 100 percent of their work time was being spent on the sponsored research. Academics were furious at the extra paperwork, the limited flexibility, and the "inhibition of scientific thought" that A-21 would entail. Heavy lobbying by scientists and universities (joined by the Department of Defense) eventually caused OMB to retreat—but only partially.

Like other policies, science and technology policies have too many components, usually intertwined with political or other policy implications, to be easily managed. In fact, it is not always desirable to have complete co-ordination if that is interpreted as the total absence of overlap. After all, redundancy is not wasteful when the potential costs of failure are unacceptable or when the potential benefits of success are great; the space shuttle's many backup computers and the many approaches constituting cancer research are primary examples. Any demands that coordination by the executive branch be strengthened should recognize that a little discord can be good.

Moreover, duplication of effort characterizes other endeavors in American society, particularly private enterprise, and it seems arbitrary to assert simply that business-like cost/benefit and efficiency criteria must apply in government research when competition is discouraged. In the absence of competition within government, only two sources of progress and change in policy are certain: the pluralist chorus of demands sung by Congress and the variety of interests, or enlightened leadership. Neither is reliable. In any case, coordination and careful management imply reliable knowledge about what is happening and what policy goals are being pursued. As long as the nation—and especially presidents—pursue policies in complex areas with goals that often conflict, presidential coordination of science and technology policies is unlikely to satisfy everyone.

Politics and Presidential Science and Technology Policy

Presidential science and technology policy making must respond to two types of political constraints: the president's own political program and political pressures from outside the White House. Political forces shape not only the president's relationship with Congress but also the tone and cohesiveness of the president's administration.

The ideological focus of a president can overwhelm other determinants of science and technology policy. The Nixon administration's attempts to politicize the institutions of science and technology policy led to a presidential apology to the National Science Board for having tried to subvert the director's job. Nixon also canceled the yearly National Medal of Science awards out of concern that scientists who had spoken out against his Vietnam policies (such as Linus Pauling, winner of two Nobel Prizes) would be invited to the White House. A White House directive (which was never implemented) indicated that the Massachusetts Institute of Technology should lose its federal funds for research because of what the document referred to as the "antidefense bias" of its president, former Kennedy adviser (and vocal opponent of Nixon's ABM proposal) Jerome Wiesner (Boffey and Nelson 1969; Shapley 1973).

No rigid hierarchy of constraints shapes science and technology policy making, so political factors do not always prevail. For example, the Reagan administration began in 1981 by slashing support for social science, science education, and applied research programs, but after 1982, "as it moved deeper into the responsibilities of governance, the administration began losing its ideological innocence" (Lepkowski 1984, 43). Contrary to the conservative tone of the administration, it supported the Clinch River Breeder Reactor, it allowed the Synthetic Fuels Corporation (Synfuels) project to continue, and it restored at least partial funding for "liberal" programs such as social science research and science education. As technology historian Melvin Kranzberg observed, we still speak in the laissez-faire, hands-off rhetoric of Thomas Jefferson, but "we live in a Hamiltonian world, where the government actively assists industry" (U.S. House of Representatives 1981g, 22).

Political reversals such as these affect the continuity of science and technology policy. When new presidents come to Washington, they need to fill thousands of policy-making positions quickly. Short sighted considerations of political loyalty and poor information about appointees' capabilities can damage ongoing science and technology programs. The nuclear fusion research program, for example, suffered during the Carter entry because of the aloofness of Carter's aides (who ignored offers of help with the transition) and during the Reagan transition because of questions of political loyalty (Heppenheimer 1984, 194, 243). The Reagan administration routinely submitted the names of nominees to science advisory committees of the Interior Department to the Republican National Committee for screening, and the Department of Agriculture used political "compatibility" tests for candidates for peer review panels (Marshall 1982).

Presidential science and technology policy making is also buffeted by political forces from outside the White House. Especially in the early days of White House science advising, "involvement in health and biomedical research policy was viewed as risky because of its avid lay following, both in and out of Congress" (David 1980, 55). During the Kennedy administration a powerful senator tried to discover the names of scientists serving on a PSAC panel that advised against developing a nuclear-powered rocket; it was reported that he wanted to deny federal contracts to the employers of those panelists (Katz 1980, 240). And, of course, members of Congress overtly press the White House to change its science and technology policies, as when Rep. John Dingell (D-Mich.) wrote to George Keyworth urging "the Executive Office to create a mechanism to quickly sort out any potentially conflicting jurisdictional issues concerning the regulation of biotechnology" (U.S. House of Representatives 1984d, 69).

Conclusion

The president has some distinct advantages over Congress in the use and manipulation of science and technology policy and in establishing priorities and possibilities for research and development. The nation's chief executives have generally been adept at finding ways to avoid fixed and vague statutory limitations on their powers, and they can often arouse enough support to change those restrictions that they cannot avoid. By the very nature of the institution the presidency has had an advantage over Congress in developing more formalized and identifiable institutions for obtaining science advice, whether from external sources or from offices within the same branch of government.

With its centralized authority the White House also has had better luck at coordinating science and technology policy than has Congress. Congressional agencies such as the Office of Technology Assessment and the Congressional Budget Office have helped the legislature compete, but it still has no institution with the power and reach of the Office of Management and Budget. Moreover, the president's science and technology policies are usually less constrained by political pressures, since he represents a far larger constituency than members of Congress. As the leader of the nation the president occasionally can be forgiven, even by many of his loudest critics, if he claims to rise above partisan politics or interest group pressures to make policy with an eye on the broader national interest. Given these characteristics, Congress will remain an important but primarily reactive part of the science and technology policy process.

Science and technology policy making in the generalist institutions of Congress and the presidency has evolved as the demands for policies have grown and changed. Both branches of government have developed specialized institutions with mandates to provide expert advice and to coordinate science and technology policy, yet neither presidents nor members of Congress have been able to find a simple solution to their need for scientific and technological knowledge.

Perhaps the most remarkable aspect of executive and legislative policy making is the rarity of the word "democratic" in descriptions of the process. Although there are 536 very important decision makers in Washington who have been elected by the public, there is practically no regular role for the general public in the actual procedures of policy making. Groups can lobby and individuals can write letters, but the internal presidential and legislative policy processes are largely nondemocratic, often relying on republican representation and experts chosen for their merit, record, or professional connections.

4

The Federal Bureaucracy in the Policy Process

Chlorofluorocarbons (CFCs) are used as refrigerants, coolants, and solvents. Until 1978 they were also commonly used as propellants in aerosol cans, but studies of the effects of CFCs on the earth's stratosphere had begun to suggest that they were interacting with atmospheric ozone, a gas that filters the most potentially harmful ultraviolet radiation from the sun before it reaches the earth's surface. Scientists suspected that the continued use and release into the air of CFCs could result in increases in skin cancer, suppression of the human immune system, decreases in crop yields and aquatic life, and fast decomposition of some plastics. Ozone depletion could even accelerate a global warming trend that would alter climate patterns and perhaps eventually melt the polar icecaps and raise the worldwide sea level.

No one was absolutely sure about the scientific evidence on CFCs. Nevertheless, with only relatively mild complaints from industry and consumers, the Environmental Protection Agency (EPA) issued regulations in 1978 to limit the use of CFCs as a propellant in most aerosol spray cans. Subsequent work has suggested that the ozone problems result from more complex physical and chemical processes than was previously suspected, so EPA and other federal and international agencies are reassessing current policies (see Figure 4-1).

This seems to be science policy working well: extreme potential dangers spark quick action, and new knowledge is used for reevaluation and adjustment. Does this mean that scientific and technological training are more compatible with bureaucratic tasks than with campaigning and compromising? Perhaps civil service laws insulate bureaucrats from political demands and allow more reasoned decision making.

In fact, politics also shape the behavior of the federal bureaucracy, though often differently from the ways it affects the president or Congress. Moreover, agencies have no constitutional status and therefore little maneuvering power when pressured by electoral institutions or the courts. The

Figure 4-1 Activities Related to EPA Stratospheric Ozone Protection Program

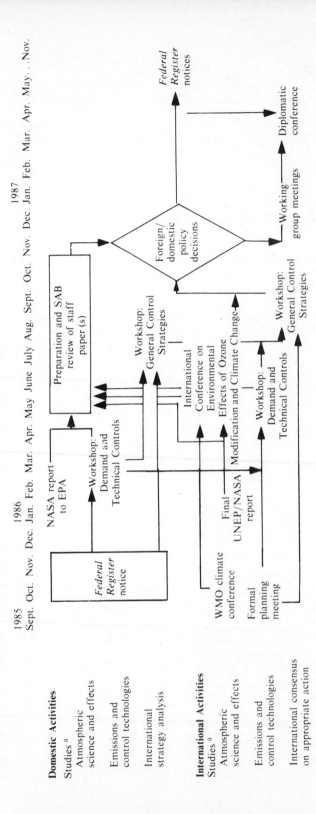

Source: Federal Register, vol. 51, no. 7 (January 10, 1986), 1260.

Note: NASA=National Aeronautics and Space Administration; SAB=Science Advisory Board (EPA); UNEP=United Nations Environmental Programme; WMO=World Meteorological Organization.

[a]Studies are ongoing in each of these categories to support major events.

bureaucracy is expected to be subservient. Yet this is the arena where scientific and technological policy questions are confronted most directly.

The essential characteristics of bureaucracies were described by German sociologist Max Weber (1864-1920):

1. "Fixed and official jurisdictional areas" based on division of labor, clear lines of authority, and consistently applied standards for hiring and promotion
2. "A firmly ordered system of super- and subordination in which there is a supervision of the lower offices by the higher ones"
3. Reliance on written documents
4. Expert training of managers
5. Relatively stable and exhaustive general rules that can be learned (Gerth and Mills 1946, 196-197).

The selection and promotion of a bureaucracy's employees and directors would not be "democratic" in the sense of allowing an equal voice for all in decision making, but that was not necessary for effective management of a bureaucracy. After all, bureaucracy is only a tool of the democratic political system, not a democracy in itself.

In Weber's characterization of bureaucracy, key features of the science and technology policy process are evident. Bureaucracies require both legal authority to act and legal constraints on their behavior. Decisions are to be well founded through the use of knowledgeable, expert managers who rely on verifiable written evidence. Coordination is implied by clear and fixed jurisdictional areas, and the ubiquitous pressures of politics are to be constrained by organizational rules and procedures.

The Science and Technology Bureaucracy

The word *bureaucracy* implies a monolithic or homogeneous organization, but a wide range of agencies make and implement federal science and technology policy according to their own mandates and styles of operation. Unlike those policy areas in which one government organization is clearly dominant (such as agriculture or defense), science and technology are affected by dozens of federal offices (see Table 4-1). Yet about 98 percent of all federal R & D is performed by just ten agencies.

Executive Departments

Each of the thirteen executive departments except Treasury includes at least one research office, and some departments have many. The Department of Health and Human Services (HHS), for example, includes the National Institutes of Health (NIH), the Alcohol, Drug Abuse, and Mental

Table 4-1 Major Federal Science and Technology Agencies and Fiscal Year 1986 Budget Outlays (Millions of Dollars)

Agency	Estimated Outlays
Department of Agriculture	
Agricultural Research Service	544.7
Cooperative State Research Service	255.9
Economic Research Service	44.3
Forest Service	105.5
Human Nutrition Information Service	10.8
Other	15.7
Total	976.9
Department of Commerce	
National Bureau of Standards	98.5
National Oceanic and Atmospheric Administration	183.6
Bureau of the Census	4.9
National Telecommunications and Information Administration	9.4
Other	0.5
Total	296.9
Department of Defense	
Department of the Army	5,028.4
Department of the Navy	10,306.2
Department of the Air Force	14,816.3
Defense Agencies	3,926.3
Director of Test and Evaluation	69.3
Total	34,146.4
Department of Education	122.0
Department of Energy	5,520.9
Department of Health and Human Services	
Alcohol, Drug Abuse, and Mental Health Administration	353.1
Centers for Disease Control	46.1
Food and Drug Administration	93.2
Health Care Financing Administration	22.0
National Institutes of Health	4,679.2
Other	69.2
Total	5,262.8
Department of Housing and Urban Development	18.6
Department of the Interior	
Bureau of Land Management	3.2
Bureau of Mines	63.3
Bureau of Reclamation	9.9
Geological Survey	213.4

(cont.)

Table 4-1 (Cont.)

Agency	Estimated Outlays
National Park Service	15.5
Fish and Wildlife Service	61.6
Other	6.3
Total	373.2
Department of Justice	25.9
Department of Labor	14.5
Department of State	1.6
Department of Transportation	
Coast Guard	23.0
Federal Aviation Administration	212.4
Federal Highway Administration	43.9
Federal Railroad Administration	17.9
Maritime Administration	12.4
National Highway Traffic Safety Administration	45.0
Urban Mass Transportation Administration	25.4
Other	8.2
Total	388.2
Department of the Treasury	26.1
Other Agencies	
Agency for International Development	267.3
Consumer Product Safety Commission	0.3
Environmental Protection Agency	317.2
Federal Communications Commission	0.9
Federal Emergency Management Agency	4.0
Federal Home Loan Bank Board	2.7
Federal Trade Commission	1.8
General Services Administration	0.9
International Trade Commission	6.3
Library of Congress	8.4
National Aeronautics and Space Administration	3,804.9
National Science Foundation	1,472.0
Nuclear Regulatory Commission	143.1
Smithsonian Institution	65.0
Tennessee Valley Authority	67.9
Veterans Administration	210.1
Other	3.8
Total, all agencies	53,550.6

Source: National Science Foundation 1984, p. 3.

Note: Discrepancies in some totals are due to rounding.

Health Administration (ADAMHA), the Food and Drug Administration (FDA), the Centers for Disease Control (CDC), and other divisions that conduct R & D. In addition, some particular areas of R & D are performed by offices in many agencies. Although energy-related R & D is centered in the Department of Energy, it is also performed by the Nuclear Regulatory Commission (NRC), the Synthetic Fuels Corporation (Synfuels, a semipublic corporation), and many government laboratories.

As the budget outlays show, the Department of Defense (DOD) is much more involved in science and technology than any other executive departments. In fact, the most significant turning point in federal science and technology policy was World War II. Forced by the outbreak of war in Europe to reconsider the American government's neglect of military matters, President Roosevelt issued an executive order in June 1940 creating the National Defense Research Committee (NDRC) to support and coordinate scientific research for military applications. NDRC included the presidents of the Massachusetts Institute of Technology and Harvard, an Army general and an admiral, and prominent industrial and academic researchers. With that leadership it was able to recruit scientists to serve on more than fifty advisory committees, responding to military requests and initiating studies on their own.

Because NDRC focused on research rather than weapons development, Roosevelt created the Office of Scientific Research and Development (OSRD) a year later. It mobilized scientists through research contracts with universities and corporations, thereby setting a pattern that continues today. OSRD eventually spent more than $1 billion, constrained in its efforts more by the lack of scientific manpower during the war than by budgetary considerations. The nation's atomic bomb research project was passed to the Army's Manhattan Project from OSRD in 1943 only after much of the basic work was finished.

The wartime agencies not only established a pattern of contracting research from universities and the private sector, but also procured enormous amounts of equipment and set technical standards that would outlast the war. Research centers such as Los Alamos and Oak Ridge were founded and funded by the federal government but operated by universities or corporations. Those relationships continue in the same general form today. During Reagan's first six years, the percentage of federal research dollars devoted to DOD grew from 56 percent to 72 percent (see Table 4-2).

Not all defense R & D is devoted directly to missiles and bombs. The Defense Advanced Research Projects Agency (DARPA), for example, which had a 1985 budget of about $770 million, conducted research for the Army that led to development of the "mouse" for desktop computers. To a large degree, its research was responsible for the development of those computers themselves, in response to the need for computational power in small spaces, such as the nose cones of missiles. DARPA innovated time-

Table 4-2   Federal Research Funds, 1960-1987

Year	Billions of Dollars			Percentage of Total	
	Total	Defense[a]	All other	Defense[a]	All other
1960	7.6	6.1	1.5	81	19
1961	9.1	7.0	2.1	77	23
1962	10.3	7.2	3.1	70	30
1963	12.5	7.8	4.7	62	38
1964	14.2	7.8	6.4	55	45
1965	14.6	7.3	7.3	50	50
1966	15.3	7.5	7.8	49	51
1967	16.5	8.6	7.9	52	48
1968	15.9	8.3	7.6	52	48
1969	15.6	8.4	7.2	53	47
1970	15.3	8.0	7.3	52	48
1971	15.5	8.1	7.4	52	48
1972	16.5	8.9	7.6	54	46
1973	16.8	9.0	7.8	54	46
1974	17.4	9.0	8.4	52	48
1975	19.0	9.7	9.3	51	49
1976	20.8	10.4	10.4	50	50
1977	23.5	11.9	11.6	51	49
1978	25.8	12.6	13.2	50	50
1979	28.1	13.6	14.5	49	51
1980	29.8	15.1	14.7	50	50
1981	33.1	17.8	15.3	56	44
1982	36.4	22.1	14.3	61	39
1983	38.4	24.5	13.9	64	36
1984	43.2	28.3	14.9	66	34
1985	49.5	33.4	16.1	68	32
1986[b]	52.0	35.7	16.3	72	28
1987[b]	60.8	44.4	16.4	73	27

Source: Office of Management and Budget 1986a, K-29.

[a] Includes military-related programs of the Departments of Defense and Energy.
[b] Estimated.

sharing and networking systems for computers, and because 40 to 80 percent of the cost of major new weapons systems is for software, it continues to push computer science.

Aside from broader concerns about the propriety of huge military expenditures and more sophisticated weapons, questions continually arise about the effect on the nation's R & D efforts of devoting large amounts of federal research funds to DOD. While total federal support for university research in the life sciences declined by 1.2 percent from 1980 to 1984, DOD support increased by 50.3 percent. Under these circumstances scientists are apt to follow the funds and alter their research interests accordingly. With such enormous sums at its disposal, DOD has the potential to reshape much of the nation's R & D effort (Wright 1985).

Executive Agencies

The many executive agencies with jurisdiction over science and technology policy deal with narrower issues than the executive departments address. These agencies include EPA, the General Services Administration (GSA), which buys and thereby sets technical standards for products and services used by the government, and the Veterans Administration (VA), which conducts medical research. (Table 4-1 lists others.) Like the executive departments, executive agencies are headed by a single administrator appointed by the president with the consent of the Senate, and they are construed as portions of the executive branch of government under the influence of the president.

The most visible executive agency with a science and technology focus is the National Aeronautics and Space Administration (NASA). Its roots go back to 1915 when Congress created the National Advisory Committee on Aeronautics (with an annual budget of $5,000) from which NASA was formed in 1958 in the aftermath of Sputnik. Apart from the military and commercial importance of space policy, NASA's fortunes have reflected the post-Sputnik fluctuations in science and technology policy. The burst of funding for the Apollo moon-landing program during the 1960s was followed by retrenchment, as popular enthusiasm for science and space waned during the 1970s. The classification of space shuttle flights in the 1980s corresponded with the military's increased interest in space and with the increasing share of federal R & D funds devoted to military purposes. The concerns raised about NASA's management and procedures following the tragic loss of the shuttle *Challenger* resembled the somewhat suspicious and cynical questions commonly raised about other government agencies, perhaps indicating that space policy had matured into just another government program.

Independent Regulatory Commissions

Congress has also established nearly a dozen independent regulatory commissions, many of which have jurisdictional responsibilities that include scientific and technological issues. Under the leadership of five or more commissioners serving long and staggered terms, these agencies are purportedly intended to issue regulations and resolve disputes without direct pressure from Congress or the White House. Yet, because the president selects—with congressional approval—the chairs of the commissions, guides their agendas, and with Congress determines their budgets, these bureaucracies are not completely free from executive and legislative politics. Those having the greatest interest in science and technology include the Federal Communications Commission (FCC), Consumer Product Safety Commission (CPSC), Federal Trade Commission (FTC), and Nuclear Regulatory Commission. Although regulatory commissions, like executive agencies, are more narrowly focused than cabinet departments, they may still have complex tasks. The NRC, for example, faces a difficult burden in coordinating the activities of more than thirty divisions and offices with such diverse responsibilities as international programs, waste management, small and disadvantaged business utilization, and reactor safety research.

Federal Laboratories

In 1901 Congress created the National Bureau of Standards (NBS). Now part of the Department of Commerce, NBS was authorized to set up the first federal laboratory to perform research on weights and measures, among other tasks. In 1904 it stepped into the realm of consumer protection when it investigated the shoddy manufacture of light bulbs in response to complaints from government offices (Kevles 1978, 73). In the 1980s NBS was involved in diverse research projects, such as computer networking standards, biotechnology measurements, and automated manufacturing techniques. Its contributions have not, however, been fully appreciated. A member of the House Rules Committee asked in 1985, "If we cannot cut [the budget of] the National Bureau of Standards, what can we cut?" *Congressional Record,* December 20, 1985, E5831) Industry officials disagreed. Betsy Ancker-Johnson, a vice-president of General Motors, complained that "U.S. science and technology policy seems blind to the critical role, which NBS plays in commercializing ... [domestic] investment in R & D" (Crawford 1985, 300).

In addition to NBS there are about 380 federal laboratories, which have a combined budget of $18 billion (about one-fourth of all federal R & D funds) and employ about one-sixth of all researchers in the United States. Some are huge, mission-oriented laboratories such as the National Institutes of Health, Oak Ridge National Laboratory, and the Marshall Space Flight Center. Others are smaller, dedicated to a wide range of particular tasks, such as new applications for lignite coal, the use of insects to control weevils and gypsy moths, and children's nutrition.

Among these federal laboratories are about three dozen Federally Funded Research and Development Centers (FFRDCs), which are operated for government agencies by universities or private firms (see Table 4-3). The government categorizes contractor-operated facilities as FFRDCs if: (1) the primary activity is performance or management of R & D, (2) the work is requested and monitored by the federal government, (3) the facility is a separate operational unit or corporation, (4) at least 70 percent of the operational expenses are federally provided, (5) the contract is for at least five years, (6) most or all of the physical facility is paid for by the federal government, and (7) the facility has an average annual budget of at least $500,000.

Because only about 5 percent of the 25,000 government-owned inventions have found commercial outlets, Congress passed several laws during the 1980s designed to encourage federal laboratories to transfer more of their results to commercial enterprises by entering into cooperative research arrangements with the private sector. The legislation provided incentives for federal laboratories to undertake research with economic potential and encouraged agencies to award cash prizes (up to $25,000 at most agencies, and $100,000 at NASA) for "meritorious work."

The National Science Foundation

Attempts by Herbert Hoover to establish a National Research Fund in the 1920s languished for lack of money, but the massive government involvement in science and technology during World War II irreversibly changed the relationship between government and research. During the war years Sen. Harley Kilgore (D-W.Va.) introduced a bill to establish a National Science Foundation (NSF). His proposal was strongly attacked as socialist and "anti-quality" because it included funding for social sciences and a geographical basis for the distribution of funds. A strong push for an NSF came in July 1945 when President Roosevelt's science adviser, Vannevar Bush, released the report *Science—The Endless Frontier,* which argued that scientific research was vital to national security, improved health, and full employment, and therefore deserved secure support from the federal government.

Congressional debate over NSF's form and functions was intense, centering on its political independence, its support for social sciences, whether research funds should be allowed to gravitate toward established research centers, and the balance of applied and basic research. Even today none of these questions has been completely settled. President Truman's veto of the 1957 bill to create NSF led to revisions of the congressional plan, and in 1950 NSF was finally formed. Legislation gave it the authority to "initiate and support, through grants and contracts, scientific and engineering research," to "evaluate the status and needs of the various sciences and engineering," to "recommend and encourage the pursuit of national policies for the promotion of basic research and education in science and engineering," and other, related tasks. A National Science Board of distinguished scientists, with a director appointed by the president and approved by the Senate, manages the NSF. It does not engage in direct military research and relies on advisory committees to judge the quality of research proposals. Divided into six directorates (shown in italics in Table 4-4), the NSF annually provides more than $1.4 billion to support science and technology.

Table 4-3 Federally Funded Research and Development Centers

Name and Type of Administering Organization	Principal Sponsoring Agency	FY 1984 R & D Budget (Thousands of Dollars)
Administered by industrial firms		
Bettis Atomic Power Laboratory	DOE, DOD	275,088
Energy Technology Engineering Center	DOE	215,944
Frederick Cancer Research Center	HHS	32,008
Hanford Engineering Development Laboratory	DOE	141,450
Idaho National Engineering Laboratory	DOE	117,408
Knolls Atomic Power Laboratory	DOD, DOE	63,519
Oak Ridge National Laboratory	DOE	297,274
Sandia National Laboratories	DOE	604,368
Savannah River Laboratory	DOE	57,956
Administered by universities and colleges		
Ames Laboratory	DOE	17,790
Argonne National Laboratory	DOE	221,239
Brookhaven National Laboratory	DOE	179,632
Lawrence Berkeley Laboratory	DOE	150,876
Lawrence Livermore Laboratory	DOE	651,537
Fermi National Accelerator Laboratory	DOE	181,683
Jet Propulsion Laboratory	NASA	261,494
Lincoln Laboratory	DOD	160,406
Los Alamos National Laboratory	DOE	513,301
National Astronomy and Ionosphere Center	NSF	6,111
National Center for Atmospheric Research	NSF	40,383
National Optical Astronomy Observatory	NSF	23,160
National Radio Astronomy Observatory	NSF	20,260
Oak Ridge Associated Universities	DOE	11,529
Princeton Plasma Physics Laboratory	DOE	130,934
Stanford Linear Accelerator Center	DOE	117,770
Administered by other nonprofit institutions		
Aerospace Corporation	DOD	203,740
Center for Naval Analyses	DOD	19,306
Institute for Defense Analyses	DOD	21,720
Mitre Corporation, C3 Division	DOD	215,640
Pacific Northwest Laboratory	DOE	69,683
Rand Project Air Force	DOD	17,806
Solar Energy Research Institute	DOE	53,399
Total		5,094,414

Source: National Science Foundation 1985c, 22.
Note: DOE=Department of Energy; DOD=Department of Defense; HHS=Department of Health and Human Services; NASA=National Aeronautics and Space Administration; NSF=National Science Foundation.

Table 4-4   National Science Foundation Divisions and Budget, Fiscal Years 1985-1987 (Millions of Dollars)

Directorates and Programs	FY 1985	FY 1986[a]	FY 1987[b]
Mathematical and Physical Sciences			
Mathematical Sciences	47.7	51.7	59.8
Computer Research	39.1	40.2	44.4
Physics	115.8	118.6	126.6
Chemistry	87.6	89.8	101.0
Materials Research	107.0	109.7	117.4
Total	397.2	410.0	449.3
Engineering			
Chemical, Biochemical, and Thermal Eng.	29.2	29.2	30.2
Mechanics, Structures, and Materials Eng.	23.3	23.7	26.3
Electrical, Communications, and Systems Eng.	25.8	25.7	26.3
Design, Manufacturing, and Computer Eng.	17.5	18.7	21.7
Emerging and Critical Engineering Systems	35.0	36.2	43.0
Cross-Disciplinary Research	19.8	29.0	38.0
Total	150.6	162.5	185.5
Biological, Behavioral, and Social Sciences			
Molecular Biosciences	60.9	62.0	67.1
Cellular Biosciences	52.4	52.1	56.6
Biotic Systems and Resources	58.1	61.0	66.5
Behavioral and Neural Sciences	44.4	45.7	48.9
Social and Economic Sciences	28.8	30.0	31.4
Information Science and Technology	8.9	9.3	11.9
Total	253.5	260.1	282.4
Astronomical, Atmospheric, Earth, and Ocean Sciences			
Astronomical Sciences	82.8	84.2	85.1
Atmospheric Sciences	95.1	96.8	100.7
			(cont.)

The NSF was to be a keystone in the array of science and technology policy institutions, shaping overall policy and drawing attention to weak spots in the nation's science and technology efforts. During its early years the NSF followed a path of self-restraint because of its shaky relationship with the scientific and political worlds, each of which saw dangers in a strong science agency too responsive to the other. In the 1960s, however, Congress pressed the agency to focus more on social problems, which resulted in two major NSF programs—Research Applied to National Needs, and Applied Science and Research Applications—and several other, smaller ones. During the 1980s Congress has required NSF to provide more support for technological R & D, such as engineering and supercomputer research.

Table 4-4   (Cont.)

Directorates and Programs	FY 1985	FY 1986[a]	FY 1987[b]
Earth Sciences	46.0	48.9	55.0
Ocean Sciences	121.3	124.1	133.7
Arctic Research Program	8.0	8.5	8.9
Total	353.0	362.6	383.2
Scientific, Technological, and International Affairs			
Industrial Science and Technological Innovation	13.4	15.9	17.2
International Cooperative Scientific Activities	12.4	10.8	12.7
Policy Research and Analysis	5.1	1.9	2.0
Research Initiation and Improvement	8.6	7.0	11.0
Other programs	4.2	4.0	4.1
Total	43.7	39.6	47.0
Science and Engineering Education			
Research Career Development	27.3	27.3	27.3
College Science Instrumentation	5.0	5.5	7.5
Materials Development, Research and Informal Science Education	22.7	25.0	25.0
Teacher Preparation and Enhancement	25.2	27.0	27.0
Studies and Program Enhancement	1.7	2.2	2.2
Total	81.9	87.0	89.0
Advanced Scientific Computing	41.4	45.2	53.6
Program Development and Management	71.9	72.5	78.0
Total research and related activities, all directorates and programs	1,393.2	1,439.5	1,568.0
NSF total	1,502.0	1,524.0	1,686.0

Source: Office of Management and Budget 1986b, I-Z81.

Note: Discrepancies in some totals are due to rounding.

[a] Appropriated.
[b] Requested.

The NSF has survived political attacks and recovered from presidential budget cuts largely because of the confidence that politicians and researchers share in its principal method of allocating funds. Through the multistage process of peer review research proposals are evaluated by other researchers in the same field, by NSF advisory boards composed of recognized experts, and finally by the appropriate NSF program director. NSF's independence (if not its budget) has also benefited from the efforts of its directors to avoid an active political or policy role (Lambright 1976). Instead, the top of the science and technology policy hierarchy is shared by Congress, the president, and the National Academy of Sciences.

National Academy of Sciences

Another major science institution had its birth in war. Created by Congress in 1863 to provide expert scientific advice during the Civil War, the National Academy of Sciences (NAS) is a private organization, not really an agency of the U.S. government. It has been described as a "political and administrative junction point of all American science and technology," the most prestigious scientific society in the nation, "science's League of Women Voters," and the scientific community's "duly delegated emissary to the U.S. Congress and the Executive Branch" (Greenberg 1967). Largely because it was established to participate in policy making by giving advice to Congress on scientific matters, the NAS has had a more unsettled history than the NSF.

The academy has often been criticized for failing to be sufficiently useful. This led to the creation of its subsidiary National Research Council in 1916 and to occasional reshufflings of priorities since then. More recently, some have questioned the academy's unwillingness to take a stand on controversial issues, such as the use of defoliants in Vietnam, airborne lead pollution, food additives, and the disposal of radioactive wastes (Boffey 1975). Part of the problem, it has been claimed, is the nature of NAS itself. Like its sister agency, the National Academy of Engineering, NAS comprises prominent researchers who are nominated and elected to the academy by its current members. A former president of NAS, Philip Handler, once declared, "This *is* an elitist organization," arguing that the careful selection of its members is its greatest asset and not, as some claimed, a source of conservatism (Culliton 1976, 543).

Because Congress is likely to assign the more difficult science and technology policy questions to NAS (more than thirty during the 1970s), the composition of panels and findings of expert panels are commonly criticized. One scientist concluded that for issues such as the safety of saccharin (which he placed "in the political social realm"), "the Academy, I'm sorry to say it, can get any kind of report out it wants depending on who they appoint to the committee." [1] Yet NAS is occasionally asked to do the impossible: to resolve disputes on scientific or technological grounds without concern for their policy or political aspects. An NAS report that found fault with the Atomic Energy Commission's handling of radioactive wastes was suppressed (Woodhouse 1983, 160); and when NAS was required by Congress to conduct a $5-million study of EPA programs and procedures, its work was reviewed by two congressional committees—one chaired by the author of EPA air pollution legislation, the other by an outspoken critic of EPA's policies (Carter 1974, 678). As a result, NAS committees occasionally have refused to answer questions that went beyond the realm of scientific fact and into the realm of untestable assumptions (McGarity 1979, 742).

The National Institutes of Health

In 1930 the Public Health Service moved its research arm to Bethesda, Maryland, just outside Washington, and renamed it the National Institutes of Health. When the National Cancer Institute was formed in 1937, NIH went beyond public health and the study of infectious diseases to use research fellowships and university grants in the pursuit of basic biomedical research (Dupree 1957, 366). Today it comprises twelve major research institutes, including those for cancer, the eye, dental research, aging, and environmental health sciences.

The growth of the nation's largest nonmilitary research organization began to accelerate after World War II when the Office of Scientific Research and Development transferred forty-four contracts to NIH, but it was during the 1950s that its role became clear. Its research budget grew by nearly 900 percent between 1950 and 1960, and by another 325 percent by 1967. About two-thirds of its $3-billion annual budget is allocated to university- and college-based researchers; only about 11 percent of its budget goes to in-house research. Such rapid growth did not occur without controversy. During the 1950s NSF worried about NIH's "imperial ambitions," and questions have been raised about its scope, role, and management (England 1982, 402 n.22). Nevertheless, NIH has been able "to utilize the consensus *against* dread disease as a means to obtain funds *for* basic research" (Lambright 1976, 148-149). This consensus is the major reason for NIH's consistently strong congressional support. In the late 1950s when NIH officials suggested changing the name of the Institute of Allergy and Infectious Diseases to the more appropriate Institute of Microbiology, one senator challenged the proposal by asking, "Who ever died of microbiology?" The idea was dropped (Racker 1979, 71).

It should not be surprising that the National Science Foundation, the National Academy of Sciences, and the National Institutes of Health have been buffeted by a variety of forces having nothing to do with science or technology. Like the other federal agencies with jurisdiction over science and technology policy, they have had to find a balance between their legislated obligations, the standards of science, and politics.

Legal Constraints on the Bureaucracy

To implement policy, the agencies, offices, and bureaus translate the words and spirit of the nation's laws into studies, contracts, construction, funding, and regulations. The bureaucracy must obey the substantive requirements imposed by the statutes that create it, and it must adhere to the procedural requirements created by Congress and the courts. Within those limits, however, there often remains considerable discretion.

Substantive Constraints

Whenever Congress makes a law, its members face conflicting pressures. As discussed in Chapter 3, political demands must be reconciled with the needs and limitations of the nation's research enterprise. As for other types of policies, in the realm of science and technology policy the lawmakers must decide how precise their instructions to policy implementors should be. Given too much latitude, an agency may be able to thwart the true intent of a law; but if the wording is too specific, the law may become irrelevant as science, technology, or political pressures change.

Under present law, for example, the Food and Drug Administration is responsible for approving new drugs and medical devices as "safe and effective" before their use. Even investigatory tests must first be approved by FDA. Congress established these regulations in 1962 in reaction to what could have been a disaster when the drug thalidomide was widely distributed before it was discovered to cause birth defects. Yet by early 1985 FDA found itself in the uncomfortable position of questioning the emergency use of an unapproved, experimental mechanical heart by doctors in Tucson. According to FDA's legal mandate the doctors had engaged in an illegal action, but few thought the law should be rigidly applied in this case. Although FDA's mandate could be criticized as obsolete or too broad, in this case it was the agency itself that received the criticism.

Some statutory mandates require agencies to pursue inconsistent goals or goals that fail to match those of other agencies. The original NSF legislation required the foundation to award grants not only on the basis of scientific merit but also with consideration of the geographic distribution of funds, though there were no guarantees that the centers of research excellence would be conveniently located. The enabling statutes of the Environmental Protection Agency, the Consumer Product Safety Commission, the Occupational Safety and Health Administration (OSHA), and the National Highway Traffic Safety Administration—agencies that regulate safety—did not give consistent guidance on what constitutes "adequate" protection or "reasonable" risk.

In addition, the formal mandates to science and technology agencies usually fail to specify the range of activities they actually undertake. The Oak Ridge National Laboratory, for example, was created to perform R & D in nuclear energy, but because it used coal to generate the electricity to separate uranium isotopes for nuclear power, it also became involved in research for ways to burn coal more cleanly (Teich and Lambright 1976). Some agencies do have specific mandates that accurately convey the complexity of their tasks. The various statutes that instruct EPA to control the byproducts of technology require it to consider air, water, noise, solid waste, and other types of pollutants, thereby bringing virtually all sectors of the economy under its jurisdiction (Regens, Dietz, Rycroft 1983).

Science and technology policies are implemented by bureaucrats who are aware of the legal limitations imposed on them. Because their actions affect individuals and firms more immediately and obviously than those of other policy makers, agencies frequently are held more specifically accountable (McGarity 1984). Judicial review of agency actions (discussed in Chapter 5) is always a threat and is usually fervently avoided. Congress and the president frequently upbraid agency heads for their failures to interpret the legislative or executive intent correctly; and because elected officials hold the potential sanctions of budget cuts, reductions in personnel, bad publicity, and even abolishment, the agencies struggle at least to appear to comply. The constraints imposed by organic statutes are the appropriate starting point for understanding bureaucratic science and technology policy, but they are only one part of the picture.

Procedural Constraints

The Constitution lays down the basic rules that govern all government institutions, such as the Fourteenth Amendment's promise of "due process" when the government takes a person's "life, liberty, or property." More specifically, Congress has passed laws governing the procedures of all agencies, including those that make science and technology policy. Most significant is the Administrative Procedure Act (APA) of 1946. APA instructs agencies on how to conduct hearings and trials, specifying the rights of people and groups to be notified of pending matters and their opportunities for presenting arguments and evidence (that is, what constitutes a "fair" procedure). It also imposes on an agency an obligation to include in final decisions its findings and conclusions of fact and law, the reasons for its actions, and the evidence to support its decisions (in other words, whether the decision can be justified if questioned in court).

More than a dozen additional laws constrain agency procedures. The 1970 National Environmental Policy Act opened a wide door for citizens' groups to affect agency decision making by requiring environmental impact statements to be prepared for all major federally funded projects, ranging from highway improvements and agricultural experiments to shuttle launches (Caldwell 1982). Other general laws applying to agency procedures include the Freedom of Information Act (public access to government data and analyses) and the Government in the Sunshine Act (requiring most agency meetings to be open to the public), both passed in 1976 to limit the extent to which agencies can act in secrecy. The Federal Tort Claims Act allows individuals and firms to sue the federal government for damages caused by its actions or inactions. This law has produced about $5 billion in claims resulting from the side effects of the federal swine flu innoculation program, and in 1985 the U.S. Claims Court ruled that the California Canners and Growers Association had suffered $8.2 million in

losses because of the government's improper handling of the ban on cyclamates in 1970.

Another law of particular importance to science and technology policy
was the 1972 Federal Advisory Committee Act (FACA), passed in reaction
to the proliferation of advisory committees (especially in environment,
health, and safety) that accompanied the increase in regulatory activity
during the 1960s: by 1971 they numbered about 1,800. FACA acknowledged
the usefulness of advisory committees but provided that they should be kept
to a "necessary" minimum and be given finite life spans, that their activities
not be entirely secret, and that they should follow uniform procedures for
their formation and operation. At the end of 1978 only 816 federal advisory
committees were in operation (Cardozo 1981).

Each agency also develops its own rules, criteria, and standard operating procedures. Given the generality of many congressional laws, agencies
have no choice but to establish their own working definitions and procedures.
Although these may evolve slowly or be deliberately changed, in practice
they can become as inflexible as statutory requirements because of their
usefulness in reducing decision-making costs.

In addition, agency procedures are shaped by their individual authorizing statutes, which may impose time limits, require particular types
of analysis, or exempt some activities from agency jurisdiction. FDA,
for example, was hampered in the controversy over laetrile (a cyanide-
containing substance claimed to be effective in preventing or curing cancer) by laws that explicitly prohibited it from lobbying state legislatures
or the U.S. Congress as they considered legislation to legalize the drug.
It could only respond to inquiries and argue informally against laetrile's
use (Rich 1980). More generally, procedural mandates affect science
and technology policy as much by what they leave unsaid as by what they
make clear. In many cases the outcome of the science and technology
policy process is determined by how agencies interpret two words: "reason," which spans law and logic, and "risk," which spans science and
politics.

Agencies that use scientific and technological knowledge in decision
making are forced to be explicit about where such evidence came from, who
presented it, how much confidence it deserves, and what weight it is
accorded. Technical data is thereby made available not only to policy makers
but also to those who want to challenge agencies' decisions. Such openness
becomes crucial in science and technology policy making when the procedures for evaluating evidence are as important as the substantive knowledge
itself. "Many disputes with high scientific content hinge more on differences
over which side should bear the burden of proof than on differences in
appraisal of the technical situation" (Brooks 1984, 41).

Because of vague mandates and the lack of certainty in data and
scientific understanding, legal procedures allow agencies considerable discre-

tion in "interpreting statutory language, balancing conflicting values, determining priorities, and answering scientific and engineering questions" (Greenwood 1984, 4). Because of judicial and legislative oversight, however, there are limits to agency discretion. Courts are particularly concerned that agency decisions should fall within a "zone of reasonableness," allowing an agency to consider the unique aspects of each case while anchoring its discretion in consistently applied criteria of evidence and justification *(Hercules Incorporated v. EPA* 598 F.2d 91, 107 [1978]). Unfortunately, discretion can be a two-edged sword. Critics complained, for example, that FDA used its discretion in decision making under statistical and epidemiological uncertainty about saccharin and cyclamates in a "stringent and unreasonable manner" when it applied the Delaney clause (Havender 1983, 31).

In summary, the legal constraints on the use of science and technology by the federal bureaucracy are cumbersome and confusing, reflecting both the complexity of technical knowledge and the variety of political forces to which all federal agencies must respond. The process can be very time consuming and therefore often appears inefficient: one study identified 160 separate steps that precede the expenditure of R & D funds (Shapley 1982). Yet federal courts have argued that procedural requirements encourage scientific debate, thereby reducing the chances of technical mistakes in public policies, and that sometimes delays are inaccurately blamed entirely on legal problems (Melnick 1983; Barke 1984). Like legal constraints, unavoidable scientific facts and engineering limitations also contribute significantly to science and technology policy making within the bureaucracy.

Knowledge in the Bureaucracy

The tasks of bureaucrats would be far simpler if all questions could be neatly distilled into their "scientific" and "nonscientific" aspects. The policy process could then be divided into two phases—identifying the facts and what society wants the political system to do—and bureaucrats could turn to elected officials for answers to the latter. In practice, however, science raises questions that may sound scientific but that cannot be answered in purely scientific terms because they involve more than science: they also involve moral issues or matters for which there is no scientific consensus. Policy disputes over health risks are typical of what physicist Alvin Weinberg described as "trans-scientific" questions. There is no established objective and scientific way to extrapolate the effects of long-term, low-level radiation on humans from the effects of quick and intense radiation of laboratory rats and then determine how much "health" the public should have. Policy makers must rely on untestable assumptions about such trans-scientific issues.

It follows that it would be helpful for bureaucrats always to know whether questions are scientific or trans-scientific. But to know whether a question is purely scientific, one must know the relevant science *and* its limitations. Regardless of their motives, bureaucrats often must decide matters beyond their authority or capabilities.

There is a large amount of scientific and technical expertise within the bureaucracy. In 1983 about 306,000 scientists and engineers worked for the federal government (about 8.8 percent of the national total), and about one-fourth of all federal R & D funds are spent on work performed by agency employees themselves and not contracted out to firms or universities (National Science Board 1985, 240; National Science Foundation 1983, 160, 14). These figures indicate, of course, only the technological capabilities of federal employees, not the science and technology *policy-making* capabilities of agency decision makers who are likely to be specialists in law, economics, business, or politics. Even agency directors who are trained as scientists or engineers cannot be experts on all topics in their fields, so policy makers frequently turn to outside advisers for help.

Advisory Committees

To gain access to scientific or technological information and useful analysis, policy makers often rely on advisory committees made up of experts or ordinary citizens. As early as 1941 the Supreme Court referred to a professional advisory group as "in reality an extra-governmental agency, which prescribes rules for the regulation and restraint of interstate commerce" and was therefore subject to procedural requirements (*Fashion Originator's Guild v. FTC,* 312 U.S. 457, 465 [1941]). As described above, the 1972 Federal Advisory Committee Act requires such groups to hold open meetings, keep careful records, and allow public participation, and it provides for membership to be "fairly balanced in terms of points of view represented." Unfortunately, there are several ways to interpret a "fair balance": by field of expertise, by level of training, or by political inclination. The Department of Health and Human Services requires that the names of nominees to FDA's sixteen drug-safety advisory committees be submitted for departmental approval, possibly jeopardizing the balance of expertise sought by FDA (Sun 1984). OSHA's advisory committees, which include both employee and employer representatives, are often confrontational and unproductive, and the "citizen" (that is, nonexpert) representatives on FDA advisory committees have been judged by Mendeloff (1979) and Friedman (1978) to have had little effect because of their lack of technical understanding.

Some advisory committees are established by law. A 1974 statute created the EPA's Science Advisory Board, for example, and requires the agency to submit proposed regulations to the board for review; the legislation also requires the board to advise House and Senate committees. In 1984 Congress formed a commission to study the evaluation of debilitating but unmeasurable pain in order to help the Social Security Administration determine eligibility for disability benefits. Agencies create other advisory committees as particular needs arise. The Advisory Committee on Technical Standards for DBS (Direct Broadcast Satellite) Service was formed by the Federal Communications Commission in response to the development of new technology that would allow television signals to be beamed directly to small, rooftop, home antennas. NIH has formed about 150 advisory committees on topics ranging from maternal and child health to aging.

The large variety of advisory groups makes it difficult to generalize about their role in science and technology policy making. Several comparisons of EPA and OSHA advisory committees have, however, reached similar conclusions: EPA advisory committees were generally effective and useful, and OSHA committees were often primarily a forum for argument (Ashford 1984; Greenwood 1984). Greenwood has identified four factors that determine the usefulness of an advisory committee (1984, 126):

1. The criteria for membership. Committees with members chosen for their expertise are more narrowly focused and are better able to resolve disputes than committees with members chosen for their professional affiliation.
2. The point in the process when advice is given. Advisory committees that review the work of agency staff (the gathering and analysis of information) rather than duplicating it can be an independent source of analysis.
3. The recipient of the advice. The recommendations of committees are most effective when submitted directly to high-ranking officials, rather than filtering through the agency bureaucracy.
4. The statutory basis for the advisory committee. An advisory committee is harder to ignore if its participation is required by law.

Advisory panels have problems apart from their composition or legal standing. They often deal with ambiguous or inadequate data, which lead to dissent among committee members or a failure to make firm recommendations. The FCC's DBS Advisory Committee was able to produce only a few voluntary technical standards for DBS television broadcasting because the technology was still evolving and demand for the service was uncertain (Barke 1985b). Even when advisory committees are able to reach unanimous conclusions, the sponsoring agency might shop for the answer it wants by turning to additional advisory committees (Melnick 1983, 284-287).

Congress, moreover, has been openly suspicious of the policy-making role of experts on advisory committees. Proposals to create an advisory panel to evaluate research on President Reagan's ballistic missile defense program were met by the objections of Sen. Phil Gramm (R-Tex.) that the experts would not act objectively "as physicists or chemists or engineers," but would assume a mandate from those opposed to the program "to supplant our committee and people who were elected by the people of the United States" (*Congressional Record,* June 4, 1985, S 7379). Even if an advisory committee can avoid political and methodological problems, its effectiveness in the policy process still depends on how its findings are coordinated with those of other advisory committees and decision makers.

Peer Review

Advisory committees are used both for the application of science and technology to policy making and for assistance in providing government support for R & D. A more specialized procedure has also aided the process of making policy for science. Although major decisions about the overall science and technology budget or large-scale R & D projects are made by Congress and the president, agency employees commonly choose which scientists or institutions will receive individual research grants. These decisions are usually based on the recommendations of relevant practitioners. The secretary of energy may rely on an expert advisory panel to rank the importance of large-scale energy research projects, but smaller grants will be allocated through peer review, the evaluation of research grant applications by fellow scientists or engineers.

Considering the importance of this topic to the scientific community and the finite size of the federal R & D budget, it is not surprising that peer review is of intense interest to researchers and elected officials (Chubin and Jasanoff 1985). Since the initial attempts to establish engineering experiment stations at land-grant colleges in 1916, there have been disputes about "best science" versus geographical criteria for funding (Kevles 1971). Recent efforts to circumvent the traditional allocation system by appealing directly to Congress were described in Chapter 2. These complaints have been fueled by a persistent pattern of funding in which about 40 percent of federal funds for basic research go to only ten institutions, nearly all on the East or West coasts. The thirty leading research universities receive about half of all public support for nonmilitary research (Goodwin 1985).

This allocation of funds results from the peer review system. It takes different forms among and within the various science-funding agencies, but two versions are illustrative. The National Science Foundation, which allocates about 30 percent of all federal research funds for universities, typically sends research proposals to six anonymous researchers in the same field as the proposer. They evaluate the scientific merit of the research, the quality of the research design, and the qualifications of the researcher to carry through on the proposal. While these ad hoc reviews are, on average, detached and objective, the reviewers do not judge proposals competitively, nor do they need to worry about budgetary constraints. At the next stage an advisory panel of established experts evaluates the proposals and their mail reviews, making recommendations whether to fund each proposal fully, partially, or not at all. The relevant NSF program director then makes the final decisions subject to review by the NSF director.

In contrast, the National Institutes of Health, which support about 40 percent of all biomedical research in the United States, evaluate roughly 20,000 applications each year through some sixty-five study sections organized by discipline (such as biochemistry, metabolism, and toxicology). Comprising fifteen to twenty members, these sections meet three times annually to assess the quality of proposals as well as safety precautions and other matters. Although their evaluations are reviewed by a separate national advisory council, the recommendations of the study sections are likely to be accepted. NSF relies more on peer advice, and the NIH process is closer to peer decision. In addition, NIH has created a "consensus development" process "which brings together scientists, practitioners, consumers, and others in an effort to reach general agreement on the safety and efficacy of medical technologies" (Kalberer 1985, 64).

Questions have been raised about whether peer review is an "old boy system" that discriminates in favor of established researchers at prestigious research centers, about its reliability, and about the large investment in time and money simply to write a detailed proposal. In defense of the system a study by the National Academy of Sciences found that "the scientific enterprise is an exceedingly equitable, although highly stratified, social institution in which the individuals who produce the work that is most favorably evaluated by their colleagues receive the lion's share of the rewards" (Cole, Rubin, and Cole 1977). Moreover, the effort required to write an acceptable research proposal is probably rarely wasted, even for unfunded projects, since the system encourages careful preparation and clear thinking, which ought to contribute to a researcher's other work.

The Meaning of Risk

No topic in science and technology policy is more pervasive in the 1980s than risk: the probability and severity of undesired effects. The word is usually applied to matters of health and safety; undesired economic effects are considered "costs" (Lowrance 1976). Risk encompasses a wide range of issues under the jurisdiction of many federal agencies, and it affects the support and use of many types of scientific research and technological development. Much of this activity was spawned by laws requiring agencies to determine the risks of industrial technologies and scientific experiments. As noted in Chapter 2, 177 bills were submitted in the 96th Congress (1979-

1980) that included the word "risk" in their abstracts, and by 1985 33 statutes required federal agencies to consider risk and ways to reduce it.

The study of risk brings into sharp focus the tensions between scientific or technological knowledge and political goals. *Risk assessment* is the interpretation of data and the selection of methods for estimating the probability and effect of undesired occurrences. Scientific principles can be applied to risk assessment because it aspires to be no more than an objective way of describing problems. *Risk management* is the evaluation and selection of policy actions based on the acceptability of risk, and acceptability requires the application of political and social values about trade-offs between health and economic goals.

Ideally, the tasks of risk assessment and risk management should be separated since political judgments should not color the establishment of facts about risks. In practice, this seems to be impossible for many reasons. First, the word *risk* is not consistently defined in law. Phrases such as "adverse effects," "adequate margin of safety," and "substantial present or potential hazard" are commonly used. Section 4(f) of the 1976 Toxic Substances Control Act (TSCA) requires EPA to act on information indicating "that there may be a reasonable basis to conclude that a chemical substance or mixture presents or will present a significant risk of serious or widespread harm to human beings from cancer, gene mutations, or birth defects." In applying TSCA to formaldehyde exposure, EPA interpreted this passage as follows (*Federal Register,* May 23, 1984, 21870-21898):

1. "Significant risk of serious harm": the exposure of persons to particularly high risks
2. "Significant risk of widespread harm": the risks to exposed individuals are somewhat lower, but the number of persons exposed is very large
3. "Reasonable basis": data from laboratory tests on animals has been extrapolated using mathematical models and common tests of statistical confidence to provide an indication of how many exposed persons would contract cancer.

A second reason it is impossible to separate risk assessment and risk management is that there may be questions about which risks agencies should consider relevant. TSCA specifies that EPA is to minimize carcinogenic, mutagenic, teratogenic (causing fetal malformations), and behavioral risks, but other laws require that FDA, in regulating food additives, is to consider primarily carcinogenic risks. Third, data on health and safety problems are often extremely poor, causing agencies to concentrate on risks that are amenable to study. An EPA planning director for air quality admitted that "we focused on cancer because that's where the data are" (Stanfield 1985). Fourth, there are no generally accepted techniques for extrapolating across species (from laboratory rats to humans), across dosage levels (is a concentration of ten parts per million ten times worse than one part per million?), or across time (is a high but short exposure to radiation less dangerous than a long-term, low dose?) (Hadden 1984). Fifth, few agencies have tried to separate those employees engaged in "scientific" risk assessment from those responsible for "political" risk management, and complete separation is probably impossible given the unavoidable mixture of science and policy in risk assessment (National Research Council 1983). Finally, risk assessors, like other policy analysts, cannot be assumed to be capable of isolating their work completely from personal or political biases (Jenkins-Smith 1982).

Many of these problems with risk analysis arise because the legal mandates given to agencies are unclear, inconsistent, and indecisive.[2] Yet it is doubtful that even the most thorough and well-founded statutes or executive orders could solve the problems of risk analysis, given its complexities and uncertainties, since neither Congress nor the president can simply declare that the gap between risk assessment and political choice is closed. Nevertheless, it might be possible to make the issues more distinct. For example, the Office of Science and Technology Policy (OSTP) drafted a framework of the general principles that guide analysis of carcinogenesis to "serve as the basis for consistent regulatory cancer guidelines that the Federal agencies can tailor to meet the requirements of the legislative acts they are charged to implement" (*Federal Register,* May 22, 1984, 21594-21661; see also Rushefsky 1985). Moreover, as a step in this direction, members of Congress have proposed the Risk Assessment Research and Development Act, which would create a "federal scientific advisory agency" to coordinate and refine risk analysis techniques.

Even if a perfectly objective risk assessment could be produced, the task of risk management is necessarily political. Given the uncertainties of data and methods that plague risk analysis, experts can usually be found to take opposite sides of an issue (Meehan 1984). Comparisons of risks (for example, living next to a nuclear plant is less risky than living in Denver because of the cosmic rays that reach high altitudes) are based upon assumptions about voluntary action and unavoidability that are not always made clear. In addition, the comparison of risks and benefits—identifying, measuring, and comparing by some common measure all of the relevant values and variables—cannot be completely scientific.

Cost-Benefit Analysis

As risk analysis seeks to balance health and safety costs against expected benefits, cost-benefit analysis is intended to balance economic costs and benefits. It has been required for "major" policy making by all executive agencies by President Reagan's Executive Order 12291, and many independent agencies have voluntarily agreed to comply with its guidelines for determining the "potential net benefits" of agency policies.[3]

In spite of its major effect on policy making, E.O. 12291 does not define *cost*. Instead, it refers to "a major increase in costs or prices for consumers, individual industries, Federal, State, or local government agencies, or geographic regions," and "significant adverse effects on competition, employment, investment, productivity, innovation, or on the ability of United States-based enterprises to compete with foreign-based enterprises." Thus, costs are significantly but only tangentially related to science and technology. The word *benefit* is also undefined, but in practice it often connotes reduced safety and health risks, so scientific questions frequently emerge in cost-benefit analyses.

As already discussed, risks are hard to measure, and converting them into a common metric, usually dollars, is often impossible; yet bureaucrats are frequently required to try. In the early 1970s FDA considered banning DES (diethylstilbestrol, a synthetic chemical, similar to female sex hormones, that promotes growth in cattle) because of studies showing, for example, that 6.25 parts per billion of DES in the diet of mice caused a significant increase in cancer. Was the chemical safe for humans? It was estimated that banning DES would cause an increase in the price of beef of 3.85 cents per pound. What could a cost-benefit analysis tell a policy maker about the *net* benefits to society of banning DES? (Hadden 1984; Wade 1972).

One of the arguments in favor of cost-benefit analysis is that it forces agencies to reveal the evidence that justifies their decisions, thereby opening the process to wider participation. In addition, it can force analysts to examine more of the consequences of agency policies, to find new ways to measure benefits and costs, and to illuminate the economic aspects of policies (Whittington and Grubb, 1984). Cost-benefit analyses may not, however, be able to escape the normative problem of setting a value on benefits (how much is a life, or a reduced risk, worth?), or even determining what constitutes a benefit, now or in the future. For example, Westinghouse found that its costly efforts to comply with environmental regulations eventually resulted in a net profit for the company after it marketed its pollution-control techniques to other firms. Cost-benefit analysis is not equipped to assess the distributional effects of policies that provide benefits disproportionately to different groups of society.

In some agencies risk analysis and cost-benefit analysis are uncoordinated, performed by different offices. The assumptions and models on which these analyses are based are likely to be forgotten as the results are put to use. Moreover, cost-benefit analysis often exacerbates the inconsistencies between agencies since different values can be attached to the loss of life or the risk of disease or injury.[4] These problems are not merely academic exercises for the agency personnel who are required by law to try to solve them, but they illustrate the critical tension between fact finding and policy making.

Constraints on the Bureaucratic Use of Scientific Knowledge

Advisory groups, peer review, risk-benefit and cost-benefit analyses are tools by which agencies attempt to make better-informed decisions. Each carries the potential for mischief. An unsuccessful analysis or inconclusive result is an incentive for regulators or legislators to rely less on analysts, and so for analysts to offer false confidence. Sometimes that false confidence is knowingly tolerated. A congressional study of EPA's air quality standards found that there was no "safe" pollution level but that the agency had used the idea of a "safe threshold" as "a necessary myth to permit the setting of some standards" (U.S. House of Representatives 1977, 111). Scientists and engineers often find it difficult to convey a complete picture of their work to the lawyers and administrators who write regulations and implement policies. A study of drinking water contamination is of little use to decision makers who conceive of underground water as fast-moving, invisible rivers and fail to understand the relatively slow (usually less than two feet per day) and three-dimensional movement of groundwater (*Environmental Science and Technology* 1984).

Analyses of bureaucratic behavior have suggested an inescapable logical conflict between the central authority of the policy maker and the decentralized expertise of the scientific professional, which results from the multiple decision-making points common to organizations. Even if homogeneous groups of professionals are used by each agency, "there will now be multiple and conflicting systems of preferences within the executive branch as a whole" (Hammond and Miller 1985, 17). Because of conflicts between analysts and decision makers, some agencies comply with the legal requirement that analyses be performed and then ignore the results. These characteristics weaken the link between knowledge and policies, and they make coordination of activities across agencies unlikely.

Coordination of Bureaucratic Science and Technology Policy

Public policies on nuclear power include (1) safety and design questions that affect construction, plant licensing, and site approval performed by the Nuclear Regulatory Commission and state regulatory commissions, (2) issues of rate bases, rate authority, and schedules reviewed by the Federal Power Commission and state commissions, (3) worker safety, supervised by OSHA, and (4) environmental impact studies performed by the EPA and state authorities. Federal patent policies fall under the scope of at least twenty-six federal laws, and fifty-four federal entities have responsibilities for research on ocean pollution. Under such arrangements, how can policy making be logical and consistent?

Agencies are constantly making decisions based on assumptions about future conditions, and it is often difficult or impossible—scientifically or politically—to be explicit about them, even if one tries. The range of scientific facts that can be applied is often unbounded, leading Rep. Claudine Schneider (R-R.I.) to observe, "I think one of the most amazing things that I have learned while serving on [the Committee on] Science and Technology is the lack of integration of scientific research on a broad spectrum of subjects" (U.S. House of Representatives 1981c, 15). Legislators are not the only ones frustrated by uncoordinated policies. In early 1982 the Consumer Product Safety Commission banned the use of formaldehyde foam in building insulation because of its cancer risk, and OSHA ruled almost simultaneously that there was insufficient evidence to limit worker exposure to formaldehyde.

Coordination of bureaucratic behavior depends in part on strong presidential leadership, clear congressional instructions, and control of agencies by their directors. It also depends on the attitudes of employees and the career incentives they face (Price 1983, 53). Henry Lambright summarized his study of science and technology policy in this way:

> What the Constitution divides and weakens at the top of government tends to be filled in the middle layers by administrative/congressional alliances about specific functions. Hence, a vacuous national policy finds itself standing opposite relatively cohesive fiefdoms of sectoral policy. Some sectors are strong, some weak; but, in the aggregate, they are a significant force opposing central, general political initiative. This is the major problem facing the governance of science and technology (Lambright 1976, 206).

With such overlap and fragmentation in the subcommunities of science and technology, how could there be anything but fragmentation and confusion in bureaucracy?

Approaches to Coordination

Solutions to the coordination problem depend on the particular causes of the discord. Doniger (1978) has identified three types of responses to failures of interagency coordination in determining health and safety policies. First, he suggests that agencies clarify their jurisdictions. Some statutes, such as laws affecting EPA, OSHA, CPSC, and other agencies, do in fact try to provide jurisdictional boundaries that precisely tell those agencies when to defer to others. These types of prescriptions often fail in practice. Second, bureaucrats can focus on cooperating on individual cases that fall within the domain of more than one agency. EPA has hundreds of interagency research agreements, such as an arrangement to use a NASA airplane equipped with lasers, computers, and spectrographs to make accurate measurements of air pollution levels (see Chapter 8).

Doniger's third suggestion—regular cooperation on general issues—touches on a promising practice that has become increasingly common. A growing number of interagency bodies have been created to provide coordination on general issues such as risk assessment and regulation.[5] Along with formal interagency agreements, "memoranda of understanding" have been used to allow agencies to share information and analyses. Particular substances, such as chlorofluorocarbons, have been the subjects of interagency "work groups" that have coordinated risk assessments and policies. A National Toxicology Program was established in the Department of Health and Human Services in 1978 to coordinate the testing of toxic chemicals in six agencies, and a Senior Interagency Group on Space works with NASA, the U.S. Trade Representative, and the Departments of State, Commerce, and Transportation on developing policies for commercial space launches. Of broader scope has been the Interagency Regulatory Liaison Group formed in 1977 to coordinate the programs of EPA, OSHA, FDA, and CPSC.

The problems in forming coordinating bodies are illustrated by the several attempts of the Office of Science and Technology Policy that eventually led to creation of the Biotechnology Science Coordinating Committee (BSCC) in November 1985. A large number of federal agencies (EPA, FDA, OSHA, NIH, NSF, and the Departments of Agriculture, Defense, Energy, and HHS) were brought together into a group intended to "serve as a coordinating forum" and to "promote consistency in the development of Federal agencies' review procedures and assessments." By the time a consensus on BSCC had been formed, however, outside scientists had been excluded from membership (to allow the protection of "confidential business information"), and the committee had been limited to receiving documentation, conducting analyses of "broad scientific issues," convening workshops, and holding "periodic" public meetings. Sen. Albert Gore observed that in this form the FSSC may be no more than a "toothless discussion group" (Sun 1985b).

A Department of Science

The idea of coordinating federal science and technology activities through a cabinet-level Department of Science first arose during the 1880s, and it has never disappeared. It was revived in the 1930s, in 1958, and again in the 1980s, each time accompanied by fears that "overcentralization" of American science and technology would stifle peacetime R & D. President Reagan's Commission on Industrial Competitiveness recommended in 1985 that the research activities of NASA, NIH, NSF, and other federal agencies be combined into a Department of Science and Technology not only to improve coordination, but also to aim research more toward fields with commercial applications. White House science adviser Keyworth expressed no great hurry to implement that suggestion (U.S. House of Representatives 1985, 54).

Many arguments have been offered in support of a Department of

Science. Scientists and engineers would have a representative in the cabinet that would give their efforts more status. Congress would have more influence over science and technology policy if activities now placed in independent agencies were centralized in an executive department. The nation's science and technology activities would be performed more efficiently, since duplication would be curtailed; and both human and financial resources could be more rationally allocated, since the department hierarchy would assign tasks and resolve conflicts within the science and technology bureaucracy (Brooks 1968; Humphrey 1960).

The potential drawbacks of a Department of Science are more compelling. As a practical political matter, existing agencies and their constituencies would not yield their programs without a fight. Much mission-oriented R & D would remain within larger departments such as Defense, Agriculture, and HHS; these bodies not only would be outside the influence of the new Science Department but could become competitors for research funding. Ongoing programs could be harmed by organizational shifts, and the NSF's focus on basic research could be lost if it were encompassed in a department more dedicated to applied research. In any case, Congress has shown no eagerness to transfer the authority of independent agencies such as NSF to the direct influence of the president.

Perhaps the most relevant criterion for judging proposals to create a Department of Science and Technology is whether this solution is appropriate for what are perceived to be the flaws in science and technology policy. The fragmentation of government efforts to support R & D cannot be completely eliminated because the problem is a manifestation of such basic principles as separation of powers, federalism, and open participation in policy making; nor can the task of policy support for science be completely separated from the application of science in policy making.

Fragmentation, duplication, and conflict are not entirely flaws in the system. Science and innovation appear to flourish when they are somewhat unplanned. Individual initiative and creativity need the opportunities of serendipity. Although better communication and cooperation would reduce the problems that plague risk assessment, cost-benefit analysis, and the ranking of research priorities, the virtues of pluralism—especially the opportunities for lay citizens to participate—in science and technology policy could be retained while the specific vices are addressed.

Politics and Bureaucratic Science and Technology Policy

The pressures on bureaucrats to use and support science and technology in politically acceptable ways are felt at least indirectly in almost all of their activities. Their interpretations of legislative mandates must be sensitive to the prevailing moods of Congress, the president, and the public. It was the

Geological Survey, established in 1879, that became the focus for the first intense political debate about science and technology policy making by agencies. Competition for research funds and the hostility of new western states, which feared massive land-use planning as a result of geological surveys, prompted the formation of the Allison Commission (1884-1886), a joint commission of the Senate and the House of Representatives, to investigate the federal organization of science.

This commission brought into the open a conflict that continues today: the accountability of scientists receiving federal funds as against the intrusion of politics into the programs of scientific research. The arguments by John Wesley Powell, the controversial head of the Geological Survey from 1881 to 1894, foreshadowed much of today's debates about the role of the federal government in science and technology. In justifying federal support for research, Powell claimed that knowledge is a public good that benefits all—"the laws of political economy do not belong to the economics of science and intellectual progress"—and that "all governmental research stimulates, promotes, and guides private research" (Dupree 1957, 227).

Although agencies do not comprise elected officials, they are hardly insulated from politics. Proposals for new regulations or legislation are constrained by expectations of what has a chance to succeed with Congress, the public, or interest groups. Reagan administration officials would not have tried to dismantle EPA's research office during Anne Burford's term had they not anticipated general public hostility toward "over-regulation," the approval of regulated firms, and congressional acquiescence. When they discovered that none of these political conditions existed, plans to transform EPA dissolved. Across agencies, the coordination that can be achieved depends on the community of interests that develops around each program.

The scientific component of bureaucrats' work is not neatly separable from the political component, either in its practice or in its resources. That is, it is not possible to simplify the picture by designating the work of scientists as "scientific" and all else as "political." Scientists can also be political actors, and they can be suspected of retaining their personal values regardless of how hard they try to exorcise them from their work. Not only must bureaucrats respond to political pressures when they apply scientific and technological knowledge to policy problems, but they are also buffeted by politics when they become involved in supporting R & D.

Given the confusion that is often found between or even within agencies, the bureaucracy is in a peculiar position. Bureaucrats have an enormous amount of influence over the formation and application of science and technology policy, but still, "the loose American system is the opposite of a strong bureaucracy" (Price 1978, 87). For federal agencies to realize their potential influence over these matters, they need an alliance with the third (and least directly political) branch of government. Federal judges have written of the "constructive cooperation" between agencies and the courts in the application of science and technology to further the public interest in health and safety (*International Harvester Co. v. Ruckelshaus*, 478 F.2d 615 [D.C. Cir. 1973]).

Lambright (1976) has identified two general patterns of administrative behavior within the federal science and technology bureaucracy. These patterns have emerged from the tension between the orientations of the government and the scientific community. First, the political and legal constraints facing some agencies have pushed them in the direction of "society-oriented administration," insofar as agency personnel respond primarily to politicians, purchase research from scientists, assume the initiative in selecting problems (usually short term) to be researched, focus the management of programs in Washington, and stress the "relevance" of research. Second, agencies that tend toward "science-oriented administration" are more likely to take their cues from the scientific community, support (rather than simply purchase) research, delegate initiative and program choices to scientists, evaluate more on the basis of "excellence" rather than relevance, look toward the long term, and downplay political accountability and responsiveness.[6] The two cases discussed in Chapters 8 and 9, hazardous wastes and the Space Telescope, illustrate the political forces that operate within each of these realms.

Conclusion

General theories of bureaucracy commonly try to explain why organizations become rigid and unresponsive, why they develop closely guarded ties with constituents, and why there is a general tendency for them to expand their jurisdictions and their budgets. Not surprisingly, evidence of such behavior is sought and can usually be found. Science and technology policy has not been immune from these purported flaws, but some aspects of this policy realm serve to remind us that not all types of bureaucratic behavior can be explained so succinctly. They can be the result of various combinations of forces. We cannot evaluate an agency's competence just by looking at how it processes information, because agencies are compelled to do more than that. What appears to be stubborn, mindless rigidity may be a form of procedural consistency—a virtue if its opposite is the only feasible alternative—in the face of analytic uncertainty. Reliance on only a few sources of support and advice may be simply a desire to rely on expertise, though it is much more tolerable for peer review of biomedical research decisions than for the selection of sites for nuclear power plants. And agencies surely have a tendency to grow, but the motivating force for expansion is not always clear. Where does laudable scientific curiosity for more knowledge end, and where does a selfish desire by bureaucrats to maximize their budgets begin?

The role of scientific and technological knowledge in the actions of agencies illustrates the essence of the conflicting forces that shape all bureaucratic behavior. Informed decision making carries a bias toward admitting complexity and waiting until more is known. Yet what actually happens is oversimplification, premature declarations of guaranteed justifications, and contradiction. The community of analytical and empirical truth continually fights a cold war with the forces of political expediency and pressure. The framework of forces discussed here serves as a reminder that, even in the unlikely chance of political consensus, conflict will eventually emerge. The inertia of laws, the organizational complexity of American government, and the fluidity of knowledge rule out the possibility of any sort of dynamic equilibrium in policy.

In all this, the bureaucracy is caught in the middle. It lacks a constitutional birthright, and it cannot claim democratic legitimacy. An agency needs, and develops, a constituency: perhaps interest groups or interested congressional staff, and maybe a group of scientists or engineers, but rarely the general public. That political constituency becomes the bureaucracy's sea anchor, allowing it to maneuver as it adjudicates, bargains, and balances the forces of science and technology policy.

Notes

1. U.S. House of Representatives 1981g, 105. The NAS Committee on Nuclear Power and Alternative Energy Systems was attacked for including among its fourteen members only one critic of nuclear power. See Carter (1975a).
2. For an illustrative example of the legal and scientific issues faced by regulatory agencies in assessing risk, see "Polychlorinated Biphenyls (PCBs) in Fish and Shellfish; Reduction of Tolerances; Final Decision," *Federal Register*, May 22, 1984, 21514-21520.
3. E.O. 12291 and the general characteristics of cost-benefit analysis have been discussed and analyzed at length. See, for example, V. Smith 1984; Viscusi 1985; Crandall and Lave 1981.
4. See the testimony by Michael S. Baram before the House Committee on Science and Technology, in U.S. House of Representatives 1981f, 54-68.
5. A 1978 report listed ten formal and a dozen informal mechanisms for interagency coordination. See National Science Board 1978, part 2, chap. 8.
6. These approaches are described as the "goal-driven model" and the "discipline-driven model" in a recent NSF report (National Science Foundation 1985a).

5

The Courts and the Legal System in the Policy Process

In 1982 two researchers at the University of California at Berkeley asked the Recombinant DNA Advisory Committee (RAC) of the National Institutes of Health (NIH) for permission to field test two genetically engineered bacteria that retard the formation of frost on plant leaves. Comments were solicited by publication of the request in the *Federal Register* and through direct notice to 3,000 interested persons on an RAC mailing list (but none offered public comments). After a public hearing, RAC voted 7-5 (with two abstentions) to approve the proposal. When additional safety concerns were subsequently raised, NIH decided to postpone the test, and the researchers revised their proposal. Once again notice was issued of RAC's consideration of the test, and again no public comments were received. A slightly altered proposal was approved at RAC's public hearing by a 19-0 vote.

One year after the original proposal was submitted, a lawsuit against NIH was filed in U.S. District Court by a group of environmental activists headed by author Jeremy Rifkin.[1] The suit alleged that NIH was required to prepare a formal environmental impact statement before approving an experiment that involved releases of recombinant DNA organisms into the environment. The court agreed and issued an injunction against NIH approval of field tests. NIH and the University of California appealed, and on February 27, 1985, the U.S. Court of Appeals for the District of Columbia vacated the district court's injunction against future deliberate release experiments, but it still required an environmental assessment for the California test.

The same activist that used the courts to delay what had been approved by an agency also had success in a court decision to halt the Army's plans to build a chemical and biological warfare laboratory in Utah and in slowing experiments under the Department of Agriculture to increase the size of livestock by recombining human genes into those of sheep and pigs. According to Rifkin, "There was little or no interest on Capitol Hill until we

framed that interest by forcing public policy to deal with court decisions"
(Malakoff 1985).

The Expanding Role of Courts in Science and Technology Policy

In a political system where electoral institutions are under constant
political pressure and where government agencies are forced to respond to
changing constraints, one might assume that the judicial system is the major
source of continuity in policy making. The courts are expected to ensure that
stable principles of constitutional and common law are observed, but they
can deal only with questions brought to them by litigants. Even constant
principles cause conflict in a changing world, so bedrock doctrines have
evolved in response to social, economic, and political changes, often wrought
by scientific and technological advances. In addition, those principles are
often mutually inconsistent; most Americans, for example, expect not only
the benefits of industrialization, but also a clean environment, healthy
workplaces, and safe products—all at low cost, of course. The courts also
enforce the more fluid statutory and administrative laws that affect (and are
affected by) science and technology. Moreover, the structure and functions
of the American legal system have changed in ways that affect all areas of
public policy.

Approximately five million lawsuits are filed in American courts each
year; in federal appeals courts the yearly filings increased by almost 40
percent between 1975 and 1980. As Americans have turned more to the
courts for the resolution of disputes among individuals, firms, and government, the inadequacies of legal responses have become more noticeable. In
spite of the lack of expertise of judges and legal institutions in science and
technology, they sit at the juncture of *all* the science and technology policy
arenas. It should not be surprising that their decisions often fail to resolve
the questions that Congress, agencies, and other policy makers cannot
resolve either. Yet whatever their shortcomings, the courts must play an
active role in policy making.

Public laws affecting science and technology have become both more
common and more complex, resulting in disagreements about congressional
intentions that the courts are often asked to resolve. The growth of nuclear
power in the 1950s and the burst of new health and safety regulations in the
1970s led to questions about the meanings of laws, the reliability of technical
evidence, and inconsistencies in government actions; so it has fallen largely
upon judges to determine such questions as what levels of risks Congress
implicitly designated as acceptable, or how much ambiguity in analysis was
permissible (Vig and Bruer 1982). Answers are rarely clear. When a decision
by the Occupational Safety and Health Administration (OSHA) to limit
worker exposure to the industrial chemical benzene was challenged because

of the agency's failure to balance workers' benefits against industry's costs, a federal appeals court ruled that OSHA had erred. Yet on appeal the Supreme Court held that Congress's failure explicitly to require a cost-benefit test in OSHA's statutory mandate should be interpreted as a legislative policy of emphasizing technical feasibility rather than economic consideration (*Industrial Union Department, AFL-CIO v. American Petroleum Institute*, 448 U.S. 607 [1980]).

Furthermore, procedural changes have made it easier for individuals and interest groups to participate in legal challenges to government actions. The Freedom of Information Act and the National Environmental Policy Act were among the most important steps in opening federal policies to judicial action. Individuals and interest groups could oppose government policies by seeking reversals, or at least lengthy delays, through the courts. Many other statutes passed since the early 1970s included explicit provisions enabling regulatory and other government actions to be reviewed by the courts. Although legal challenges are expensive for intervenors, they are usually cheaper than grass-roots organizing to lobby Congress, or intervention in agency proceedings, so tactics such as Rifkin's challenge of genetic engineering testing became more common.

Finally, changes in science and technology themselves have spawned entirely new legal questions and reinterpretations of old ones. As capabilities to reshape nature and avoid (or create) risks have grown, courts have had to adjust their traditional interpretations of legal responsibility. A federal district court judge in Boston ruled in 1984, for example, that the National Oceanic and Atmospheric Administration was liable for the loss at sea of three lobstermen because it had been negligent in failing to repair an Atlantic Ocean weather buoy whose data was necessary for forecasting storms. In May 1986 a federal appeals court overturned that decision, ruling that "a weather forecast is a classic example of a prediction of indeterminate reliability, and a place peculiarly open to debatable decision, including the desirable degree of investment of government funds and other resources" (*Houston Chronicle* 1986). Furthermore, new medical technologies are forcing the courts to consider basic ethical questions such as the constitutional rights of fetuses and infants unable to survive without medical treatment. The judicial system has moved from acting retrospectively (requiring proof of actual injury before taking action) to acting prospectively when scientific and technological evidence points to future risks that can be avoided (Vig 1984, 63).

Courts are, however, basically conservative institutions, relying on precedents whenever possible. They are limited in how they can respond to new problems because changes in legal doctrines and practices tend to come along more gradually than the rapid changes in science and technology. Courts are expected to be reactive, helping to navigate the course set by the Constitution, Congress, and president, rather than exploring new territory.

Legal Constraints on the Courts

Like all institutions of American government the courts must be able to justify their authority before they become involved in the science and technology policy process. That authority flows from the Constitution, from statutes, and from the public's belief in the legitimacy of the judicial system. As each of these sources provides power to judges and courts, it also sets limits on how far that power extends.

The Sources of Law

The ultimate source of law for the judicial system is the Constitution. Because *constitutional law* includes such a wide range of topics—the structure of government, the Bill of Rights, civil rights, and so on—and because it takes precedence over common, statutory, and administrative law, it affects the role of the courts in science and technology policy in many ways. For example, disputes over the extent to which Congress's "legislative power" can be delegated to experts at the Environmental Protection Agency (EPA), the Food and Drug Administration (FDA), and OSHA in health and safety matters turn on interpretations of the intentions of the Constitution's framers regarding separation and sharing of powers. As technology has advanced, the courts have been forced to apply provisions of the Fourth and Fifth Amendments on privacy and self-incrimination to questions of whether firms can require potential employees to undergo genetic screening for susceptibility to occupational diseases, whether that information can be shared with insurance companies, and whether employees have a right to see these medical analyses. Judges generally are reluctant to raise disputes to the level of constitutional interpretation, preferring to find answers in other sources of law, but fundamental questions about the powers of government and individual rights can often be resolved only by invoking the supreme source of American law.

Another authority for judicial involvement is *common law,* which draws upon a series of judicial precedents whenever possible for the purpose of consistency across courts and over time. Included in common law are concepts such as property, contract, and tort (a wrong or injury). Examples of adjustments of common law to scientific and technological advances are plentiful. Neither legislative statutes nor the Constitution answer such questions as to whom in vitro embryos "belong"—the donors of the original egg and sperm or the parents to whom the embryo is transplanted—and what are their inheritance rights. Until a legislative body passes a law that establishes, for example, the property rights of a homeowner with a rooftop solar collector that is being shaded by a neighbor's tree, judges must turn to similar past cases and try to apply the earlier logic to the current problem. Only if a judge cannot find an identical precedent to such a case can the common law be expanded by establishing a new interpretation of property rights.

The third source of legal principles is *statutory law,* consisting of the laws made by local, state, or national legislatures. The growing complexity of industrial society has increased the importance of statutory law. Because it is more comprehensive and flexible than common law, statutory law enables policy makers to respond to new information or new problems in ways for which common law precedents are missing or inappropriate. It is also vital to a growing commercial society since it allows individuals and firms to make plans with advance knowledge of legality. And because statutory law always prevails over common law, the common-law discretion of the courts is reduced as statutory law expands.

Often, however, statutory laws require interpretation and judicial review of their constitutionality, thereby tending to increase the role of the courts. Since statutory limits on judicial power are actually implemented by the judges themselves, a judge's discretion ultimately is "constrained only by the court's own self-restraint and by the possibility of Supreme Court review" (McGarity 1984, 97). Although the Constitution allows Congress to limit the appellate jurisdiction of the Supreme Court and to expand or restrict the jurisdiction of other federal courts, Congress rarely uses this power.

The fourth source of laws and legal limits on judicial participation in science and technology policy making is *administrative law.* Administrative law is intended primarily to constrain the procedures and powers of administrative agencies, but it also constrains the courts. The Administrative Procedure Act (APA), for example, requires agencies to give advance notice of decision making, to allow interested parties to argue and present evidence, and to provide reasons to justify their decisions. The courts may then review whether the agency's decision was "objectively" supported by evidence and whether its procedures were fair, but the courts cannot require agencies to follow stricter guidelines than Congress imposed.

The importance of this constraint is illustrated by the Supreme Court's landmark decision in the *Vermont Yankee* case (*Vermont Yankee Nuclear Power Corp. v. Natural Resources Defense Council, Inc.,* 435 U.S. 519 [1978]). The Court of Appeals for the District of Columbia Circuit had decided in favor of environmental groups in a dispute over nuclear power plant licensing. It ruled that the procedures of the Atomic Energy Commission—later the Nuclear Regulatory Commission (NRC)—had not allowed intervenors sufficient opportunities to question technical evidence on the disposal of radioactive wastes. But the Supreme Court unanimously reversed the appeals court's decision, finding that courts should be very cautious in requiring administrative procedures that go beyond those established by Congress lest they enter the realm of policy making. When the data are uncertain and their interpretation questionable, the judiciary's reading of administrative laws regarding evidence and substantiability is crucial for the direction of policies.

Judicial Review

The most important function of the courts in the policy process is to review the actions of Congress, the president, agencies, and state and local governments. Established by the 1804 Supreme Court decision in *Marbury v. Madison,* the Administrative Procedure Act, and many other specific statutes, judicial review allows federal courts to make certain that the federal and state governments act in accord with the U.S. Constitution and with relevant laws. This power has its greatest effect on science and technology policy when the courts are asked to determine an agency's compliance with laws and regulations governing its actions: whether it has correctly interpreted congressional statutes, followed the proper administrative procedures, and established sufficient evidence to justify its decisions.

Judicial review of agency *procedures* for science and technology policy often focuses on compliance with requirements for open meetings and notice of pending actions. If an agency, for example, relies upon a scientific advisory group that failed to comply with the provisions of the Federal Advisory Committee Act regarding public access, the agency's decisions may be overturned by a court on procedural grounds. In addition, courts may review the completeness of an agency's records or its adherence to rules regarding peer review, consistency of criteria, and so on. During the 1970s new laws imposed more specific fact-finding procedures on agencies (such as EPA's obligation to consult its Science Advisory Board), and as the *Vermont Yankee* radioactive waste case illustrates, procedural review has also been used by some judges in attempts to influence the substance of agency decisions.

The power of judges to second-guess agencies' procedures is constrained by specific statutory limitations (for example, the Veterans Administration is protected by law from judicial review of its decisions on medical disability) and by appellate decisions that sometimes tell judges that they have gone too far. The Supreme Court reversed a decision of the D.C. Court of Appeals concerning an NRC ruling on underground radioactive waste disposal, telling the lower court to "remember that the Commission is making predictions, within its area of special expertise, at the frontiers of science. When examining this kind of scientific determination, as opposed to simple findings of fact, a reviewing court must generally be at its most deferential" (*Baltimore Gas & Electric Co. v. Natural Resources Defense Council, Inc.,* 103 S.Ct. 2246 [1983]).

Judicial review may also focus on the *substance* of agency decisions. It is in this arena that questions of science and technology policy are most troublesome for judges. If the courts are to determine whether agency actions are "based on a consideration of the relevant factors and whether there has been a clear error of judgment," it must be assumed that judges are able to determine what is relevant and what is a clear error (*Citizens to Preserve Overton Park, Inc. v. Volpe,* 401 U.S. 416 [1971]). In some cases judges have been willing to delve into an agency's methodology; the Fifth Circuit Court of Appeals faulted the Consumer Product Safety Commission (CPSC) for its failure to conduct a study of randomly selected homes in its decision banning urea-formaldehyde foam insulation. In a case involving the pollution of Lake Superior from an iron mine, the Eighth Circuit Court of Appeals retained its own expert medical witness to evaluate evidence of health risks, and a Fifth Circuit panel recalculated the figures submitted by Texas in support of its estimates of regional photochemical oxidant concentrations (*Gulf South Insulation v. Consumer Product Safety Commission,* 701 F.2d 1137 [5th Cir. 1983]; *Reserve Mining Co. v. EPA,* 514 F.2d 492 [8th Cir. 1975]; *Texas v. EPA,* 499 F.2d 289 [5th Cir. 1974]).

The delicacy of substantive judicial review has been recognized by the Supreme Court in its repeated instructions to lower courts to avoid substituting their judgments for those of agencies, but the top court has not been immune to the practical problem of trying to separate procedural and substantive review. In its 1980 decision on the industrial chemical benzene (known to cause leukemia and other diseases), the Supreme Court divided on the question of whether OSHA was justified in lowering the occupational exposure standard for benzene from ten parts per million (ppm) to one ppm. Had OSHA interpreted its statute to mean that zero risk was required, or had the agency proven that the new benzene standard was adequately supported by epidemiological evidence? The Court ruled 5-4 (with four separate concurring opinions) that OSHA had failed to meet the burden of proof required by Congress; Justice William Rehnquist wrote that the deliberate ambiguity of the statute was an unconstitutional delegation of power. The Supreme Court was unable to avoid reviewing the scientific evidence for OSHA's decision, causing the four dissenting justices to criticize their colleagues for assuming the expertise and authority to make scientific judgments.

Judicial review of science and technology policy illustrates the unavoidable entangling of procedural and substantive issues. A scientifically correct answer is not legally valid if discovered by incorrect procedures, and procedures cannot be correct if they produce scientifically unsupportable answers. The dilemma for the courts is to try to separate the "science" from the "law" while evaluating both. Because the courts are assumed to be expert in only one of those arenas, the introduction of scientific and technological expertise into the courtroom is crucial to the way the legal system affects science and technology policy.

Scientific and Technological Knowledge in the Courts

The natural and engineered worlds of physical and biological processes affect the courts' participation in public policy in several ways. First, the legal system must either possess or borrow the expertise to interpret the science- or technology-based claims of contending parties. Second, courts must reconcile unavoidable scientific uncertainty with legal doctrine, which requires near-certainty. Third, the judiciary must adjust to changes in scientific and technological knowledge that affect laws and their implementation. Fourth, the legal system itself has gradually evolved in response to changes in its scientific and technological environment.

Judicial Expertise

Judicial review raises an important question about the role of judges in examining the scientific and technological substance of cases. Very few judges have formal training in technical matters, so are they able to be educated enough to distinguish conjecture from scientific fact? Chief Judge David Bazelon of the D.C. Circuit Court of Appeals once stated:

> Socrates said that wisdom is the recognition of how much one does not know. I may be wise if that is wisdom, because I recognize that I do not know enough about dynamometer extrapolations, deterioration factor adjustments, and the like to decide whether or not the government's approach to these matters was statistically valid (*International Harvester Co. v. Ruckelshaus*, 478 F.2d 615 at 650-51 [D.C. Cir. 1973]).

Therefore, Bazelon argued, "technically illiterate judges" should be content to review the process by which agency decisions are made, making sure that decisions are based on all relevant factors subject to public scrutiny. In contrast, his colleague Judge Harold Leventhal argued that judges cannot abdicate their responsibility to examine all of the substantive facts of cases before them because of the impossibility of avoiding scientific and technological issues, even if judges intend only to review administrative procedures (*Ethyl Corp. v. Environmental Protection Agency*, 541 F.2d 1 [D.C. Cir. 1976]).

It is likely that some judges are capable of learning as much science as is necessary for particular cases before them, but in practice their abilities will be limited by the need for them to master the substance of other policy areas, such as economics or finance, since judges typically rule on a panoply of types of cases. Yet the question of judicial competence depends less on the intelligence of judges than on whether it is possible and appropriate—or inevitable—for judges to try to distinguish between scientific and political analysis, or between "good" science and "bad" science. Even scientists are reluctant to pass such judgments, primarily because of the unreliability of knowledge and the data on which it is based.

Scientific Uncertainty

One constant aspect of the legal system will always shape the courts' role in science and technology policy: information is presented to judges and juries, and courts must decide on the basis of facts. The problem is for courts to find a basis for bestowing the label of "fact" on the evidence. To determine which of several competing hypotheses is best supported by the evidence, courts must assess the reliability of the evidence. Recognizing that all empirical knowledge is inherently uncertain, a court evaluates evidence by tests such as "preponderance of the evidence" in civil cases or "beyond a reasonable doubt" in criminal cases. Ideally, on this basis a court accepts or rejects arguments or demands further studies. In practice, courts also avoid uncertainty by reformulating disputes, or they defer to the expertise of agencies (Abraham and Merrill 1986).

This process, in ideal form, sounds somewhat familiar: it is also a rough description of the scientific process. Like scientists, judges see their task as taking a look at the evidence to see if there is a "rational basis" for making a decision—in effect, using their reasoning and the rules of their discipline to make connections between concepts and what can be known about events. Judges and legal scholars, however, are less unanimous in their approach to interpretation than are scientists. One major tendency in modern jurisprudence, derived from the nineteenth-century English jurist John Austin, is "legal formalism" (or "logical positivism"), which attempts to separate law from morals. It "embodies a methodology consciously taken from a Newtonian view of natural science that makes the judicial process a matter of the deductive application of pre-existing rules within the context of fixed institutional constraints" (Biden 1985). This approach stands in contrast to "legal realism," which recognizes the subjective and indeterminate nature of judicial interpretation. Whichever model applies, the criteria used by scientists and lawyers are different. Scientists, moreover, can wait for years to accumulate additional data, but courts are constrained by the necessity of making timely decisions and by the hard fact that a court's ruling usually imposes a cost on someone. In the end scientific uncertainty must be converted into a justification for a decision and a policy.

The Changing Scientific and Technological Bases for Law

The task of ensuring consistency between facts and decisions would be hard enough in a world with scientific uncertainty and slow change, but when breakthroughs in techniques and understanding occur frequently, the courts are ill-equipped to keep up. The statutes that the courts must apply are slow to change. When Congress passed the Delaney Amendment to the Food, Drug, and Cosmetic Act in 1958, it included a mandatory ban on food additives "found to induce cancer when ingested by man or animal." Since then not only have great advances been made in determining carcinogenicity and in measuring extremely small concentrations, but also more is known about the possible benefits of substances with minuscule but measurable carcinogenic effects. Until the law is changed, the courts are limited in incorporating such new knowledge in their decisions.

In addition, the "rational basis" discovered by judges can be wrong, or at least not entirely correct. While scientific knowledge about cause-and-effect relationships progresses, the courts are largely bound by the legal tradition of relying on precedents whenever possible. Scientists expect themselves to revise basic theories when necessary, but judges are expected to allow only gradual and reluctant change. In 1985 a Rhode Island Superior Court judge ruled that the cordless-phone conversations of an alleged drug trafficker (which a neighbor had first overheard on her AM radio) were not illegally recorded by police. Like metal detectors, these new devices raised new questions about privacy and illegal searches, and court rulings that incorporated the new technology have been criticized on constitutional grounds.

Getting Knowledge into the Courts

Considering the complexity of the subject matter, the peculiar rules and norms of legal institutions, and the importance of the outcomes, it should not be surprising that the conflicts between science and the courts have not been settled. Judges may be somewhat better informed about science and technology than their predecessors, but there have been few institutional changes to reduce the inherent tensions between law and science.

To take only one of many possible examples, water policies of federal and state governments are shaped by a tension between the natural world and the legal world. There are basically three types of water in nature: water in the air, water on the surface of the earth, and water under the surface of the earth. In law, however, water on the surface of the earth is defined as (1) "diffused surface water," (2) "surface water in watercourses," (3) "surface water in lakes or ponds without connection to a stream system," (4) "spring water," and (5) "waste water"; surface water in watercourses is further subdivided into "water flowing in well-defined channels" and "water flowing through lakes, ponds or marshes, but part of a stream system" (Templer 1976, 24). Each of these legal classes of water is treated by different rules of law.

The hydrologic cycle described by meteorology and geology comes into conflict with legal logic when the law tries to define ownership rights for water. Clouds (which may be seeded to cause precipitation), surface water, and ground water usually move horizontally and cross property lines, while precipitation and soil moisture move primarily vertically. Because water rights developed under common law when little was known about the science of hydrology (and especially the vertical movements of water), courts find themselves in quandaries when asked to determine who has a better legal claim to water as it moves through the hydrologic cycle (Templer 1976).

There has been no lack of suggestions about reforming the legal system to improve the ability of courts to apply scientific and technological knowledge. The adversarial procedures used in courtrooms have been criticized as inappropriate for the determination of scientific fact. There is no guarantee that a court will hear all sides of each issue in any case, and in complex scientific and technological cases it is often difficult to know who is on which side or whether all affected parties are represented (Jasanoff and Nelkin 1981). Furthermore, an adversarial decision process is likely to distort facts: "no process that forces the parties into logically indefensible positions, and depends for important information upon the testimony of self-interested advocates, is conducive to reasoned decisions" (Yellin 1981, 531). The clash of extreme opposites is much more tolerable in those policy settings where bargains can pacify each side, but when courts must produce all-or-nothing decisions, the choice of whose "facts" to believe becomes hard to compromise.

To improve the courts' ability to assess competing claims, new mechanisms have been proposed to bring more expertise into the legal process. A formal role for outside experts immediately raises questions about which experts and how they are to be chosen. Contradictory expert opinion is hardly rare. A range of testimony, for example, about possible genetic tendencies toward antisocial behavior for males with an extra male chromosome ("XYY" males) has led to conflicting legal opinions about the proper punishment for accused "supermales." This particular issue came to light in an Australian murder case in which a defendant was acquitted because of his genotype (Blank 1981). Even in a world of scientific certainty it would still be possible for experts to tailor their advice to nonscientific factors: expertise is a necessary but not sufficient basis for reasoned decision making.

Another possibility for improving the flow of legally useful scientific and technological knowledge would be the institutionalization of expertise within the courts. Courts could hire science clerks in addition to law clerks, or they could create standing committees composed of scientists, engineers, and lawyers, perhaps to be appointed by the president with Senate confirmation. The courts' science experts would try to separate the technical questions in complex cases from the legal questions and would offer judgments only on the former (Leventhal 1974). There have also been calls for permanent scientific "special masters": experts brought into a court, usually on an ad hoc basis, to provide advice on matters such as school desegregation and water pollution.

A frequently mentioned possibility for improving the courts' consideration of scientific and technological evidence has been a "science court" in which impartial and expert scientists from disciplines "adjacent" to a particular dispute would act as judges, hearing testimony from other experts who would be allowed to cross-examine one another in a courtlike setting. The scientist-judges would then offer opinions of the scientific evidence (but *not* questions of public policy), which could then be more usefully absorbed by real judges (Task Force 1976; Casper 1976; Abrams and Berry 1977).

Experience with facsimiles of science courts do not offer much hope. The term *science court* was bestowed on meetings held between EPA officials and representatives of firms that manufacture di-(2-ethylhexyl) phthalate, a carcinogenic component of plastic products, but opposing points of view were not invited (Sun 1981). An attempt by the FDA to use a public board of inquiry with procedures roughly similar to those of a science court led to delays, disagreements over procedures and substance, and finally the FDA administrator's rejection of the board's recommendation that the artificial sweetener aspartame not be approved. In spite of the practical problems with science courts—among them, the utility of adversarial processes and the ability of judges to use the recommendations of science courts—the general concept has definite appeal. In 1985 the Administrative Conference of the United States urged that "agencies with regulatory programs that depend on scientific determinations consider experimental use of a process similar to the FDA's Board" (*Federal Register*, December 27, 1985, 52893).

The practicality of most proposals for reforming science and technology in the courts depends on the contentious question of whether technical and legal issues are indeed separable. One advocate of a new legal advisory committee on scientific matters commented hopefully that "it would be best if members of such a committee were trained in both technical matters and law," and that they would be consulted only when a judge chose to use their expertise (Yellin 1981, 555). But these suggestions merely skirt the issue of whether science and law can be—or should be—separated. A structural reform works only if it fits the requirements of the system in which it is installed.

Something like a science court could be useful in exposing issues and allowing judges and others to be educated about scientific and technological knowledge. But just as there are trans-scientific issues with fuzzy areas between the scientific and the political realms, there are "trans-legal" questions in which issues are presented as legal controversies but for which the methods of law are inappropriate (Weinberg 1972). These are likely to be questions of science or politics, not law. A study of the role of the courts in clean air regulation found that what the courts need most is a better understanding of *administrative* issues, not technical ones. The courts have gotten into trouble when they have relied on general impressions and sketchy evidence to conclude that an environmental or administrative problem exists and then issued haphazard instructions on how the EPA should deal with it (Melnick 1983, 388).

The courts run into these problems not only because of their lack of scientific expertise but also because of political constraints and the lack of common rules and criteria within government.

The Courts and Coordination

The courts are in an awkward position in judging science and technology policy, for they can claim little expertise. All federal and many state judges are unelected, yet they claim the authority to review the actions of elected officials. Moreover, their decisions can be final. It would be amazing if they ever pleased everyone.

Nevertheless, there are some minimal standards to which courts, like other policy makers, are held. For one, they must obey the law. They should also be expected to be sensitive to scientific and administrative feasibility. In addition, their decisions are constrained by the need to coordinate with other policy makers. If courts were regularly in conflict with agencies or legislatures over science and technology issues, the policy process would have a serious and blatant flaw. Similarly, legal procedures and standards are expected to be consistently applied both within a court and across the entire legal system.

Coordination with Agencies

In the discussion of judicial review it was stated that courts usually defer to lawmaking institutions on the substance of policies. Decisions of Congress and the president are not casually contradicted by judges. Judicial institutions may follow procedures different from those of agencies, but like agencies they are ultimately bound by due process, the need for justification, and the substantive intent of specific statutes. In fact, Federal Judges Bazelon and Leventhal have agreed that in some areas of science and technology policy Congress created a "partnership" between agencies and courts to promote "reasoned decisionmaking" (*International Harvester Co. v. Ruckelshaus*, 478 F.2d 615 at 647 [D.C. Cir. 1973]).

Although agencies and courts tend to pull in the same direction, they also have some significant differences that lead to coordination problems. Like all government institutions, courts have supporting constituencies (most notably the legal profession) whose interests and perspectives may differ widely from the scientific, economic, and political constituencies of government agencies. Furthermore, the functions of courts and agencies in the science and technology policy process differ in ways that make coordination difficult. Agencies must formulate, adopt, and implement policies—all requiring a sensitivity to political factors and, consequently, a willingness to balance interests and find compromises. Yet the courts that review these actions are expected to apply "objective" and "reasoned" criteria based on hard law, not the give and take of politics. This distinction is not always strictly observed; the plurality of Supreme Court justices in the *Benzene* case based their assertions about OSHA's interpretation of congressional intent on "a replacement of the balance between risks, costs, and benefits attempted by Congress" (Matheny and Williams 1984, 438).

Finally, coordination between agencies and courts is sometimes weakened by the differences in the standards of "burden of proof" found in scientific, regulatory, and legal arenas. Scientists commonly apply a statistical standard of 5 percent error probability (that is, their results would have been accidentally found less than 5 percent of the time). Regulators also commonly apply such scientific standards to their decision making, but they are usually not required to do so by law. In practice, the level of certainty that agencies adopt is likely to be influenced by political factors such as pressure to delay decisions or the need for compromise. The courts fall somewhere between the scientific and political poles: they need not apply strictly scientific standards, but neither can they arbitrarily choose the most convenient tests of burden of proof.[2] Thus, much of the lack of coordination between courts and agencies on science and technology matters can be attributed to differences in structure, functions, and procedures. Separation of powers ensures that the lack of coordination will continue.

Coordination among Courts

There are 50 state court systems in the United States and more than 100 federal district and appeals courts. Under the Constitution's supremacy clause the federal government can dispose of part of the coordination problem by preempting the jurisdiction of state courts and agencies where "Congress has taken the particular subject matter in hand" (*California v. Zook*, 366 U.S. 725, 729 [1949]). Although there are some structural and procedural differences between these courts, the legal norm of consistency should provide a high level of uniformity among courts. There are occasions, however, when judicial coordination fails.

Sometimes coordination problems in the courts are clearly revealed. A lower court's decision may be overturned on appeal, indicating a failure to adhere to precedent or to anticipate correctly the attitudes of higher courts. In those courts in which rulings are made by panels of three or more judges, such as federal courts of appeals, judges may openly disagree or apply contradictory logic to a case, as in *Ethyl Corp. v. EPA* (discussed above in the section Judicial Expertise). The *Benzene* case, also discussed above, illustrated how badly divided even the Supreme Court can be. Although the majority's decision has the force of law, separate concurring decisions or internal contradictions within the majority decision will leave doubts about how similar issues will be decided in the future.

Similarly, a court may fail to apply the same reasoning from one case to another. For example, in its 1971 *Overton Park* decision the Supreme Court encouraged courts to scrutinize strictly the substance of the evidentiary records of administrative proceedings; in the 1978 *Vermont Yankee* case it unanimously instructed lower courts to defer to agency expertise; in the 1981 *Benzene* case the Court became entangled in assessing "significant risk"; and in the same year it deferred to the judgment of Congress on the balancing of risks on a case involving standards for exposure to occupational cotton dust (*American Textile Manufacturers Institute, Inc. v. Donovan*, 452 U.S. 490 [1981]).

The lack of coordination among courts provides an incentive for lawyers to "forum-shop," that is, to choose courts that are more likely to produce favorable decisions. For example, the Ninth Circuit Court of Appeals in San Francisco has been more sympathetic to questions of environmental and civil liberties than other courts; in mid-1984, it had lost all twenty-two Supreme Court appeals of its decisions. There have been other indicators of the lack of judicial coordination, such as "races to the courthouse." Litigants who expect certain courts to be more agreeable than others sometimes go to extremes to be the first to file a petition for review in one of the twelve U.S. courts of appeals, since subsequent petitions in other courts usually must be forwarded to the court where the first petition was filed. When the EPA was about to issue a final rule banning the chemical Compound 1080, used in the control of predators, one law firm continuously occupied the only public telephone near the issuing office so that a colleague at the Tenth Circuit Court in Denver could be notified immediately. Other would-be litigants have used walkie-talkies and human signaling chains. Some laws such as the Clean Air Act, the Resource Conservation and Recovery Act, and the Safe Drinking Water Act provide for exclusive judicial review in the D.C. Circuit Court of Appeals, but races to courthouses have plagued attempts to issue some types of regulations in a calm and coherent manner.

The Effects of Incoordination

Not all of these problems of courts in coordinating their decisions are unique to science and technology policy, but they illuminate one of the most important reasons that there is *no* single science and technology policy. The policy-making system is fragmented, with no central guidance and with various institutions pursuing different goals. "Consistency and neutral principles are not problems until there are many occasions for decision; the reach and complexity of contemporary administrative law have made them problems" (Rodgers 1981, 302).

Some may be willing to tolerate poor coordination of courts' decisions since it weakens them as a major source of direction in science and technology policy. Moreover, coordination problems not only facilitate, but also reflect the role of political forces in the legal system.

Politics in the Courts

At no time during American history has there been a serious direct assault on the judiciary's independence. The Constitution's framers and their descendants attempted to insulate the federal courts from public opinion, popular passions, and interest group pressures insofar as federal judges are not elected and serve for life. Nevertheless, the courts are unavoidably a part of the political system if only because they are active in policy processes that give people incentives to complain.

Politics and Judicial Appointments

The president's power to nominate federal judges and the Senate's customary willingness to confirm nearly all presidential nominees has meant that the federal bench can be ideologically tilted by an active president. Presidents as dissimilar as Jimmy Carter and Ronald Reagan have been accused of trying to mold the federal judiciary into a long-lived legacy of their administrations. Because the political effect on science and technology policy is greatest in the realm of social regulation, such as health, safety, and environmental policies, this is the arena in which ideologies are most likely to affect the application of knowledge in the policy process. For example, Richard A. Posner, a recognized economist and legal scholar and an articulate advocate of applying cost-benefit analysis to legal questions, became an intellectual leader in the federal appeals courts following his appointment to the bench during the Reagan presidency. Posner wrote compelling arguments to support a sharply constricted public role in regulating risk.

The Court as a Political Forum

Because citizens have the right to petition the government through the courts, the judicial system has always been a mechanism for taking political action. Since the mid-1960s, however, the courts have been used more and more often as a political forum. The National Environmental Policy Act, the Freedom of Information Act, the Government in the Sunshine Act, and other agency-specific statutes have made it far easier for private citizens and interest groups to use the legal process to intervene in government decision making. Moreover, many specific statutes have included provisions that allow private citizens and groups to bring suits against violators of federal laws. For example, in 1985 Public Service Electric & Gas Co. of New Jersey reached a $100,000 settlement with the Friends of the Earth and the New Jersey Public Interest Research Group, which had sued for pollution violations under the federal Clean Water Act.

Administrative law has undergone a gradual reinterpretation in an attempt to improve the legitimacy of the administrative process (Stewart 1975). Largely in response to the perceived over-representation of regulated interests (primarily businesses) in agency proceedings, there was a slow but steady move toward increasing public participation in decision making. As "public confidence in the scientific accuracy of agency decision making has diminished," participation in health and safety matters has been broadened both in agencies and in courts (Breyer 1982, 351). A large part of this change has occurred in the realm of "standing": the legal right of individuals and groups to enter a court action (Orren 1976). Legal standing to challenge agencies also became easier for intervenors to gain as the courts gave broader interpretations of environmental laws requiring "adequate consideration" of effects on the quality of human life (*Calvert Cliffs' Coordinating Committee, Inc. v. AEC,* 449 F.2d 1109 [D.C. Cir. 1971]). Similarly, as private actions (those in which the government is not a party) have become more involved with scientific and technological issues, the courts have been used to enforce notions of "social responsibility" on scientists and technologists (Tribe 1971).

The use of the courts for political purposes has extended beyond intervention in agency decision making. Since the early 1970s the judicial system has been increasingly exploited as a device for educating the public or for steering the public agenda. The example that began this chapter illustrates one way the system works. While Rifkin's use of the courts was a direct attempt to alter government actions, many citizens groups emphasize public education as a goal in their efforts to affect public policies through court actions. A study of legal maneuverings on nuclear power plant licensing found, however, that the courts were probably an ineffective educational forum because of limited publicity and debates over incomprehensible technical data (Ebbin and Kasper 1974, 192). Because the legal process is better at reacting than anticipating, its usefulness as a forum for guiding future actions is indirect and limited.

Conclusion: Responsibility and Accountability of the Courts

The American judicial system was designed on the premise that judges should not be held accountable to or be dependent upon the general public for their decisions. Instead, they were to be responsible to the legal canons of objectivity, consistency, and dispassion. Yet it has become increasingly impossible for the courts to avoid political questions about science and technology policy. Their political entanglement is practically guaranteed by constitutional and legal ambiguities, by difficulties in applying static principles to a rapidly changing world, and by the political content of every public policy question. These factors led David O'Brien to call for restraint in relying upon the courts in science and technology policy:

> The chilling effects of judicial independence, as much as the limitations of judicial competence, the institutional structure of the judicial forum, and the adjudicatory process, dictate a modest role for the judiciary when intervening in science-policy disputes and when reviewing legislative and administrative assessments of technology and the promulgation of health, safety, and environmental regulations (O'Brien 1982, 103).

The courts have an unavoidable responsibility, however. The statutes passed by Congress and the regulations issued by executive agencies are not always well designed for managing science and technology policy. They may be very general, allowing adaptation to scientific or technological change but requiring interpretation by courts. Or the laws may be very specific, reducing the need for interpretation but requiring the courts to oversee their applicability as advances in knowledge make problems slide away from old statutory or regulatory solutions. Because science and technology often affect economic and social life immediately, the participation of the courts in the policy process is legitimate.

This role must be bounded, however, because of the undemocratic structure of the courts and because of their limited expertise. Congress, the executive branch, and agencies are capable of providing both legitimacy and expertise to the policy process; but when they are unable or unwilling to judge scientific and technological issues, the responsibility becomes that of the courts. Thus, no one has been able to suggest a precise formula for determining the optimal role of the courts in the science and technology process. Those who call for reforms such as science courts will continue to ask, How can expertise and democratic values be balanced? This may be one of many political questions that, because of its implied premise of simplicity, has no answer.

Notes

1. *Foundation on Economic Trends, Jeremy Rifkin, Michael W. Fox, Environmental Action, Inc., Environmental Task Force, Plaintiffs, v. Margaret Heckler, James E. Wyngaarden, Richard Krause, Defendents,* Civil Action No. 83-2714, U.S. District Court for the District of Columbia.
2. See the argument of Judge J. Skelly Wright in *Ethyl Corp. v. EPA,* 541 F.2d 1, 23 n. 58 (D.C. Cir. 1976), and McGarity 1979.

6

The Public in the Policy Process

In March 1811 bands of masked rioters began a five-year wave of nighttime terrorism throughout England. The Luddites burned textile factories, smashed machinery, and sometimes murdered the factory owners who supported mechanization. Their violence was sparked by their opposition to job losses caused by the new manufacturing technology, and they felt threatened by the transition from old customs and work habits to mechanized factory systems (Thompson 1963).

In recent times those who see their livelihoods and life styles threatened by new technology have raised similar concerns. Workers and unions worried about automation of assembly lines in the 1950s and about industrial robots and ubiquitous video display terminals in the 1980s. Social activists have warned of the dangers of scientific research and forecasted a technological wasteland in which individuals would lose their identity. Political protest techniques have become more refined, however; the frame breaking of the Luddites has been replaced by the more chaste practices of the legal profession.

Throughout the history of conflicts between the public and technological innovators, there have been waves of hope and discontent—from the technological utopias of Francis Bacon and Edward Bellamy to the warnings about technical servitude of Thorstein Veblen, Jacques Ellul, and Theodore Roszak. The decade following World War I was an era of rapid growth industry and in consumer technology, when science and technology entered the home through radios and refrigerators, and even basic research became familiar to the general public as Einstein was elevated to a celebrity. Yet during the next decade the Depression caused many to suspect that the technological economy was largely responsible for their misfortune.

Some scholars, corporate officials, and politicians see Americans in the 1980s turning against science and technology in ways that damage the nation's economic strength,[1] yet never in American history has there been widespread public opposition to science or technological progress in general.

Nevertheless, public opinion in the United States always has the potential to affect science and technology issues.

Scientific Disputes and Public Controversy

There has been no clearer illustration of the general public's potential role in science and technology policy than the dispute in 1976 in Cambridge, Massachusetts, over the safety of a new laboratory at Harvard University. The issue was raised because the laboratory would be used for experiments in recombinant DNA (deoxyribonucleic acid), about which some Harvard scientists and nonscientists had deep concerns. After an inconclusive campus forum to debate the safety question, the mayor of Cambridge took up the cause. The city council declared a short moratorium on recombinant DNA research and established an Experimentation Review Board of lay citizens. The review board heard testimony from opposing sides and after several months produced a report that strengthened but did not radically change existing federal safety guidelines.

The Cambridge experience has been described as a turning point in the participation of the public in science and technology policy. Although it has never been repeated, it illustrates the wide variance to be found in the factors that affect meaningful public participation. First, no legal restrictions affected the ability of average citizens or politicians to decide the issue. There were rancorous public hearings where legal standing was not an issue, and the city's authority to regulate local research as a health hazard was not likely to be preempted by the federal government. Second, the problems of lay participation in scientifically complex issues were clearly laid out: "scientists continued to control the scope of the debate, the underlying assumptions, and the composition of the opposing sides" (Goodell 1977, 37). Third, it was difficult to define which part of the public was participating because those opposed to DNA research "had no institutional basis to provide support and no matrix for organization" (Goodell 1977, 38). Finally, the scientific issue was thoroughly intertwined with nonscientific (in this case, political) questions. Many of the opponents of DNA research had been outspoken antiwar activists and were perceived as habitual radicals, and the mayor of Cambridge openly clashed with researchers over who had the power to make decisions.

Several aspects of the Cambridge case will reemerge later in this chapter. For example, it is typical for the public to become involved only after scientific experts are unable to reach agreement; and on those unusual occasions when members of the general public do become involved in science or technology policy, because of their dependence on experts for information they frequently act more as jurors than as direct participants. In addition, as the four general categories of policy factors—law, knowledge, coordination, and politics—are discussed, it becomes obvious that for each case of science and technology policy "the public" is usually irrelevant. What matters are the many small and shifting subgroups of the general public as they enter the policy process at different stages, in different ways, and with varying effect.

Who Is "the Public"?

It would be grossly misleading for anyone studying the policy process to think of all American citizens as simply "the public." In no area of policy does the American public think or act completely homogeneously, and given the nature of science and technology, widespread involvement in these policy issues is hardly likely. Participation in science and technology policy may come ·from environmental and consumer organizations, practicing scientists, and scientific or medical associations, but only occasionally from the general public (Culliton 1978, 149). More than a half century ago John Dewey sought this illusive "public":

> Legislatures make laws with luxurious abandon; subordinate officials engage in a losing struggle to enforce some of them; judges on the bench deal as best they can with the steadily mounting pile of disputes that come before them. But where is the public which these officials are supposed to represent? . . . Just as philosophers once imputed a substance to qualities and traits in order that the latter might have something in which to inhere and thereby gain a conceptual solidity and consistency which they lacked on their face, so perhaps our political "common-sense" philosophy imputes a public only to support and substantiate the behavior of officials. How can the latter be public officers, we despairingly ask, unless there is a public? (Dewey 1927, 117).

Drawing upon Gabriel Almond's work, Jon Miller has described a pyramid of publics relevant to science policy (Almond 1950; Miller 1983). At the top are a very few decision makers who interact with the more numerous "policy leaders" at the next lower level. Policy leaders are outside the government (at least temporarily), perhaps heading interest groups, teaching at universities, or publishing on science and technology issues, and lobbying for policy changes. At the third level of the pyramid comes the "attentive public" comprising interested and somewhat knowledgeable people (see Table 6-1). At the bottom of the pyramid is the huge mass of inattentive people who are neither interested nor informed about science and technology matters. Their influence over policy has the potential of becoming significant only if they are sufficiently aroused, which seldom happens. Even spectacular events such as the explosion of the space shuttle *Challenger* or the destruction of the Soviet nuclear power plant at Chernobyl captured the attention of the mass public for only a few months, and very few appear to have become active in science and technology policy as a result.

Each science and technology policy question will have a separate pyramid of publics since each issue will involve different combinations of

Table 6-1   Attentiveness of the U.S. Public to Science and Technology
Issues, 1979-1983 (Percentage of Population)

Extent of Interest and Knowledge	All Adults			College Students, 1983
	1979	1981	1983	
Attentive[a]	19	20	24	25
Interested but inadequately informed	21	18	28	22
Not interested or attentive	61	62	47	53

Source: National Science Foundation 1985b, 146.

[a] Includes those "very interested" and "very well informed" about science or technology.

decision makers, policy leaders, and the attentive public. Those who were
mobilized into involvement in genetic research policy in the 1970s were not
identical to those who opposed nuclear power plants. Even similar issues will
be decided by slightly different sets of participants. Hazardous waste and
acid rain may both involve some of the same officials at the Environmental
Protection Agency (EPA), members of Congress, and interest groups, but
the participating industrial and environmental personnel will be determined
by the nature of their business, or by what part of nature they see as their
business.

Policy issues spark different degrees and types of participation by these
portions of the public pyramid. Dorothy Nelkin (1984) has suggested four
types of controversies that are likely to motivate individuals and interest
groups: (1) local projects that are believed to impose heavy costs on a
community (such as an airport or a nuclear power plant), (2) threats to
health or environment, (3) limitations on freedom of choice (such as banning
saccharin or laetrile), and (4) conflicts with traditional or religious values.
Not all participants are motivated by a public-minded desire to become
active in policy making. Some individuals or groups are attracted to an issue
because they have coinciding responsibilities; a mayor, an architect, or a
seismologist may be brought into the "policy leader" stratum when asked to
testify to a congressional committee following a large earthquake. In
addition, when policy leaders disagree among themselves or fail to convince
decision makers, they may try to mobilize the attentive public for support
(Miller 1985). In some rare but significant cases (for example, fluoridation
and nuclear power), scientific issues have been presented to the local or state
electorate for their judgment by referendum.

What Is "Participation"?

A definition of *participation* is somewhat simpler than a definition of
public but also necessarily imprecise. A study of science and technology

policy in western democracies by the Organization for Economic Cooperation and Development defined public participation as "any activity by any
person, group of persons or organization, other than elected or appointed
officials of government or public corporations, that directly or indirectly is
aimed at taking part in or influencing the affairs, decisions, and policies of
the government or public corporation" (Nichols 1979, 15). This could
include writing to members of Congress or local newspapers, picketing
nuclear facilities, or commenting on proposed regulations. The discussion in
this chapter will be confined to attempts to participate *directly* in the science
and technology policy process since indirect participation is hard to identify,
describe, and explain. Nevertheless, it should be remembered that participation can serve other functions besides influencing policy—such as group
strategy and communications, conflict resolution, or even personal therapy
(Wengert 1976).

Law and Public Participation

As befits a nation that proclaims democratic principles, the United
States has few laws that constrain its citizens' attempts to influence science
and technology policies. To the contrary, the American legal system has its
greatest effect on public participation in its provision of opportunities, not
obstacles. Nevertheless, as members of the public try to affect science and
technology policy, they may confront several types of legal impediments.

Legal Limitations

One of the most fruitful paths for the public to pursue in affecting
science and technology policy is the judicial system. As discussed in Chapter
5, the courts impose the constraint of standing on those wishing to
participate. Not only must an activist be able to prove an "interest" in a
pending matter, but that interest must be covered by a statutory or
constitutional guarantee of protection.

Traditionally, this doctrine required proof of personal economic loss, but
major changes occurred after World War II. The 1954 Atomic Energy Act
promised standing to "any person whose interest may be affected" by
nuclear power plant licensing proceedings, and a 1957 amendment *required*
a public hearing before issuance of a construction permit or operating
license. The movement toward liberalization of standing before agencies and
courts accelerated during the 1960s. Since then a large number of court
decisions, primarily on civil rights and environmental issues, have expanded
the doctrine of legal standing to include those who claim to represent the interests of the public (Orren 1976; Stewart 1975). For example, because the
environment affects all citizens, anyone might claim standing to challenge
government policies affecting the environment.[2] In fact, more lenient policies

on legal standing are likely to increase the participation not only of private citizens and interest groups but also of business firms, state government officials, and any other group that can claim to be affected by science and technology policies with a broad (that is, health, safety, or environmental) impact. Although this may appear to be movement in the direction of democratic participation, narrower guidelines on standing would move many controversies from courtrooms back to the traditional representative policy-making arenas (Melnick 1983).

Another legal practice that constrains public participation in science and technology policy is the availability of information. Individuals or groups wishing to challenge a policy must be able to know why it was chosen or how it is to be implemented. In a legal proceeding the "discovery" phase can be crucial since it is the opportunity to obtain relevant information. During discovery an intervenor can request an inspection of facilities, reproduction of documents, and even interrogation of agency staff. A group seeking to block a nuclear power plant needs to know about the plant's design, construction, and operation—information contained in the utility company's application and supporting materials. In practice, however, not all of the required information may be accessible. An agency may have allowed some of the applicant's materials to be designated as "confidential" because they contain proprietary business information. An agency's internal discussions may be relevant but may fall outside the protections of the government in the Sunshine Act. Moreover, statutory deadlines intended to reduce regulatory delay may limit the availability of information; the procedures at many agencies allow as few as sixty days for intervenors to prepare their cases before a public hearing.

Finally, an important constraint facing many would-be participants in the policy process is imposed not by specific laws but by the legal system itself. Intervention can be extremely expensive, especially when it involves courts or agencies and the required attorneys, reproduction or transcript fees, filing costs, and so on. The financial costs to participants in agency or judicial proceedings can far exceed the capacity of most individuals or even interest groups, running to hundreds of thousands of dollars.

Legal Opportunities

Many of the legal barriers to participation in science and technology policy have not changed or have even worsened over the past decades; but others have evolved, disappeared, or become avoidable. In some cases individuals and groups have found increased opportunities for participation in state and local government, and changes in laws and judicial procedures have created additional paths for affecting science and technology policies of the federal government. Many of these mechanisms for participation—advisory boards, study groups, lawsuits, and so on—are better at providing the appearance of influence than real effectiveness. Moreover, some participatory initiatives, such as the movement toward public funding for indigent intervenors in the late 1970s, have been short-lived or largely rescinded.

In recent years individuals and groups have turned to local and state governments for help in their attempts to influence science and technology policies. Also, local governments have tried to restrict scientific and technological research in weapons development. Cambridge, Massachusetts, for example, has tried referenda, ordinances, and lawsuits to ban the testing of chemical warfare agents and the construction of nuclear weapons within its city limits (Krimsky 1986). More generally, in recent years cities and states have been passing "right-to-know" laws to help them monitor risky activities such as the production and transportation of hazardous materials. In 1985 at least nine states passed or considered bills requiring companies to disclose workplace or environmental hazards.

Other changes in the federal policy process have increased public participation. Beginning with the 1964 Economic Opportunity Act's mandate for "maximum feasible participation" of the poor in the formation and implementation of social policies, there was a trend toward greater opportunities for individual and group participation that accelerated with the passage in 1969 of the National Environmental Policy Act (NEPA). NEPA embodied the principle of pluralist participation as it gave citizens, interest groups, and firms the chance to block proposed federal actions (Caldwell 1982). Before the end of the 1970s, federal agencies had prepared more than 10,000 environmental impact statements, and nearly 1,200 lawsuits had been filed under NEPA's provisions (Liroff 1981). NEPA was not the end of the push for a larger public role: "of the more than 200 public participation programs in place in federal agencies at the end of the seventies, 61 percent had been created during that decade" (Petersen 1984, 5). Not surprisingly, those favoring speedy decisions or particular actions protested that such changes would allow spurious intervention by those wishing only to delay or obstruct federal policies. The Reagan administration responded by cutting back on many federally sponsored citizen participation programs.

Similarly, other laws that were aimed at facilitating participation by opening more of the policy process to public scrutiny were often criticized for their unintended consequences. The Government in the Sunshine Act was designed to reduce secret decision making by public officials, but it has been attacked for impeding the private collegial discussions that sometimes efficiently produce good policies. Some agencies have tried to take advantage of the law's loopholes. The Nuclear Regulatory Commission attempted to redefine the word "meeting" (or to call its meetings "gatherings") to avoid Sunshine Act provisions (Large 1985). Nevertheless, Congress created a presumption in favor of openness, shifting the burden of proof to agencies to explain why they wished to close their meetings to the public. Another law aimed at increasing public participation, the Freedom of Information Act

(FOIA), allows the public to examine most agency data and records. Scientists have complained, however, that data on publicly funded research, to which the researcher expects the right of first interpretation, have become subject to FOIA raids by other researchers or by business firms (Raven-Hansen 1983). Lobbyists and those pursuing their private interests have used FOIA more than have the members of the public, for whom increased access was supposedly intended.

Other aspects of the science and technology policy process allow individuals and public groups to participate. Cost-benefit analysis provides evidence and arguments that serve as targets for interested groups wishing to challenge agency decisions (Whittington and Grubb 1984). Administrative hearings allow groups the opportunity to publicize their complaints and solicit support (Ebbin and Kasper 1974, 254). And scientific practices such as clinical research, experimentation, and safety procedures have been shaped by liability suits—or the threat of them—filed by individuals or groups (Nelkin 1984, 30).

The use of law and legal rights by individuals and groups wishing to affect policy is often revealed in actions commonly lumped together and called "bureaucratic bottlenecks," "the invasion of the Washington lobbyists," or "the litigious society." These are the effects of a devolution of political power, for better or worse. Whether the legal opportunities for public participation have overextended the public's role in science and technology policy depends on their effects, and those effects must be judged not only by their contribution to "good" policy but also by their compatibility with political requirements. Optimal policies produced in the most efficient manner can be irrelevant in a political system where legitimacy is equated with easy political access for individuals and groups.

The Public and Scientific and Technological Knowledge

If the public has a valid claim to participate in science and technology policy making, and if policy is to be judged by its ability to improve society, then it makes sense to examine whether the public is able—or willing—to make a useful contribution. How well do average citizens understand the causal connections that are so fundamental to scientific knowledge and, therefore, science issues? How do they get their information, and is it reliable and sufficiently complete? In other words, one needs to examine the link between the "real world" of scientific or technological knowledge and the policy role of the public.

What Does the Public Know?

The general public's ignorance of science and technology has provided the raw material for superstitions, astrology, and even literature. In 1921 the play *R.U.R.* premiered in Prague. The Czech playwright Karel Capek had written about a world in which artificial men, or "robots" (from the Czech word *robota,* meaning "servitude or forced labor"), revolted against their creators, leaving only one human alive. *R.U.R.* ran for 184 performances in New York. Ironically, when a worker at Diecast Corporation in Jackson, Michigan, suffered a heart attack after being pinned between an industrial robot and a safety pole in July 1984, the first recorded case of a robot-related fatality was hardly noticed (Bulkeley 1985).

Nevertheless, the public has had a rather accurate sense of the effect of science and technology on social values and economic well-being. There probably has been no "typical" period of public knowledge about science and technology. During waves of popularization, such as the 1920s and the post-*Sputnik* decade, there have been bursts of awareness of scientific and technological exotica, such as Einstein's theories and space travel; but this interest was usually on thrilled observation and not real insight. The cycle of attention and inattention has continued, with indifference and suspicion replacing fascination and support.

Even among the tens of millions of Americans who are attentive to science and technology policy, very few follow a broad range of issues. A 1979 study found that only 7 percent of the adult public could be considered "scientifically literate" insofar as they understood the scientific approach, basic scientific constructs, and major science policy issues (Miller 1983). Surveys have shown that even on broad basic questions about science and technology most Americans are simply uneducated and uninformed. An ABC News/*Washington Post* survey in September 1985 found that 29 percent of the public thought that the number of diagnosed cases of AIDS (Acquired Immune Deficiency Syndrome) was closer to one million than 10,000 (at the time the actual number was 13,000), and 36 percent believed AIDS was at least as contagious as the common cold. Soon after the nuclear power plant accident at Three Mile Island in 1979, only one-third of the respondents to a survey knew that a reactor could not explode like a bomb (Mitchell 1982). Another study revealed that about one-fourth of American adults believe that humans have lived on earth less than 100,000 years, and another 21 percent had no idea about the age of the human species (Nelkin 1982). A Harris Poll found that a majority of Americans agreed with the *New York Times* in favoring the legalization of the purported cancer cure laetrile in spite of overwhelming opposition from the medical community (Rich 1980). Figure 6-1, which compares the public perception of death rates and their causes with actual rates, shows the flaws in the general public's perception of technological risks. In an analysis of studies of how consumers incorporate risk choices into decisions, Susan Hadden (1986) showed that even when provided with adequate information about risks, costs, and benefits, most consumers—especially the poor and poorly educated—do not act rationally. They usually fail

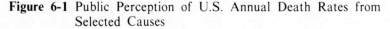

Figure 6-1 Public Perception of U.S. Annual Death Rates from
Selected Causes

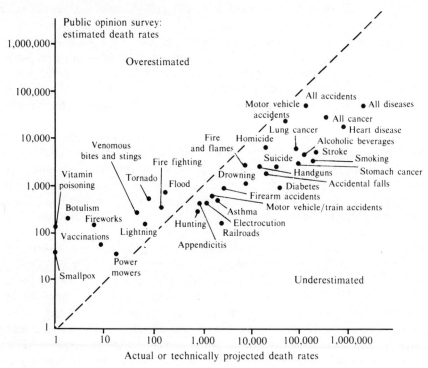

Source: P. Slovic, B. Fischhoff, & S. Lichtenstein. Rating the Risks, *Environment*, 1979,
21 (3), 15-20; 36-39. Reprinted with permission.

either to understand the information or to use it to minimize their costs or
risks.

Informing the Public

The role of schools and universities in educating the public about
science and technology is well documented. A presidential task force
concluded in its 1983 report *A Nation at Risk* that science education in
public schools was woefully inferior to that of many other industrialized
nations (National Commission on Excellence in Education, 1983). Only one-
third of all American high schools, for example, require graduates to have
taken more than one year of mathematics or science, and educators and
business leaders have voiced concerns about the relaxation of college
admission standards and of requirements in core scientific and mathematics

curricula. Once citizens have finished their formal education, what chance do they have to become well informed?

The Mass Media.   The major provider of science and technology information for the public is the mass media. Popular science magazines reach the attentive public, and even weekly news magazines and daily newspapers commonly carry feature articles on science and technology. Similarly, television programs, such as "Nova" and National Geographic Society specials, reach many viewers; and some scientists, such as Carl Sagan and Stephen Jay Gould, have the skills to communicate with large lay audiences. Of course, members of the public who buy the books of Sagan or Gould or watch their television shows are self-selected members of the small attentive public.[3] And none of these sources is intended to create a scientifically "savvy" citizen: "a person who understands how science and technology impinge upon public life" (Prewitt 1983, 56). News items are usually brief, requiring some previous knowledge for a useful understanding of the significance of the identification of a new protein or why the discovery of subatomic W and Z particles is important. They seldom place innovations in a broader context, rarely explain the methods by which science proceeds, and almost never relate the science news to policy questions.

It is not clear that "more science news" in the popular press will make a significant difference. There are fundamental differences in attitudes and ideology between scientists and journalists, who are often trained and rewarded for minimizing ambiguity and for emphasizing conflicts. By oversimplifying policy issues journalists fail to provide the public with the knowledge necessary for participation in science and technology policy. Even worse is the news media's resultant contribution to the "corruption" of science by focusing on dissenting scientists, thereby short-circuiting the peer review system and the normally self-regulating institutions of science (Rothman 1983). At times the public is exposed to lurid exaggerations, such as columnist Jimmy Breslin's description of the Three Mile Island accident in the *New York Daily News:* "steam drifted out of the tops of the four cooling towers and ran down the sides like candle wax. The steam was evil, laced with radiation."[4]

Government Information Programs.   The public might expect to receive better information about science and technology policy from government agencies. In addition to those established expressly for the purpose of providing technical information (albeit primarily to business firms), such as the National Technical Information Service, many agencies have congressional mandates to share information with the general public. (Agency officials would, however, probably recognize their self-interest in publicizing their activities anyway.) The National Aeronautics and Space Administration (NASA), for example, is required by law to publicize space flight and its spinoff benefits. Some government offices have made concerted efforts not only to inform the public but also to increase participation. As part of its mid-1970s study of Coastal Effects of Offshore Energy Systems, the Office of Technology Assessment conducted a large experiment in public participation involving public workshops, brochures, interviews, and other activities that eventually reached more than 15,000 people.

Agencies sometimes approach their informative tasks with too much zeal. Federal statutes prohibit the use of federal funds to influence federal legislation, but agencies nevertheless usually have offices of "congressional relations." Federal agencies have also tried to influence state elections and referenda. The General Accounting Office found that the Department of Energy (DOE), for example, had tried to influence the outcome of a 1976 California referendum on nuclear power through an expansion of its "information" programs in California in the months just before the vote. In 1981 DOE was pressured into canceling a $2-million pronuclear program that would have included "arranging public appearances and interviews with friendly journalists for DOE officials, hiring writers to prepare articles for popular magazines, arranging meetings with local government officials and private civic organizations, and holding seminars for the press" (General Accounting Office 1978; Holden 1981, 527). Because no distinct boundary exists between education and persuasion, a precise legal prescription for agencies' roles in educating the public is impossible.

The National Science Foundation (NSF) also has attempted to increase public understanding and participation in science and technology issues. In the early 1970s NSF established the Ethics and Values in Science and Technology program (EVIST), intended to support research on value assumptions and ethical implications in the use of science and technology, on public participation, and on democracy and accountability, among other topics. An attempt by the Reagan administration to eliminate EVIST was averted in 1985 when Congress instructed NSF to devote $1 million annually to the program. Although EVIST sponsored studies of public participation, it was not intended to increase it directly. For that purpose NSF created another program, Science for Citizens, in 1977 to try to correct the imbalance in expertise between business and government on the one hand and less-affluent or less-organized groups on the other. Congress prohibited the program from providing financial support for "public interest" groups or intervenors (Hollander 1984), and in 1981 Science for Citizens died from a lack of funds. In contrast to other western democracies (most notably, Sweden and Austria) the American federal government has made only minor attempts to go beyond mere opportunities for public participation and directly provide the information and funds necessary for broad public involvement in science and technology policy.

Proposals for improving the public's knowledge about science, technology, and related issues usually either avoid or fall at the question of how this is to be accomplished. In 1985 an NSF advisory panel recognized that the "education and participation of the public will require an immense amount of effort by scientists, educators, citizens, and public representatives," but could find only weak mechanisms for creating improvements: community college programs, scientists' training in ethics, adult education programs, press briefings by the NSF director, and a quarterly NSF newsletter on science and technology issues (National Science Foundation 1985a).

Perhaps the most important evidence on the ability of the general public to influence science and technology policy comes from the public itself. A survey taken soon after the Three Mile Island accident found that 38 percent of the respondents believed that public officials should "keep back information if they're afraid people will panic" (Mitchell 1982). In a 1979 survey for the National Science Board, people were asked whether most citizens were well enough informed to set scientific research goals or to decide whether new technologies should be developed; about 85 percent responded that most citizens lacked sufficient knowledge (Miller, Prewitt, and Pearson 1980). Those who promote widespread participation in the science and technology policy process must reconcile their ideals for democratic government with the fact that most Americans lack not only the capability but also the desire to participate.

Coordination of the Public

As discussed above, there is not one "public" for science and technology policy, but many. The degree to which citizens are well informed and politically active depends, among other things, on the issue and the locale involved; and not all of those who participate agree on ideology, substance, or tactics. Because the cost of information about issues and methods of influencing policies can be enormous for the individual, organizations form to reduce these costs by sharing them. Yet organization implies coordination of individuals, and even organizations face problems of minimizing conflict and costs of information. Thus, coordination is vital not only to those individuals who want to have more than a minuscule effect on policy as single voters, but also to groups.

The Problem of Collective Action

Why are there not more coordinated activities to encourage public participation in public policy? The answers are to be found in the incentives and constraints that affect cooperation. Political economist Mancur Olson has offered a compelling argument: "Unless the number of individuals in a group is quite small, or unless there is coercion or some other special device to make individuals act in their common interest, *rational, self-interested individuals will not act to achieve their common or group interests*" (Olson

1965, 2; emphasis in the original). Instead, they will ride for free, knowing that they can enjoy some of the benefits to which their efforts would have contributed only a small increment.

Yet groups do form. Some groups that affect science and technology policy are able to skirt the collective action problem by drawing upon business profits, religious tithes, or other resources. Other groups offer their members individual benefits such as magazines, professional meetings, or group insurance rates. The only large groups of nonscientists or nonengineers affecting science and technology policy are environmental groups, such as the Natural Resources Defense Council (NRDC), the National Wildlife Foundation, and the Sierra Club, whose interest in science or technology is somewhat one-dimensional: research and regulation to protect the environment. The research concerns of scientists are too diffuse and esoteric for the general public, and the methods of applying scientific knowledge to the policy process are usually important to lay individuals or groups only insofar as they aid more concrete goals such as health, safety, and prosperity. Moreover, even the "public" environmental groups usually engage the policy process through their lobbying or legal staffs that hardly resemble (though they may claim to represent) the general public. For example, in its efforts to initiate and promote policies relating to chlorofluorocarbon aerosol propellants and their effect on atmospheric ozone, the well-trained, professional NRDC staff filed petitions with the Food and Drug Administration and the Consumer Product Safety Commission and received funding from the West German government for a twelve-country comparative study of fluorocarbon regulation (U.S. Senate 1981).

Although many obstacles hinder the formation of "public" science and technology policy groups, some organizations do overcome them. In the realm of space exploration policy, for example, there are groups such as the L-5 Society and the Planetary Society, composed of members of the attentive public who attend meetings and write letters on behalf of their favorite policies. The Viking Fund was organized by the American Astronomical Society for the purpose of raising funds to allow NASA to continue operating the *Viking* lander on Mars. Although NASA had some trouble finding a legal way to accept contributions for such a specific purpose, it received $60,000 that had been collected from more than 10,000 space enthusiasts. Yet in spite of occasional bursts of activity, "the attentive public for science policy is less internally organized" than other attentive publics, such as those interested in foreign policy (Prewitt 1982, 9).

The Effects of Public Incoordination

Poor coordination of public activity is an important element in understanding why individuals and public groups generally have little influence on science and technology policy. The effectiveness of citizens and organizations in the policy process depends on their ability to provide incentives to policy makers to adopt their positions. These incentives may be career oriented, such as electoral benefits for legislators. Groups, whether friendly or hostile, can mobilize the public or other groups, generate publicity, and raise campaign funds. When a group has the potential for causing conflict in agency rule making or implementation, the incentive may be the prospect of cooperation throughout these stages of the policy process. For groups wishing to influence either legislators or administrators, the most persuasive tool may be the promise of expert information, analysis, or arguments. These incentives depend upon coordination of the public.

Even if individuals are able to form groups, they may present a confusing image of disagreement to policy makers. Some activists join the policy process to promote science, while others oppose science or its applications. The saccharin controversy illustrated the possible effects of a lack of coordination:

> Those who claimed to be the spokesmen for consumers were divided. Some viewed governmental intervention as an unjustifiable infringement on private enterprise and the free market. Others were particularly incensed because saccharin played an important role in the control and reduction of bodily weight. . . . Still others viewed the positions of the Food and Drug Administration as correct; they asserted that the saccharin industry was trying to deny a possible link between saccharin and cancer (Priebe and Kauffman 1980, 564).

Similarly, two of the largest technology-policy movements—activists opposed to nuclear power and those opposed to nuclear war—began to form organizational links only after the Three Mile Island accident (Nelkin 1981). Thus, in many cases the efforts of activists will sum to zero or be lost in the confusion.

Politics and the Public in Science and Technology Policy

The public is the ultimate origin of politics in the United States, so in one sense, there are no formal political constraints on public participation in science and technology policy. Unlike presidents, legislators, judges, and bureaucrats, the public is accountable to only itself. Only when political groups are forced to enter coalitions with one another or temper their arguments for strategic purposes are they limited by political constraints. Nevertheless, relatively few members of the public exploit this freedom. Their influence on science and technology policy is constrained primarily by their attitudes and ideology.

In contrast to the doubts of many social activists and analysts, the general public's attitudes toward science and technology have been consistently positive and optimistic. During the early days of the Republic, science and technology were discussed as moral and religious values or as manifesta-

Table 6-2   Public Perceptions of Risks and Benefits of Science and Technology, 1972-1985 (Percent)

Year	Do More Good Than Harm	Do More Harm Than Good	About the Same Amount of Each	Don't Know/ Not Sure
1972	54	4	31	11
1974	57	2	31	10
1976	52	4	37	7
1983	73	3	21	3
1984	63	5	27	5
1985	58	5	32	5

Source: National Science Foundation 1985b, 153.

tions of the American freedom to inquire (Meier 1957). Even during the bursts of antitechnology sentiment aimed at the military and industrial establishments of the 1960s and 1970s, public confidence in science remained high relative to other American institutions (Prewitt 1982).

Surveys in the early 1980s found that only a very small percentage of the American public believed that the costs of scientific research outweigh the benefits (see Table 6-2). The scientific community continued to elicit more support than organized religion, political institutions, the business and financial community, and the press; only medicine ranked higher. Americans also continue to be optimistic about the future benefits of scientific research, particularly those attentive individuals who are most likely to try to influence policy (National Science Foundation 1985b; Miller 1985).

Still, this vote of public confidence is qualified on some science and technology policy issues. About one-third of the public is willing to prohibit research that might enable people to live more than 100 years or that might discover intelligent beings in outer space (National Science Foundation 1985b, 153). These concerns have been aggregated and articulated by some activists who are unwilling to defer completely on all such questions to scientific experts (see Goggin 1984; Lappe and Martin 1978). There have always been and will always be people—lay individuals and groups, as well as many within the scientific community—who doubt the net benefits of some research and development or who worry about the implications of science and technology for democratic values.

Because modern science and technology are pervasive, expensive, and centralized, it is difficult, however, to disentangle other attitudes and ideologies (such as opposition to nuclear war, the capitalist state, or specific technologies) from antiscience and antitechnology feelings. Those groups and individuals who advocate cautious policies toward science and technology run the risk of being discounted as liberal antiwar, back-to-nature Luddites. In addition, there is an element of social class distinction in public attitudes toward science and technology since those who are most likely to follow, comprehend, and participate in these policy matters are those with more education, income, and leisure time (Yankelovich 1982).

The relationships between knowledge and ideology as determinants of policy choices have been studied by political scientists interested in voting decisions based on new complex issues. An investigation of knowledge and attitudes on nuclear power questions found that knowledgeable citizens "relied heavily on their political ideologies but did not draw on their generalized outlooks toward technology," while the less knowledgeable relied more on cues from reference groups (such as business, labor, and environmental groups):

> To be informed is to scan the full range of policy outcomes accruing from the use or nonuse of nuclear fuel, to choose consistently with the calculated costs and benefits of those consequences, to eschew group cues (but accurately perceive them), and to invoke a core political value. To be uninformed is to account for fewer consequences, to choose less consistently with the presumed balance of costs and benefits, to follow group cues (and less accurately perceive them), and to invoke a value having little to do with ideological policies. . . . [Nevertheless] all people draw on long-held values when forming preferences on technical policy matters (Kuklinski, Metlay, and Kay, 1982, 634).

If the role of politics in public decisions on science and technology issues is pervasive and unavoidable, prescriptions for changes in the policy process must take into consideration the effects that political values will always have on policy outcomes. Those effects must be reconciled with demands for policies that are more effective at producing desired changes. Political values may not be mistaken, but policies can be.

Conclusion: Virtues and Vices of Public Politics

A common argument of those who favor the popularization of science and technology policy is that the voter is as qualified as a Nobel laureate to make decisions involving value judgments.[5] All policy decisions—even those rare nonconflictual and unanimously supported decisions—involve value judgments, whether by the allocation of public funds, the granting of privileges or opportunities, or the endorsement of ideas. Some have tried to finesse the issue of public participation in science and technology policy by arguing that "the public should have no role in pure science," but as Sheldon Krimsky has observed, "pure science" (with no public funds, no prospective applications, and no threat of harm) is very rare (1984, 49). All other science, and all technology, requires public accountability insofar as it uses public resources or threatens the public welfare. Unfortunately, "accountability" is no more simple a concept to put into practice than "participation."

The debate over the separability of scientific and value components of policy questions will continue as long as any government professes to follow democratic principles, so any proposal that can be condensed to leaving science to the scientists and politics to the public will hardly be an enforceable solution. Yet it has been argued that widespread participation in science and technology policy by diverse groups both within and outside government—even if it is wrong-headed or doomed to failure—is valuable insofar as it enlightens the public about policy questions (del Sesto 1979, 135). Participation also conveys information about social values to the experts and endows policy outcomes with legitimacy. Moreover, it "is an intrinsic political value in its own right. Not only is participation good for the soul of the citizen, but it is also necessary for the viability of democracy as a form of government" (Brooks 1984, 46). In any case, the right to participate is guaranteed by the Constitution. Therefore, the question should be not whether the public should participate but how they can participate.

Lyndon Johnson may have encapsulated the potential vices of public participation in science and technology policy at an award ceremony for the National Medal of Science: "An aggrieved public does not draw the fine line between 'good' science and 'bad' technology.... You and I know that Frankenstein was the doctor, not the monster. But it would be well to remember that the people of the village, angered by the monster, marched against the doctor" (Kevles 1978, 400). The public has been wrong, as in the case of laetrile. It can act out of self-interest, as in the "not-in-my-backyard" syndrome plaguing the issue of nuclear waste disposal. And there is little evidence that those organizations that wear the cloak of "public interest group" actually do always represent the public interest, no matter how sincere their intentions (Lowi 1979).

Regardless of such arguments, the public does participate. Sometimes, as in the cases of recombinant DNA or antinuclear referenda, members of the public are active, with a voice both unified and clearly heard. At other times public participation is loud but has no discernible effect (Casper and Wellstone 1981). Usually members of the public participate by default, tacitly endorsing the decisions of others by their silence. Ironically, the same generalizations apply to those policy participants who are in many ways most unlike the general public: the scientific community.

Notes

1. See, for example, Kimura (1985).
2. *Scenic Hudson Preservation Conference v. Federal Power Commission,* 354 F.2d 608 (2d Cir. 1965). See Carroll (1971) and Stewart (1975).

3. Ironically, mass-marketing techniques can distort even the most effective popular science. The artist's eye-grabbing illustration for the cover of Sagan's *The Dragons of Eden* shows dinosaurs and early humans cohabiting a verdant landscape, when in fact the nearest that the human species has been to a dinosaur was a 65-million-year-old bone.

4. Cited in Machalaba 1983, 1. For analyses of media coverage of science, see Dunwoody (1980), Goodfield (1981), and Altimore (1982).

5. See, for example, the discussion of this conclusion by the California state legislature on nuclear power debates in Nelkin and Fallows (1978).

7

Scientists in the Policy Process

In the 1860s scientists took the first steps toward understanding that there was a discoverable, chemical basis for heredity. During the years 1944-1953 microbiologists discovered the existence and structure of the DNA (deoxyribonucleic acid) molecule, which allowed them to tie their understanding of the workings of the cell to the process of evolution and even to life itself. Scientists soon realized that they were on the threshold of a radically new technique: the ability to snip and splice—that is, recombine—genes from one organism to another. This turning point for biological science created a turning point for science and technology policy as the researchers began to recognize that their work raised safety questions that could not be ignored or postponed. Accordingly, in July 1974 they declared a temporary moratorium on experiments believed to carry some risk. Never before had scientists taken such a major self-regulatory step.

After several meetings and the circulation of letters among researchers, a large conference was planned. About 140 scientists from the United States and other nations met in February 1975 at the Asilomar conference center in California. For four days they discussed scientific risks, methods of containment for recombinant DNA experiments, the onerous possibility of drastic government regulation, and the ethical and legal liability implications of their research. A rough consensus formed around a set of general guidelines that would classify particular types of experiments according to their estimated level of risk. Some types of experiments were deemed too risky for current safety techniques, and appropriate biological and physical containment methods would be used for other experiments (Wade 1977; Rogers 1977).

The history of recombinant DNA regulation did not end at Asilomar. The National Institutes of Health (NIH) labored over regulatory guidelines for NIH-supported research. These safeguards have undergone many revisions as more has been learned about risks. Industry became very interested, and largely because NIH had no jurisdiction over private-sector research,

Congress and local governments became involved. Members of Congress introduced at least thirteen bills to regulate recombinant DNA research, but none passed, largely because it was widely perceived that the scientists had done an adequate job of regulating themselves.

This experience cannot be translated into a simple prescription for a generally "proper" role for scientists in science or technology policy. The potential risks were speculative; the potential benefits (such as disease prevention and improved food production) were enormous; the science was almost completely unfamiliar and invisible to most citizens and policy makers; there was no clear government jurisdiction; and, at least at the crucial beginning, the number of interested scientists was small enough that coordination was possible. The actions of the microbiologists are relevant to most science and technology policies not because they provided a formula for the role of scientists in the policy process but because they clarified many of the questions about how, when, and why scientists become policy actors.

Another example suggests a more typical relationship between scientists and the policy process. In 1979 a group of scholars began to design a survey of public attitudes on science. They intended to ask the general public about their knowledge and attitudes on three complex but not obscure scientific and technological issues: food additives, nuclear plant siting, and genetic engineering. But the researchers received requests from members of the National Science Board and the staff of the National Science Foundation (NSF) for three other issues—nitrogen fixation, black holes, and plate tectonics—to be included in the survey. These esoteric suggestions led Kenneth Prewitt to suggest that perhaps "the public knows more about science than the scientists know about the general public" (1982, 6).

In spite of these uneasy relationships between science and the political arena, scientists and technologists have been allowed a remarkable amount of autonomy. There have been greater incentives for political leaders to use or exploit scientists and their work than to limit their research. As a result, some writers have worried that scientists have become a "new priesthood" whose words are endowed with awesome authority and whose actions are vital to politics and society yet beyond common understanding (Lapp 1965). Although this is hyperbole, scientists do play an unusual role in the policy process, not only when they are brought into the policy process as science advisers, but also when they decide to participate as policy advocates.

In 1970 Daniel Patrick Moynihan referred to our time as "the age of 'the great simplifiers' " and worried that "the essence of tyranny was the denial of complexity" (David 1975). But while some simplification may be necessary—to Plato, even lies could be "noble"—complexity divorces the public from its government. As policy actors, scientists must choose a comfortable balance between comprehensibility and comprehensiveness.

More than three million men and women are employed as scientists or engineers in the United States (with men outnumbering women by more than seven-to-one. Most of these people participate in the political system like other well-educated citizens: by voting. Relatively few scientists take to public life—whether out of a personal interest or a technocratic version of noblesse oblige—cloaked in scholarly robes. When they do, they behave as a meritocratic extension of the civil service, more competent and therefore more influential on some issues than either the public or elected officials (Brooks 1984). For example, scientists have met in international forums to decide whether their nations' ministers are capable of understanding and acting upon uncertain data, such as the relationship between carbon dioxide in the atmosphere and global warming (U.S. House of Representatives 1981d). For most scientists, however, direct intervention in the policy process is rare. Any description of political activity beyond casting a ballot will apply only to a relatively small number of scientists or technologists.

Even among those identifiable as policy leaders, direct political activity is far from common. Miller (1985) compiled a list of about 3,500 science and technology policy leaders based on criteria such as whether they were science journalists, were officers of scientific associations, were members of the national academies, had testified to Congress, or had served on an executive branch advisory committee. When surveyed they indicated that personal contact is the most effective way to influence federal policies (53 percent), followed by group response (23 percent), formal communication (11 percent), electoral activity (4 percent), and using the media (2 percent). More than one-third of these science policy leaders had, however, made no contacts with federal decision makers during the preceding year, and only 18 percent had been in touch more than a dozen times.

Although the political activities of individual scientists and engineers may be significant for an occasional issue, activists are most likely to exert influence when they act through a group, for the same reasons that organized participation by average citizens is more effective than solo efforts. In groups scientists can hope to have more than an incremental effect as they monitor, comment on, and lobby for policies. Engineers and architects organized for Woodrow Wilson's election, and scientists and engineers formed an election committee for Lyndon Johnson. After World War I, the American Chemical Society took an active role in the debate over chemical warfare, and in 1983 the American Physical Society passed a formal resolution opposing President Reagan's approach to nuclear arms control. Their stature as scientists, however, is no guarantee of success; the chemists' efforts to block the Geneva Protocol failed, and there has been no evidence that the physicists have slowed the pace of weapons research. Even the highest scientific award cannot be equated with political influence. During the 1970s nineteen Nobel laureates unsuccessfully tried to persuade California authorities to exclude biblical creationism from school curricula (Jones 1980; *Physics Today* 1983a; Keyworth 1983; Zuckerman 1977, 24; Primack and von Hippel, 1974).

Given the training of scientists and the resources of their groups, it is not necessarily intellectual arrogance that causes them to concentrate their efforts on direct lobbying rather than trying to educate the public about policy-relevant issues. A concerted educational campaign by activist scientists would probably be criticized for unfairly exploiting expertise, university prestige and tenure, or public research funding. In any case, no one expects economists, defense experts, or the business community to abandon their lobbying efforts in favor of mass education.

Law and Scientists in the Policy Process

In one sense, the most significant legal influence on the political activity of scientists and technologists is not any particular set of laws but simply the law itself. Few citizens outside the legal or political communities adequately understand the substance and procedure of law. In fact, in spite of their education and presumed intelligence, scientists are at a peculiar disadvantage because they have been trained to think about problems in a fashion very different from that of lawyers. Naturally, both are inclined to prefer their own paradigms: Sen. Paul Tsongas (D-Mass.) commented that "only doctors show a greater disdain for the legal profession" than scientists (U.S. House of Representatives 1979, 73).

Legal Limitations on Scientists

There is a lengthy, albeit erratic, history in the United States of government actions that have the effect (deliberate or not) of hindering scientific and technological research. During the nineteenth century, a 25-percent tariff on imported books and periodicals hindered American scientists' abilities to keep up with their more advanced European counterparts, and bills were submitted in Congress to prevent the Geological Survey from spending funds for the publication of research (Kevles 1978, 56). Yet any suggestion that scientific research be subjected to public controls raises the spectre of anti-intellectualism, exploitation, or malversation—and for good historical reasons. The persecution of Galileo by the Catholic church, the endorsement of Lysenko's absurd critique of classical genetics by Stalin's Central Committee, and the Nazi persecution of Jewish scientists (and the persecution of Jews in the name of "science") are never far from the minds of those who worry about the manipulation of science for nonscientific purposes (Cole 1983). Nevertheless, the scientific community has accepted, or occasionally even encouraged, some limitations on research.

Self-imposed Regulations.   Although the meeting of microbiologists at Asilomar in 1974 was remarkable, it was not unique. There are more than 2,000 scientific organizations and groups in the United States, many of which have adopted guidelines, ethical codes, and procedural standards for their fields of study. These range from the Oath of Hippocrates for medical practitioners to the 1975 Declaration of Tokyo, the "World Medical Assembly Guidelines for Medical Doctors concerning Torture and Other Cruel, Inhuman or Degrading Treatment or Punishment in Relation to Detention and Imprisonment" (Dickinson 1984). Engineering groups have adopted enormous numbers of self-regulatory guidelines for technical standards to ensure that equipment and measurements are compatible and interchangeable (Barke 1985b).

Protection of Experimental Subjects.   Self-regulatory guidelines may be inadequate or obsolete, or the potential risks from research may be seen as significant public health or moral questions. Consequently, controversies may result in statutory or regulatory limitations on scientific research, intended either to minimize risk to the public or to protect national security.

The unsuspecting public is protected from nefarious or careless scientists by laws and regulations involving research on living subjects. The Constitution itself has been invoked to forbid "cruel and unusual punishment" of prisoners, who have been attractive to medical and psychological researchers as likely subjects (Delgado 1977). In 1985 the Public Health Service, the National Science Foundation, and the Office of Science and Technology Policy responded to public concern about cruelty to laboratory animals by issuing policies on humane care and use of vertebrate animals in testing, research, and training. In addition, agency regulations and congressional statutes (for example, the National Research Act of 1974) have been created in response to gross abuses of human subjects. Among these were the infamous Tuskegee study in which black men were given placebos in the treatment of syphilis to determine the effects of the disease (Jones 1981) and a 1964 experiment in which researchers injected live cancer cells into elderly patients without their knowledge (Katz 1972). Of particular concern to ethicists in recent years has been research on embryos and fetuses. A 1974 decision by the Department of Health, Education, and Welfare has had the effect of preventing NIH from supporting studies of in vitro fertilization.

Under current regulations all federal agencies that conduct research on human subjects are required to have proposed biomedical projects evaluated and approved by an institutional review board (IRB). Universities and other institutions receiving federal funds are also subject to federal regulations that require statements of "informed consent" from human subjects of biomedical and social scientific projects in which potential harm might result. Scientists and others objected to the first draft of regulations on the use of human subjects as being too extreme, but they have generally accepted the amended regulations as legitimate, with the condition that researchers and universities be able to preserve some independence from federal controls (Pool 1983). The criteria for approving research on human subjects include:

1. Minimization of risks to the subjects
2. Reasonable risks in relation to anticipated benefits
3. Equitable selection of subjects
4. Assurance of informed consent
5. Adequate provisions for monitoring data
6. Provisions for protecting the privacy of subjects
7. Assurance that decisions to participate in research will not be coerced (Office of Technology Assessment 1984, 38)

The informed consent requirement poses profound problems for some researchers. Those who are investigating the debilitating effects of Alzheimer's disease, for example, are likely to find that the ailment makes their research subjects either incapable of being fully informed or unable to give meaningful consent.

National Security Limitations.   Restrictions on scientific activities because of national security concerns are hardly new, but as technological competition with the Soviets has become more intense, so have concerns about technological "leakage." Whether because of leaks of American technology in computers, lasers, communications, and materials science through international trade or technical publications, or because of orchestrated Soviet attempts to acquire western technologies through bribery or indirect purchases, since the mid-1970s American officials have intensified their attempts to control the flow of technology from West to East (National Academy of Science 1982b; Central Intelligence Agency 1982). Under the Atomic Energy Act, the Arms Export Control Act, the Export Administration Act, and presidential executive orders, federal authorities can regulate the dissemination of information, forbid foreigners at American universities from participating in "sensitive" research projects, and control the international sale of technical devices.

Not surprisingly, university, business, and public officials have expressed doubts about the net costs and coordination of stringent secrecy rules, in part because nearly four dozen federal offices have some jurisdiction over technological leakage. The chairman of the National Science Board (and a corporate official for R & D at General Electric) warned that "an obsession with preventing leakage of our technology will cripple our ability to remain the leader" in research (Clark and Hall 1984, 80). Others have raised questions about the unavoidable confrontation between constitutional protections of free speech and policies designed to protect national security (Ferguson 1985). These doubts are to be expected given the conflicting social and political goals incorporated in science and technology policies.

Legal Protections of Scientists

Because laws exist in hierarchies, legal limitations on behavior must be consonant with higher laws. A regulation affecting scientific activity must be made in accordance with procedures prescribed by statutes, and statutory provisions must be permitted by the Constitution. In this way the legal system affects science and technology not just through its restrictions but also through its guarantees. Both constraints and protections have prodded scientists and technologists to become active in public policy.

Freedom of Inquiry. The most fundamental of these protections is implied by the Constitution. Although the First Amendment mentions only speech, press, and assembly, the Supreme Court has interpreted the clause to mean that the government is also prohibited from limiting freedom of expression. The Court has never ruled specifically on "freedom of research," but it has acknowledged that free inquiry is a prerequisite for freedom of speech and belief (Emerson 1979). There is consensus on some appropriate restrictions on speech, such as publication of nuclear launch codes or instruction for brewing biological weapons, yet most jurists reject government censorship through prior restraint except in cases involving the most direct threats to public safety or national security.

Although agreement may exist on the cultural importance of free scientific expression, scientific inquiry may occasionally fall more within the realm of "action" than "expression." In other words, just as "science" and "policy" each refer to both process and outcome, so does "inquiry." If the act of scientific research itself poses a potential threat to the public, is it still constitutionally protected from government interference? Harold Green (1979) has concluded that "where scientific research involves experimentation with human or animal subjects or where it impinges upon the community, it would clearly become subject to regulation," but there will always be fuzzy areas where it is far from certain whether, when, and how an experiment will impinge on a community. Albert Einstein's work in theoretical physics early in the twentieth century eventually had a major effect on social and political life, and some feel that the implications of recent work on recombinant DNA should be viewed in the same manner. Do the threats to social order or public health, however unlikely, then make *all* basic research susceptible to restriction? No court has gone so far.

Once again, the only feasible solution—vague as it may be—is a balancing of interests, a solution the Supreme Court has applied in other types of cases.[1] In the end, the question, How much protection does the Constitution give scientific research? is not strictly answerable, because of conflicting and changing social norms, constitutional vagueness, and empirical uncertainties about the effects of research. Although balancing may be the only realistic approach, it is troublesome to many because of its unreliability and possible inconsistencies, and because balancing frequently occurs in the unrepresentative judicial system. Yet, there is no evidence that the courts have been frivolous or uneducable in their defense of scientific inquiry.

Patents.   Another fundamental legal protection for science and technology is derived from the only mention of science in the Constitution. Article I, Section 8 grants Congress the power to "promote the progress of science and the useful arts by securing for limited terms to authors and inventors the exclusive right to their respective writings and discoveries." The intent was clear: to reward and provide incentives for creativity. Patents provide exclusive rights for seventeen years on "new" and "useful" inventions, including processes, methods, machines, composition of matter, and, since 1980, forms of life carrying a manmade, genetically engineered component. (*Diamond v. Chakrabarty,* 447 U.S. 303 [1980]). They may not be renewed, but new patents can be issued for improvements.

The economic importance of legal protections on "knowledge as private property" is obvious, so it follows that questions about how the system operates have always been controversial. There have been long-lasting disputes about patent ownership (the dispute over patent rights for the laser lasted twenty-three years) and the patentability of innovations created by firms under government contract (if the public paid for the research, should the benefits be private?). The legal issue of ownership of "intellectual property" can be very complicated. For example, the Supreme Court has depicted the patent grant as a legitimate "monopoly" but one to be "narrowly and strictly confined" to avoid the "evils of an expansion of the patent monopoly by private engagements." [2]

Another related issue that has plagued science and technology policy has been whether universities can claim patents on research funded by the federal government. The Patents and Trademarks Act of 1980 answered this question affirmatively, which caused many researchers to worry that academic inquiry and freedom are on the verge of being subordinated to commercial hungers. Harvard University president Derek Bok spoke of "an uneasy sense that programs to exploit technological development are likely to confuse the university's central commitment to the pursuit of knowledge and learning by introducing into the very heart of the academic enterprise a new and powerful motive—the search for utility and commercial gain" (Dickson 1984; Culliton 1982). Nevertheless, in an era of federal budget cutbacks and an aging university research infrastructure, a change in patent laws appeared to many to be an acceptable way of encouraging businesses to invest in university-based science and technology.

Whistle Blowers.   A less common but often conspicuous legal question about the work of scientists concerns those researchers who feel an obligation to express doubts about what their employers—government or private sector—are doing. These "whistle blowers" run considerable risks not only because of the economic incentives for them to keep quiet but also because they, like so many others, may be relying on uncertain or incomplete data about risks or abuses and therefore could be wrong. Studies of the dilemmas facing whistle blowers have concluded that scientists have a moral obligation to warn of potential risks but that they are understandably reluctant to speak out (American Association for the Advancement of Science 1975; Cole 1983; Chalk 1980). Some business firms and federal agencies have devised procedures to protect whistle blowers, but the threat of informal sanctions against them will continue to make formal due process protection largely irrelevant.

Changes in Legal Constraints on Scientists

The fact that American science and technology have flourished indicates that legal protections have outweighed legal prohibitions on scientific activity. This relationship may be slowly changing. Although the nation has a history of eventually transferring even the most sensitive military research (nuclear energy, computers, and radar, for example) to the private sector, the potential effects of new scientific breakthroughs and technological applications will continue to become more relevant to national security, so challenges to the legal autonomy of science will become harder to deter. It has been recognized since the time of Archimedes that scientific knowledge can turn the tides of battles, but it has never before been so important to defense.

At the same time, recent breakthroughs in the biological sciences suggest that scientists are on the brink of transcending the metaphor "the new priesthood." As they perfect their abilities to alter the basic mechanisms of life itself, they will soon be capable of combining the roles of a *demiurge:* to Homer, an artisan or physician; to the Peloponnesians, a higher magistrate; and to Plato, the creator of the world. Even if it can be hoped that genetic engineering will progress carefully, the real and imagined risks will be reflected in an altered relationship between science and law that could spill over into other areas of research. Just one mistake, no matter how minor, will escalate into a political outcry for reckless scientists to be made publicly accountable for their behavior. Only the most optimistic scientific libertarian could imagine that the legal autonomy of science will not change.

The Constraints of Scientific Knowledge

During the negotiations in 1959 over the Nuclear Test Ban Treaty, there was intense debate among American seismologists. The scientific study of earthquakes had promised a technique for distinguishing between underground nuclear explosions and earthquakes in the Soviet Union, but no consensus was reached on the reliability of the test ban control system, less because of political disagreements than because of "opposed definitions of the issue at stake, differing definitions of qualitative terms, and the use of *ad hoc* hypotheses" (Gilpin 1962, 267).

In the mid-1980s the United States was involved in a similar dispute, this time over the Comprehensive Test Ban Treaty. Once again, seismologists were asked to guarantee that their study of seismic waves could reliably detect clandestine Soviet nuclear tests. Once again, the scientific community disagreed. Seismic experts at the U.S. Geological Survey claimed that they could, while earthquake scientists at Lawrence Livermore National Laboratory argued that the Soviets still might be able to disguise their violations of the treaty.

At one extreme, scientific debates "based on no evidence are among the most revealing in the history of science, for in the absence of factual constraints, the cultural biases that affect all thought (and which scientists try so assiduously to deny) lie nakedly exposed" (Gould 1977, 210). Yet too many facts, passed to an inexpert policy maker through formal advisory channels, inhibit the discretion and maneuvering vital to political decision making (Price 1983, 181). Scientists who involve themselves in the policy process always fall somewhere between the extremes of omniscience and complete ignorance, but regardless of which end of this scale they occupy their discretion in choosing advocacy roles is limited. The scientific method ascribes a particular approach for coping with uncertainty. It implies hierarchies of expertise and authority, and it carries its own perspective of the world and its problems. The same can be said of democracy, and neither guarantees correct results.

It is easy for casual observers of science, among both the public and policy makers, to misunderstand the peculiar function of uncertainty for scientists, largely because of confusion over concepts such as "theory" and "law of nature." This has been most clearly revealed by the attacks of religious fundamentalists on evolutionary theory as "merely a theory." As Judge William Overton found in his 1982 decision overturning the Arkansas "creation science" law, "a scientific theory must be tentative and always subject to revision or abandonment in light of facts that are inconsistent with, or falsify, the theory." [3] That is, uncertainty and falsifiability are not only common to science; they are fundamental to it. Scientific theories, therefore, are rather common. In contrast, a scientific "law" is a formulation of a sequence of events that has been found to occur with unvarying uniformity under the same conditions. Thus, there is the law of gravity (everything in the universe attracts everything else with a force dependent on mass and distance) and the second law of thermodynamics (no engine can be completely efficient), but only theories of evolution, relativity, and so on.

Scientists are trained to treat uncertainty as both a problem and an opportunity to advance knowledge. This perspective makes them ill-suited for the realms of politics and law. Imagine a fastidious scientist being considered as a potential juror in a criminal case, with its standard of "beyond a reasonable doubt," telling an attorney that "all empirical knowledge is inherently uncertain." It should hardly be surprising, then, that the political personality despairs of, or even taunts, scientists who seem unable to assemble their data and produce simple judgments. The lengthy public debate over whether the "yellow rain" reported by Southeast Asians was evidence of Soviet chemical warfare or bee feces may have persuaded some scientists to avoid becoming involved in any similar controversies in the future.

This inability of many scientists to adjust their perspective to that of politics is a major factor in what are often labeled science policy "failures." For example, the surgeon general's advisory committee on smoking and health in the early 1960s had vigorous debates about the "various meanings and conceptions of the term *cause*," but it offered no clarifications. In fact, the committee used four variations: "a cause," "a major cause," "a significant cause," and "a causal association"—all referring to "a significant, effectual relationship" (Reiser 1966, 298-299). Many scientists, however, are aware of the effects of such confusion. The American Society for Clinical Nutrition adopted a code of ethics, which pledges members to "present information in a manner or style that minimizes misinterpretation by a person untrained in nutrition" (Orlans 1980, 523).

Unfortunately, that caution can itself be a cause of confusion. In the process of deciding whether to undertake a nationwide program of vaccinations against the swine flu in 1976, scientists

> were uncomfortable expressing subjective estimates, even if based on expert knowledge and experience. They resented having to quantify their judgments. Indeed, they think that it is unprofessional to express judgments in terms they cannot call scientific, worse still to express them in the presence of laymen. They see placing precise numbers on uncertainties as an incitement to public misunderstanding (Neustadt and Fineberg 1978, 88).

Or, in the words of a physicist who served as a Congressional Fellow, "scientists typically know a great deal about very little. Politicians, particularly good ones, tend to know very little about practically everything. Although the areas under the curves may be identical, to the scientist who measures everything through a narrow-band filter they may not seem so" (Horwitz 1976, 32).

In 1950 Eugene Wigner predicted that as science inevitably becomes fragmented with each researcher pursuing narrower questions, levels of hierarchy would develop with "bench scientists" overseen and linked together by the next higher level. Scientific spokespersons are recognized by their record of publication, administrative duties, or awards. This hierarchy has an effect on political activity by scientists inasmuch as lay people (politicians, judges, and so on) hear more from—and give greater credence to—those with better credentials. At the same time, Wigner hoped, these prominent individuals would develop greater experience in dealing with the nonscientific world. Don Price recently observed that "the experienced leaders of the scientific elite are troubled by the approach of their less sophisticated colleagues to policy issues," because of their inability to adjust to the norms of politics (Price 1983, 56-57). And realism about what to expect from politics and policy colors attitudes. There is evidence (discussed later in this chapter) that those scientists higher in the hierarchy tend to be ideologically distinct from the rank and file.

These effects of science on scientists' participation—the influence of uncertainty, contrasting paradigms, and hierarchy—are manifested not only when scientists intentionally try to change policies but also when they are invited to join the policy process as science advisers.[4] In fact, the self-motivated, politically active scientist or technologist will be perceived as having stepped farther outside the strictly professional role than the expert who waits to be asked for advice. Not only will "public interest scientists" receive little credit from their peers for writing in a style accessible to the general public, but they may even face disciplinary disincentives to do policy work (Primack and von Hippel 1974). This is true even of Nobel laureates:

> Except when advocacy is in the cause of science—when, for example, the teaching of creationism along with Darwinian evolution was publicly denounced by a number of laureates—such activities are apt to be criticized by scientific colleagues as publicity seeking and unscientific. . . . This makes the majority of laureates leery of making public statements on issues not directly connected with their scientific expertise, and a small fraction refuse to lend their names to political causes of any kind, even those they privately support (Zuckerman 1977, 235-236).

Coordination of Scientists in the Policy Process

In the 1980s the world was privileged to see the first close-up photographs of Jupiter, Saturn, and Uranus (and expects to see Neptune before the decade's end), after two *Voyager* spacecraft traveled billions of miles in quiet flight. To appreciate the type of scientific and engineering effort that this project required, consider just one aspect of its planning. When planetary scientists began to design the flight paths for the two spacecraft, they first considered 105 possible trajectories based on navigational, scientific, and budget constraints. Then about eighty scientists working in ten teams (magnetic fields and infrared radiation, for example), met to consider whose particular research interests would prevail as exact trajectories were chosen. At stake was not only an investment of hundreds of millions of dollars, but also once-in-a-lifetime opportunities to advance each researcher's scientific and career goals (Dyer and Miles 1976).[5]

In similar ways, administrators and policy leaders must coordinate their efforts as they set priorities for the expenditure of funds, often relying on the advice of scientists whose preferences cannot be assumed to be completely objective. The importance of scientific coordination and consensus has been demonstrated several times in the field of space science. In 1972 a panel of prominent astronomers conducted a survey and produced a set of recommendations for expensive astronomy projects in the 1970s, including the Hubble Space Telescope (Chapter 9), the Gamma Ray Observatory satellite, and the Einstein X-ray satellite. Similarly, in 1982 another committee, chaired by astronomer George Field of Harvard, gave the National Academy of Sciences (NAS) a new report on research priorities for the next decade, which reportedly earned for the committee members "enormous credibility in official Washington" and "an inside track on funding" (Waldrop 1985, 283-285).

Scientific Associations

Occasionally an individual scientist such as Carl Sagan or Paul Ehrlich attains enough prominence in the popular media to be regularly heard on policy issues and perhaps even influence some voters' attitudes (Goodell 1977). Or a singular, well-timed or well-publicized event might have a small, incremental effect on policy. When David Parnas, a computer scientist at the University of Victoria in British Columbia, resigned a $1,000-a-day position as a defense expert on "battle management" computers, his complaints about the Strategic Defense Initiative program were given prominent but short-lived attention in newspapers and magazines.

In general the policy efforts of lone scientists or technologists are relatively ineffective. Yet even when scientists coordinate their activities in organizations or groups they confront the same logical obstacles facing collective action by the public: who pays the information and organization costs, and why should anyone choose not to ride free?

Unlike the public, the scientific community has been able to avoid the problem somewhat by forming associations ostensibly for collective scholarly purposes but which produce individual benefits to members, such as journals and meetings. These groups also may influence science policy by aggregating and articulating the interests of individuals (Almond 1960). By far the largest of these is the American Association for the Advancement of Science (AAAS), formed in 1848 and today comprising about 130,000 members.[6] The AAAS sponsors meetings and workshops, and it publishes several periodicals (including *Science*). The director of AAAS has some claim to be the spokesperson for the entire scientific community, especially on matters relating to the defense and promotion of scientific research; but the association limits its policy role to rather safe and consensual issues, such as R & D budget cuts, government intrusions into laboratories, the rights of Soviet scientists, and threats to open scientific communications.

Many other scientific and engineering societies, arranged by particular discipline, may occasionally take an active role in policy issues beyond routine self-defense or responses to requests for advice (see Cahn 1974; Primack and von Hippel 1974). As discussed earlier, the American Chemical Society took a forceful position against the 1925 Geneva Protocol banning chemical weapons, and the governing council of the American Physical Society adopted a formal resolution calling for a reduction in nuclear weapons. Taking such positions is not simple or risk-free. Some members are likely to object to adoption of policy stances as threats to the scientific "objectivity" of their organizations, and an association's governing body (presumably higher in the hierarchy than most members) might not consult the rank and file before endorsing a policy.[7] In addition, groups are limited in their political efforts by two formal constraints: they may lose their tax-exempt status if they actively lobby, and many scientific associations are forbidden by their own self-governing constitutions to take stands on political issues.

In contrast to these professional associations are the policy-active scientific and technical groups that have been formed, especially since World War II. Several are particularly prominent. The Federation of American Scientists (FAS) was formed in 1946 by researchers concerned about the policy implications of atomic energy; in the 1980s its major focus was on arms control and SDI. The Union of Concerned Scientists (UCS) claims a membership of 5,300, including 530 members of the National Academy of Sciences, and also has been active in opposing nuclear arms and SDI. It has organized campus workshops on nuclear weapons policy, obtaining endorsements from fifty-four Nobel laureates for its anti-"Star Wars" efforts. The FAS, UCS, League of Women Voters, Friends of the Earth, and other groups have coordinated their efforts on national security policies through a Space Policy Working Group with the primary aim of affecting congressional votes (Glen 1985).

Conflicts Among Scientists

Progress in science and technology is not always smooth and peaceful. Conflicts are common when issues such as prestige or funding are at stake. Even American heroes are not immune: Thomas Edison fought an unsuccessful battle against Nikola Tesla's alternating-current electrical system, at one point arguing that AC experiments should be outlawed in the interest of public safety. Disputes also arise when the scientific basis for a policy recommendation is unreliable. For example, the National Academy of Sciences revises dietary guidelines (used in package labeling and food stamp allotments) every four or five years, but in 1985 it was unable to avoid an impasse resulting from "scientific differences of opinion" on the large pool of nutrition data.

In addition, the same data may be exploited in different ways depending on the personality or politics of the scientist. During the test ban treaty debate in the late 1950s, Linus Pauling (a strong advocate of a test ban as a first step toward disarmament) presented evidence on the projected number of deaths among children due to fallout; Edward Teller (the "father" of the hydrogen bomb) compared the risks of fallout to the dangers of smoking cigarettes—using the same data (Gilpin 1962, 167). Some difference of opinion is permissible, even vital, for scientists as scientists, but it confuses nonscientists and jeopardizes the application of scientific knowledge by policy makers.

The coordination problem is exacerbated when policies are fragmented or when the size of the federal research budget is decreasing. The biomedical research lobby, for example, is divided between those who support research for its own sake and those who promote it as a tool of public health. Similarly, health policies are implemented by many federal agencies, so even a solitary, united association of biomedical researchers from all subdisciplines would face a challenge in coordinating their efforts to affect policy. And when researchers who are dependent on public money find that the funding pie is shrinking, competition for funds can lead to dissension that threatens programs. During the 1970s the worries of space scientists about the opportunity costs of the space shuttle were exploited by those opposed to the program, and the same phenomenon occurred when President Reagan proposed a space station. The effect of such disagreements can be subtle but significant. Alice Kimball Smith wrote:

> Because scientists have claimed to provide the medium for revelation of truth about the physical world, one answer to any given question is expected of them, as, indeed, they have come to expect it of themselves; and when they disagree in public, the authority of science is undermined to a greater degree than is that of other disciplines (Smith 1970, 367).

Conflict in the scientific community about public policy is inevitable given scientific uncertainty, competing disciplines, and the inseparability of facts and values—even by scientists. Therefore, any hope (or attempt) to cure the coordination problem runs the risk of squelching the legitimate concerns of scientists who, after all, are also citizens. Moreover, conflicts in opinion and advice are not always bad for public policy. They can force issues onto the public agenda or expose a proposal to more complete scrutiny. Finally, consensus carries no guarantees of truth. The physical world is not required to be accountable to simple or democratically revealed answers. Furthermore, the most significant progress in science (and perhaps in politics) is often marked by revolutionary shifts in ideas that are stubbornly resisted (Kuhn 1970). Ernest Rutherford, the discoverer of the electron, predicted in 1933 that energy would never be obtained from the transformation of atoms, but no committee was required to approve Einstein's 1939 letter to Franklin Roosevelt urging the United States to develop an atomic bomb before the Germans.

Politics and the Scientist

The government abounds with people doing jobs for which others are overburdened or unqualified. Congressional staff, regulatory commissions, and advisory groups act as agents under contract to their principals who have the authority to make public decisions. According to this model of organizational behavior, problems are inevitable because principals are often unable to judge whether their agents are promoting the principals' agenda or their own personal plans; yet if a principal had the time or resources to oversee an agent, the agent would not be needed (Moe 1984).

In the case of science and technology policy one might ask, who is the principal and who is the agent? Because the generalists in the White House, Congress, and courts lack the expertise to compete with scientists on their own terms (that is, within their own terminology), it can be difficult to determine whether the political system serves the interests of science, or vice versa. Consider publicly funded science, which requires huge investments in research where no immediate payoffs are demanded or expected, only the self-evaluated progress of scientists. When Energy Secretary James Schlesinger referred to the fusion energy program as a "scientific sandbox" costing hundreds of millions of dollars for the amusement of scientists, he was complaining of being the agent, not the principal (Heppenheimer 1984, 199).

In this sense, science policy resembles social policy—where few demand that the poor, aged, and handicapped produce something tangible in return for public dollars—more than defense or economic policy. This leads to the source of considerable confusion about the politics of science policy: science is both an end and a means to an end. As an enterprise undertaken for its own sake, little accountability is required of research; as agents of public policy, scientists are held responsible. It was this conflict to which Franklin Roosevelt referred in his second inaugural address when he called for the federal government to "create those moral controls over the services of science which are necessary to make science a useful servant instead of a ruthless master of mankind" (Kevles 1978, 264).

The Accountability of Scientists

The public obligation of the scientist has been among the most vexing questions in science policy. Its very real importance was revealed by the anguish of Manhattan Project atomic scientists after the bombing of

Hiroshima and Nagasaki and by the self-imposed caution of genetic scientists in the 1970s. Few scientists would say they have no responsibility to the public. But how is that obligation to be operationalized? Of course scientists must respond to the letter of the law and, in a looser way, to social norms and their own consciences. Yet they may lack a direct personal stake in the policy implications of their work, which may not manifest problems for a generation.

Similarly, scientific findings may be used in unanticipated ways that have social implications. For example, the current debate over genetic screening (testing fetuses or prospective employees for their genetic susceptibility to defect or disease) is being constrained by the memory of an earlier debate. Around the turn of the century many scientists, social philosophers, and even President Theodore Roosevelt promoted "eugenic" theories of racial improvement by the selective mating of humans (Kevles 1985).

Scientists also sometimes discover that they have unearthed information that the public would prefer not to know. Seismologists who have warned of a potentially devastating earthquake in the New Madrid area of southeastern Missouri have found their efforts resented or largely ignored by local officials. In such a situation they must decide whether to be content publishing their findings in geophysics journals or whether they are "responsible" for protecting a cowering public.

Although the terms *responsible* and *accountable* are sometimes used interchangeably, *accountability* seems more appropriate for researchers because it is more tentative. Being asked to account for one's actions or for the expenditure of public funds is less morally imposing, and probably more fair, than being held responsible for the outcomes of one's actions. Yet even a consensus among scientists that accountability is appropriate would beg the question that haunts many policy-active scientists: as the effects of the work of today's researchers cascade through the years or decades, might they regret their lack of foresight and humility? The answers to such doubts are not found in statutes or political platforms but are shaped by the attitudes and beliefs of scientists themselves.

The Ideology of Scientists

In 1982 a panel of the National Research Council completed a four-year study of policy options on marijuana use, concluding that criminal penalties for possession of small amounts of the drug should be ended because of the ineffectiveness of such measures. The committee's recommendations had undergone several reviews and revisions by the normal procedures, yet they were publicly attacked by the president of the National Academy of Sciences, Frank Press: "I am concerned that the Committee may have gone beyond its charge in stating a judgment so value-laden that it should have been left to the political process" (Walsh 1982, 228-229).

Although it was unusual (but not unique) for the head of NAS to question a panel's findings, ideological bias usually is not imputed so explicitly. No one should doubt that scientists and engineers have political attitudes and beliefs, but they are generally adept at appearing to exorcise their personal ideologies from their professional work. Furthermore, it is often impossible to disentangle the ideological and pragmatic positions of scientists on policy issues. For example, the American Chemical Society's attempt to block a ban on chemical weapons by the League of Nations was based on an argument that chemical warfare was "comparatively humane," that the United States could not be sure that other nations would comply with a treaty, and that the American chemical industry should be free to compete without international controls (Jones 1980).

The most complete study of the politics of scientists and engineers was a 1969 survey of 60,000 college and university professors. It found that the average academic was slightly more liberal than conservative, but there were distinct differences among scientific disciplines. The only academics that were significantly liberal were those in the social sciences, humanities, law, and fine arts. Professors in nearly all subfields of physical and biological sciences were markedly conservative, and engineers were particularly so; the only subfields among the natural sciences and engineering that tended to be slightly liberal were physicists and biochemists. Faculty at "elite, cosmopolitan, research-oriented" colleges were more liberal than their colleagues at other schools, as were the "achievers" who had published more recent works (Ladd and Lipset 1972).

These attitudes have been manifested in overt ways. The group Scientists and Engineers for Johnson was active in the 1964 presidential campaign; researchers openly opposed American policy in Vietnam; and scientists demonstrated on the streets of Washington against the anti-ballistic missile system proposed by President Nixon. As a result the Johnson and Nixon administrations blacklisted particular researchers from serving on government advisory committees. Although some significant changes in the ideological tilts of scientists and engineers have surely occurred between the height of the Vietnam War and the Reagan era, the differences between subgroups probably remain. Perhaps because of the mantle of the atomic bomb (in the words of Robert Oppenheimer, "the physicists have known sin"), physicists continue to be among the most politically active scientists and are usually most visible in opposition to development and reliance upon nuclear weapons or to policies that they see as destabilizing (Oppenheimer 1948).[8]

In addition to the left-right leanings of scientists and engineers, they have other personal interests that are likely to color their policy preferences and shape their political activity. Because of the increasing dependence of scientists on public funds since World War II, "members of Congress now tend to look on them as just another selfish pressure group, and not as the

Table 7-1 Industry's Expenditures for R & D in Universities and Colleges, 1960-1985 (Millions of Dollars)

Year	Current Dollars	Constant 1972 Dollars	Year	Current Dollars	Constant 1972 Dollars
1960	40	58	1973	84	79
1961	40	58	1974	96	83
1962	40	57	1975	113	90
1963	41	57	1976	123	93
1964	40	55	1977	139	99
1965	41	55	1978	170	113
1966	42	55	1979	193	118
1967	48	61			
1968	55	67	1980	235	132
1969	60	69	1981	288	147
			1982	326	157
1970	61	67	1983[a]	370	172
1971	70	73	1984[b]	425	190
1972	74	74	1985[b]	485	209

Source: National Science Foundation 1985b, 262.

[a] Preliminary.
[b] Estimated.

wizards of perpetual progress" (Price 1978, 75). Moreover, the trend of the past decade for scientists and technologists to become more intertwined with the business world (either through university-industry "relationships" or by becoming business entrepreneurs themselves) will also affect their political behavior as they lobby, for example, for changes in patent laws and regulations on the proprietary classification of research. Table 7-1 shows the growing financial investment of industries in university-based R & D. These ties could limit scientific progress if researchers become reluctant to share potentially profitable information with their colleagues, but the ideals of academic freedom and the free market will probably prevent the "academic-industrial complex" from climbing high on the science and technology policy agenda.

The Political System of Active Scientists

Another type of constraint facing policy-active scientists is the system of institutions and networks that funnel their opinions and demands to decision makers. The scientific associations and interest groups discussed above must use compromise and bargaining as tactical weapons on political battlefields. Their strategic efforts (directed at the adversary's homeland—in this case, the general public on which policy makers depend) are limited by factors that isolate the scientific community from the average voter.

Because of the likelihood that political preferences will be reflected even unintentionally in scientific advice, the system by which that advice is produced also shapes the political activity of scientists. After the White House science adviser's office was abolished in 1974, Henry Kissinger observed:

> Intellectuals are now divided into essentially three groups: those that reject the government totally; those that work on pure, abstract intellectual models which are impossible to make relevant; and a third group that's too close to power and that sees its service to the government as residing primarily in day-to-day tactics. No outsider can be very helpful on the day-to-day business because he doesn't know enough of the current situation to really make a contribution (*Science* 1974, 617).

This trichotomy reveals a dilemma facing policy-active scientists. Many of them who may wish to promote or attack policies fail to do so because their time and energy are consumed by their own work or because they see the political system as hopelessly irrational and therefore unresponsive to their legitimate demands. Although many scientists are dependent upon the political system because of public funding of their own research or the research infrastructure or because of the legal protections that it provides, they see their interests as "pure" or "abstract," and so they fail to recognize their own interests in their attempts to influence policy.

The third group of scientists—Kissinger's insiders—becomes susceptible to a special set of political constraints. Primack and von Hippel (1974) questioned the legitimacy of the science advisory system because it enables the president and Congress to exploit scientists' expertise while discouraging dissent. In effect, it attempts to rigidify the principal-agent relationship with the scientist tightly confined to the role of a dutiful servant. As Garry Brewer (1973) discovered in his study of expert advice in urban planning policies, the political constraints imposed on advisers can limit the scope of their inquiry to only those aspects of a problem or solution that are "politically acceptable." This can lead the "users" of the advice to wonder whether scientists are contributing anything new and useful to the policy process, yet if the experts fail to recognize the political necessities, their principals are likely to dismiss their suggestions as unrealistic and irrelevant. Any broad prescriptions for improving the role of scientists and technologists in public policy must either tolerate or resolve these political dilemmas.

Conclusion

In the opening chapter of this book it was suggested that science and technology policy can serve as a critical test of the general policy process since this is the policy arena in which self-conscious attempts at objectivity in analysis and advice are most likely to be found. It was also acknowledged that there are other forces at work in the policy process, so objectivity—the attempt to maximize the consistency between policies and the "facts" of the real world, as well as one can know them—will be tempered by the limitations of laws, organizational procedures, and politics.

Chapters 2 through 7 examined the science and technology policy process in the formal institutions of government and the roles played by a wide range of policy actors. The fourfold framework of constraints has been used to illustrate and analyze much of what occurs and to offer some explanations of why the process sometimes fails to work well. A general discussion of the forces that buffet science and technology policy does not offer a parsimonious set of predictive variables and relationships. A framework can suggest hypotheses that could predict which types of policies will be created, and it can be used to explain the influence of a particular type of policy actor in the policy process.

Whether these four types of constraints are applied to science and technology policy or to some other realm of public action, they encompass enormous variations and interrelationships. Devising a formal theory of public policy with strong explanatory power is analogous to the attempts of nuclear physicists to discover a grand unified theory of the four known forces of the universe. In some ways it would be even more difficult to unify the forces that affect the policy process, since it is more feasible to create experiments and measures of gravity, electromagnetism, and the strong and weak nuclear forces than to replicate and measure experimentally the effect of dissension among scientific witnesses at a congressional hearing on the formulation, adoption, and implementation of acid rain policy.

The inability of those who study public policy to make general theoretical statements that allow predictions could be, and often is, taken as evidence that the social sciences are not very scientific, or that they never can be. Progress has indeed been slow, but because no phenomena—social or physical, no matter how complex—are beyond the scope of scientific inquiry, it is possible to look ahead to the development of a science of public policy.

Notes

1. For example, *Bigelow v. Virginia,* 421 U.S. 809 (1975). Balancing, in this context, is logically similar to the "rational basis" test discussed in Chapter 4.
2. *Mercoid Corp. v. Mid-Continental Co.,* 320 U.S. 661, 665-666 (1944). In other cases federal courts have suggested that patents do not fit comfortably in a free market economic system; see *United States v. Paramount Pictures, Inc.,* 334 U.S. 131 (1948) and *United States v. Studiengessellschaft Kohle, m.b.H.,* 670 F.2d 1122 (D.C. Circuit 1981).
3. Judge William Overton, U.S. District Court, Eastern Division of Arkansas Western Division, "Memorandum Opinion on *Rev. Bill McLean et al. vs. the Arkansas Board of Education, et al."* (1982).

4. Science advice, discussed in earlier chapters as it affects decision making by government institutions, is the most common topic in the science policy literature. For a representative sample of approaches and points of view, see Brooks (1968); Clark (1974); Mazur (1973); Gilpin and Wright (1964); and Reagan (1969).
5. The implications of the choice of procedure are discussed in Riker (1982).
6. With such a large membership, AAAS has been compared with the "lower house of the parliament of science," in contrast to the "research peerage" of the National Academy of Sciences (Price 1978, 83).
7. Or the rank-and-file may simply be ignorant of the activities of their societies. An attempt in 1981 by the American Society of Mechanical Engineers to establish a Washington office received wide support before local and sectional groups learned that the society's five-person Washington office had been in existence since 1972 (Solnick 1983).
8. The *Bulletin of the Atomic Scientists* and *Physics Today* present the attitudes of today's physicists toward nuclear arms and the Strategic Defense Initiative.

8

Using Science and Technology in Policy: Hazardous Wastes

Every year about one ton of hazardous wastes is produced for each man, woman, and child in the United States, that is, about 250 million tons a year. Hazardous wastes come in the form of uranium mine tailings, byproducts from the chemical industry, spent dry cleaning fluid, used crankcase oil, dry sludge from air pollution control devices, and thousands of other forms. Most of it is stored or disposed of in tanks, waste piles, and landfills; more than eight billion gallons of hazardous substances are injected into the ground annually. The fate of Times Beach, Missouri, where the Environmental Protection Agency (EPA) spent $33 million to buy the dioxin-contaminated town from its 2,200 residents, may someday be repeated at one of the thousands of hazardous wastes sites around the United States.

Hazardous wastes are not new—they are the unshakable shadow of an industrial society—but they have become much more of a *public* problem. Well-publicized disasters such as Love Canal, New York, and Times Beach have helped to draw attention to what many environmentalists and some policy makers have known for years: there is a limit to how much can be thrown away, if for no other reason than sooner or later there will be no more "away."

Technological progress created the supply of raw materials, the demand for manufactured products, and the chemical capacity to improve the American standard of living, but the full price of that progress was hidden since there were few incentives for producers of hazardous wastes to do more than store the wastes in landfills or in forgotten mountains of chemical drums. Without government sanctions, producers paid little attention to the long-term consequences of hazardous wastes and invested little money in technologies for recovering, recycling, or neutralizing the wastes.

Hazardous waste is not only a technological problem. It involves scientific phenomena such as the movement of water through soil layers, chemical reactions, and relationships between exposure and disease. It is also an economic problem since hazardous wastes involve failures in the market system to include the total costs of production in the decisions of producers and consumers. And it is a political problem, for hazardous wastes impose health and property costs on people who then seek government protection.

The confusion of legal, technological, economic, and political forces is revealed by the short but busy chronology of federal hazardous waste policy. Since the first major hazardous waste statute was passed in 1976, there have been lawsuits filed by state governments against federal agencies, disputes about the true meanings of congressional statutes, analyses of the costs and benefits of a variety of taxes and penalties intended to discourage dangerous disposal practices, and front-page headlines as EPA administrator Anne Burford was driven from office and her assistant administrator for hazardous waste, Rita Lavelle, was jailed for perjury in congressional testimony.

These factors have combined to make the task of hazardous waste management one of uncommon scope and complexity. As a result, it serves as a useful example of the application of science and technology to public policy: scientific and technological knowledge must compete with other considerations, it is often uncertain and therefore exploitable, and its utility is constrained by many legal, organizational, and political factors.

Moreover, hazardous waste policy illustrates not only the effect of science and technology on policy, but also the indirect effect that policies can have on science and technology. Any policy that is even partially dependent on science and technology will soon run into the limits of current knowledge and thereby stimulate research. This chapter focuses primarily on the use of science and technology in policy making, but it would be misleading to ignore the reverse effect.

Law and the Policy Use of Science and Technology

Some laws directly determine which technologies may be used as tools to implement policy. These include legal requirements and prohibitions, such as the use of catalytic converters in automobile exhaust systems and the elimination of lead additives from gasoline. More generally, procedural laws prescribe the roles that scientific and technological knowledge can play in agency decision making, and in particular cases, litigation can alter the speed or direction of agency actions. Because of the incompatibilities between the legal paradigm and scientific or technological methods, legal constraints are under stress. This section examines how they can evolve.

Laws That Affect Hazardous Waste Technology

The first attempt by the federal government to reduce the environmental dangers posed by hazardous waste disposal came in 1965 with the Solid Waste Disposal Act, which established a minor program to study the hazardous waste problem. By 1970 there was growing recognition that the most prominent pollution control programs of the era—those for water and air—were actually increasing solid hazardous wastes; under these programs hazardous substances were not destroyed but merely converted into solid form. The 1970 Solid Waste Act called for the new EPA to study hazardous waste technologies, but air and water pollution problems continued to dominate the environmental agenda.

Outside events delayed serious congressional attention to hazardous wastes in the mid-1970s. The appropriate congressional committees were kept busy by concerns about the Arab oil embargo and whether to relax Clean Air Act requirements because of fuel shortages. During the same era the Nixon administration was cutting its budget requests for solid waste pollution programs by 82 percent and shifting enforcement responsibilities to state and local governments. Much of the debate over the federal role in hazardous waste programs involved definitions: the White House wanted to designate only a few substances as sufficiently hazardous to require federal regulation, but environmentalists and some members of Congress insisted that the threat was much larger. The legal mandate for research and development to resolve the dispute remained insignificant.

The Resource Conservation and Recovery Act.   In 1976 Nixon was gone, the power of Democrats in Congress had been strengthened by Watergate, and a consensus was growing, even among chemical firms, that some type of hazardous waste legislation was needed (Epstein, Brown, and Pope, 1982). After relatively little debate, the Resource Conservation and Recovery Act (RCRA) was passed overwhelmingly by Congress and signed by President Ford on October 22, 1976. It required EPA to (1) publish criteria for identifying hazardous wastes, (2) establish a system for "cradle-to-grave" record keeping on the generation, transportation, and disposal of hazardous wastes, (3) develop standards for disposal facilities, and (4) defer to states with hazardous waste programs at least as strict as EPA's rules. Most of these provisions were to go into effect within eighteen months. RCRA also limited the coordination of hazardous waste policies by prohibiting EPA from applying its hazardous waste regulations under this law to wastes covered by other laws, such as the Atomic Energy Act, the Clean Water Act, and the Marine Protection, Research, and Sanctuaries Act. Finally, RCRA required EPA to support research into hazardous waste "conservation and recovery" technologies that would be used as the bases for its regulations.

Problems with EPA implementation of RCRA soon became apparent. As deadlines for promulgating regulations passed, state agencies were joined by environmental groups in lawsuits to force EPA to take action, and a series of investigations by the General Accounting Office (GAO) documented EPA's lack of understanding of health risks and waste treatment techniques. It was obvious that the scope of the hazardous waste problem was much larger than had been realized in 1976. The 1980 reauthorization of RCRA strengthened some of EPA's enforcement powers, but because Congress was more concerned with EPA's failure to meet, or even come close to, the statutory deadlines for issuing regulations, there was no new mandate for hazardous waste research and development.

The scheduled reauthorization of RCRA in 1982 failed to pass Congress, so it was necessary for the 98th Congress (1983-1984) to address the glaring problems that RCRA had failed to solve, and in some ways had exacerbated. For example, though many other environmental laws required a balancing of costs and benefits, RCRA simply said that EPA regulations should "minimize the risk to public health and the environment," leaving the agency confused about how stringent Congress intended it to be. Other provisions, such as the exemption of firms producing less than 2,200 pounds of hazardous wastes per month, had turned out to be loopholes through which enormous amounts of hazardous wastes were passing.

How was scientific and technological knowledge used in the first set of attempts to reduce the hazardous waste problem? The simple answer—not very well—must be qualified: RCRA was passed before Congress or EPA had undertaken a careful analysis of the problem or available policy options. In 1976 policy makers had assumed that the scope of the hazardous waste problem was understood and that EPA would be able to determine the optimal methods of tracking, treating, and disposing of hazardous wastes. Most of the assumptions were wrong. In 1980 EPA estimated that 41.2 million metric tons (MMT) of hazardous wastes were being produced annually. By mid-1983 the estimates were up to about 150 MMT, and in mid-1984 an EPA survey estimated that the total was about 264 MMT. Similarly, it was several years before EPA and the Congress were fully aware of the inherent dangers in land disposal of hazardous wastes, particularly liquid wastes. RCRA did not require EPA to minimize the use of landfills or liquid injection into underground wells, although both techniques pose significant risks to ground water; and the law included only a weak mandate for EPA to study and implement alternative disposal techniques, such as incineration or biological treatment.

The Hazardous and Solid Waste Amendments.   On November 9, 1984, President Reagan signed into law a comprehensive revision of RCRA, the Hazardous and Solid Waste Amendments (HSWA). The House had passed its version of HSWA in November 1983, and the Senate passage by a 93-0 margin was a clear indication of the legislators' attitudes toward EPA's progress. The provisions of this statute were shaped not only by new scientific and technological knowledge, but also by considerations of economics, environmental protection, public health, and politics.

The two most significant aspects of HSWA were its treatment of landfill disposal and its alteration of EPA's discretion in issuing hazardous waste regulations. Regarding landfills, the House-Senate conferees announced their intention "to convey a clear and unambiguous message to the regulated community and the Environmental Protection Agency: reliance on land disposal of hazardous waste has resulted in an unacceptable risk to human health and the environment." Therefore EPA was to take steps to assure that land disposal would be used only as "a last resort" (*Congressional Record,* October 3, 1984, pt. II, H 11126). HSWA established deadlines for EPA to adopt rules for land disposal of hazardous wastes, but it went far beyond earlier mandates. If EPA missed the deadlines, a statutory "hammer" would descend upon the agency: all land disposal of hazardous wastes would end. The first effects of this provision were felt in November 1985, when about 500 of the nation's 1,600 hazardous waste facilities were ordered to begin closing because they had failed to certify that they were complying with federal standards.

Some of the relevant provisions of HSWA were very precise. The law prohibited land disposal of certain substances in specified concentrations: for example, "liquid hazardous wastes containing polychlorinated biphenyls [PCBs] at concentrations greater than or equal to 50 ppm" (parts per million). HSWA also required that new land disposal facilities incorporate a system for detecting leaks, defined as "a system or technology which the Administrator determines to be capable of detecting leaks of hazardous constituents at the earliest practicable time." Congress was uncharacteristically exact about its intent, declaring that any interim landfills meet certain standards:

> The requirement for the installation of two or more liners may be satisfied by the installation of a top liner designed, operated, and constructed of materials to prevent the migration of any constituent into such liner during the period such facility remains in operation (including any post-closure monitoring period), and a lower liner designed, operated, and constructed to prevent the migration of any constituent through such liner during such period. For the purpose of the preceding sentence, a lower liner shall be deemed to satisfy such requirement if it is constructed of at least a 3-foot thick layer of recompacted clay or other natural material with a permeability of no more than 1×10^{-7} centimeter per second (Hazardous and Solid Waste Amendments of 1984, Title II, Section 202).

Obviously, something had been learned about the promises and shortcomings of technologies for hazardous waste management. Some of the specific provisions of HSWA were borrowed from regulations in states such as California and Rhode Island, where hazardous waste policies had been more energetic than at EPA. Other technical details were based on studies by EPA, the Office of Technology Assessment (OTA), and the National Academy of Sciences (NAS), and on reports from environmental, industry, and academic sources. The new statute effectively used scientific and technological knowledge not only because Congress had more reliable information available to it, but also because there were *political* incentives for the lawmakers to pay attention to that knowledge (Barke 1985a).

The Effects of Legal Constraints

The evolution of hazardous waste policy from 1976 to 1984 illustrates the widely varying effects that laws can have on the use of science and technology in policy making. There were no legal constraints on the ability of Congress to incorporate such information in either RCRA or HSWA, and Congress was free to require EPA, NAS, OTA, or other institutions to study health risks or to develop new technological solutions for the hazardous waste problem. Yet these laws themselves affected the use of science and technology in EPA and state agency policy making.

A legislature can prescribe or forbid the consideration of certain types of data in the implementation of its policies. Unfortunately, the 1976 RCRA was extremely vague; it did not require EPA to undertake a comprehensive survey of the scope of hazardous waste contamination, nor did it establish a program to develop new recovery or disposal technologies as alternatives to landfills. The 1976 law also left the agency confused about how it was to balance costs and benefits of alternative regulatory strategies. In addition, the lack of a clear statutory definition of the term "hazardous waste" led to such confusion that EPA could estimate 1980 hazardous waste generation at 41.2 MMT, while at the same time states estimated the total at about 250 MMT (Office of Technology Assessment 1983, 121-122). EPA's attempt to redefine "solid waste" under RCRA began in 1983, lasted twenty-one months, and drew more than 100 comments from businesses, state and local officials, and environmental groups. Because RCRA failed to resolve such questions, and since the data on the generation and disposal of hazardous wastes were so poor, the nation's hazardous waste policy was unimplementable.

The 1984 revisions did not entirely eliminate all ambiguities about hazardous waste policy, if for no other reason than much uncertainty remained about health risks, the hydrology of landfill leakage, and effective techniques for storage, treatment, and disposal. Nevertheless, the new law showed that something had been learned: some aspects of hazardous waste policy were more tightly defined and controlled by Congress, especially the regulation of land disposal facilities. Still, those provisions that allowed flexibility in enforcement reflected remaining technological uncertainty. For example, HSWA extended hazardous waste regulation to the hundreds of thousands of leaking underground storage tanks that pose a threat to ground water, but Congress allowed EPA's regulations to take into account such factors as soil and climate conditions, history of maintenance, age of the tanks, current industry practices, hydrogeology, the water table, and "the technical capability of the owners and operators."

Standards or Lawsuits?

Disputes over technological policies—especially safety, health, and environmental policies—often revolve around the issue of technological flexibility. Laws or regulations may ordain *design standards,* which determine precisely which machines or processes may be used, or *performance standards,* which establish specific goals and allow firms or regulators to choose the best method for achieving them. Design standards are simpler to enforce, but may require expensive redesigns of equipment on the basis of unproven assumptions about health or safety problems, and they are a disincentive for innovation. Performance standards, by contrast, are technologically flexible but more difficult to enforce because of the wide variance in processes that regulators may have to evaluate (Stewart 1981).

EPA has had to contend almost continuously with issues of flexibility in the setting of technological standards. For example, the Clean Air Act established precise standards for EPA to implement regarding automobile emissions of carbon monoxide, hydrocarbons, and oxides of nitrogen, but the National Academy of Sciences criticized the act for being overambitious in the prescribed design standards. The same law empowered the EPA administrator to promulgate additional technical standards if other pollutants were judged to endanger the public health or welfare. When it was found that diesel engines emit from thirty to seventy times the particulates of gasoline engines, EPA issued regulations in 1980 requiring that diesel engines produce only 0.60 grams of particulates per vehicle mile by 1982, and only 0.20 grams by 1985. The courts had to decide whether EPA was allowed to project—and thereby force—future technological advances and the time required to attain them.[1] Similar issues may be raised by the 1984 HSWA because that statute combines precise design standards with some discretion as EPA considers new technologies.

To minimize the problems caused by design and performance standards, it might be desirable to turn away from both general regulations and precise statutory prescriptions and rely instead on case-by-case judgments. RCRA and other environmental laws allow any citizen or organization to seek court injunctions against activities that violate the law or agency rules, and the 1984 HSWA added provisions that allow ordinary citizens to bring actions against companies engaging in hazardous waste management or disposal practices that "may present an imminent and substantial endangerment" if neither a state nor EPA is "diligently" pursuing the same culprit.

Unfortunately, the usefulness of liability and tort law as a method of controlling hazardous wastes is complicated by enormous technological and legal ambiguities (Grad 1985). A comprehensive study of legal remedies for compensating victims of hazardous wastes was fraught with dissension among the group of attorneys and legal scholars over questions of proof of causation, apportionment of damages and liability, and legal standing (U.S.

Senate 1982). In addition, EPA's approach to regulating hazardous wastes has been buffeted by inconsistent court rulings on the liability insurance that the agency required hazardous waste facilities to have under RCRA. Ambiguities in the "pollution exclusion clauses" of general liability policies have allowed insurers to claim that they had no responsibility for damages resulting from hazardous wastes. As a result, EPA was forced to consider issues such as the reliability of technical data that could be used to allocate liability or to estimate the likelihood of "sudden and accidental occurrences" (*Federal Register,* August 21, 1985, 33902-33909).

Law and Technology: Uneasy Partners

In an address to the National Academy of Sciences in 1983, EPA administrator William Ruckelshaus cited the "conflict between the way science really works and the public's thirst for certitude that is written into EPA's laws. . . . EPA's laws often assume, indeed demand, a certainty of protection greater than science can provide" (Ruckelshaus 1983, 245). As more is learned about the risks and techniques of hazardous waste management, the language becomes more complex and further removed from the understanding of lawyers, citizens, and policy makers. Moreover, as discussed in Chapter 5, the fundamental principles of law are sometimes in logical conflict with real phenomena (for example, the two-dimensional perspective of property rights versus the three-dimensional movement of ground water and wastes).

If the application of scientific and technological knowledge to policy is to be successful, the legal constraints on its application must be congruent with several unavoidable characteristics of science and technology policy. First, such knowledge, no matter how precise and communicable, cannot be expected to resolve disputes arising from economic and political trade-offs. When lawmakers attempt to shift the focus to scientific and technological fixes (which are usually imperfect or doomed to obsolescence), they may be skirting the hard choices. Yet while such "trans-scientific" (or "trans-technological") debates may be costly or illogical, they can serve as the necessary distractions that allow policy compromises to be made. In other words, the inappropriate use of science and technology for making policy may be a very appropriate use of science and technology in politics. Thus, there is no "correct" type of legal constraint on their use in policy making, since there is no political incentive for lawmakers to limit their political tactics and resources.

This point is illustrated by Rep. Bob Edgar's (D-Pa.) amendment to the 1985 reauthorization for "Superfund" (the Comprehensive Environmental Response Compensation and Liability Act). It required firms that handle hazardous substances to report routine releases of not only acutely toxic substances, but also those "known to cause or are suspected of causing cancer, birth defects, heritable genetic mutations, or other chronic health effects in humans." The breadth of the language raised unanswerable questions about the number of substances covered by the amendment (Edgar suggested 150, others cited 2,500) and the capability of regulators to comply, given the difficulty of establishing what constitutes a chronic health threat. One legislator claimed that "one drop of dioxin in an Olympic-sized swimming pool makes it lethal for living things," but researchers have found that although it is extremely toxic to experimental animals, there is no evidence of dioxin's serious long-term effects on human health (*Congressional Record,* December 5, 1985, H 11204; Tschirley 1986).[2]

Furthermore, laws, policy goals, scientific evidence, and technological tools are seldom unambiguous. It is unlikely that the multiple goals in government programs will be explicitly stated, yet it is certain that the political demands they manifest will be difficult to ignore. At the same time, the appropriate scientific basis or technological method for designing and implementing a policy will generally be at best a vague set of loosely connected principles and techniques whose usefulness for a specific policy problem is unproven. Sometimes knowledge is firm, allowing specific statutory prescriptions or prohibitions, such as the minimization of land waste disposal; but legal requirements of certainty are usually as scientifically inappropriate as they are politically futile.

Finally, even if policy goals and their technological bases could be clearly defined, they are rarely static. The RCRA was established to prevent hazardous waste problems from becoming crises, but within a few years the disasters at Love Canal, Times Beach, and other locations demonstrated that RCRA would not suffice. Superfund was created in 1980 to finance the extremely expensive task of cleaning up past hazardous waste abuses. The preventive goal of RCRA became entangled with the remedial problems of Superfund, and the implicit cost-benefit assumptions that underlay hazardous waste policies were reevaluated. During the same period, scientific and technological knowledge about disposal problems was changing and thereby altering the ways in which it could be applied to RCRA. The scientific and technological information that was logically applicable to the policy problem could not have been frozen by a statute.

Thus, in spite of the democratic ideal of having representative legislatures make precise policies, for science and technology—and laws about how science and technology are to be used in making laws—should be expected to strive for no more than three realistic virtues. First, laws should state the *general* policy goals as clearly as possible (for example, landfills should only be used as a last resort). Second, they should allow flexibility in implementation by permitting agencies to make exceptions case by case. Third, because of the inherent difficulties in reconciling these two goals, legal constraints should be tempered by built-in mechanisms for revision, whether by reauthorization or by regular oversight, based on improved knowledge about policy goals as well as about science and technology.

Obtaining and Using Knowledge about Hazardous Wastes

If policy makers' understanding of the hazardous waste problem ever becomes sophisticated and stable, their task will then be to confront the political and economic trade-offs that each technological option would create. Because hazardous waste policies have been developed under conditions of technological change and scientific uncertainty, however, those economic and political choices have been unbounded. An evaluation of high-temperature incineration of wastes at sea, for example, had to begin with assumptions about the costs, safety, and effectiveness of not only that technology but also alternative methods of hazardous waste disposal, such as the disincentives that sea incineration would provide for recycling or destruction at the source.

Obstacles to Using Technological Knowledge

The use of science and technology in policy making is inhibited by obstacles that derive from scientific and legal norms and methods. Of course, it also depends on the body of knowledge that exists when a policy issue reaches the institutional agenda of a legislature or an agency and on how that knowledge changes. The application of science and technology in public policy is shaped by the degree to which policy makers recognize the fluidity and gaps in knowledge and allow legislation and regulations to adjust accordingly.

Definitions and Assumptions.   Preceding chapters have addressed some of the problems of policy implementation that narrow legal definitions can cause, such as technological rigidity or irrelevance. Legal definitions are often vague or inappropriate. RCRA defined a *hazardous waste,* for example, as

> a solid waste, or combination of solid wastes, which because of its quantity, concentration, or physical, chemical, or infectious characteristics may—(A) cause, or significantly contribute to an increase in mortality, or an increase in serious irreversible, or incapacitating reversible, illness; or (B) pose a substantial present or potential hazard to human health or the environment when improperly treated, stored, transported, or disposed of, or otherwise managed (Office of Technology Assessment 1983, 116).

With this sort of a statutory definition, words such as *significant, serious, substantial,* and *improperly* must be given working definitions that will allow available science and technology to be applied. Agencies and courts will have their chances to interpret these terms, but a lack of agreement on

definitions by the relevant scientific and technological practitioners themselves will jeopardize their chances of providing useful advice. At the same
time, until researchers know what the law means (for example, the difference
between "hazardous" and "toxic" wastes or the permissible level of risk from
exposure to dangerous substances), their findings will be applicable only by
conjecture.

Scientific and Technological Change.   Former EPA administrator William Ruckelshaus told an audience in 1983 that none of the
assumptions that underlay the environmental laws of the 1970s had been
totally correct. He observed that, contrary to common beliefs at the time, no
one had identified all of the bad pollutants, their health effects, the
dangerous levels of exposure, or how to regulate them at reasonable costs.
Furthermore, it turned out that it was more difficult than expected to change
the environmental laws in response to new knowledge about these assumptions (Miller 1984). The techniques of hazardous waste incineration, for
example, had begun during the 1950s and were spurred by the Water
Quality Act of 1966, since wastes could no longer be discharged into sewers
and streams; but at first, little attention was paid to the implications of
hazardous waste incineration for air quality. Then the Clean Air Amendments of 1970 prompted the development of advanced incinerator designs
that could remove more of the hazardous emissions. By the time RCRA was
passed in 1976, there were many incineration technologies under development, but there were also new types of wastes to be incinerated. In 1978
EPA proposed the first detailed design requirements for incineration, then
suggested rules—finally adopted in 1981—that allowed technological flexibility in developing and using incineration (for example, a performance
standard for organic wastes of 99.99 percent destruction and removal).

Statutory flexibility permits technological progress, which, ironically,
can make it more difficult for policy makers to know how to establish
requirements. Periodic reassessments should therefore be built into statutes
that are based on scientific or technological knowledge. Fixed mandates are
dangerous not only because they often are based on a snapshot of knowledge
that exists during the short period of policy makers' attention, but also
because as the world changes, so may policy makers: they learn.

Learning about Hazardous Waste Science and Technology

Legislators and regulators show a common tendency to minimize
psychological and political discord by overemphasizing the more easily
acquired and understood data. Herbert Simon (1947) wrote of the "satisficing" behavior of individuals in organizations: rather than maximizing the
gain from each decision, which would require long and costly studies of all
alternatives and their implications, people ratify the first acceptable solution

they find. This generalization is never more accurate than when persons face decisions dependent on information that is arcane and uncertain.

Scientists and technologists are trained to treat satisficing behavior as an anathema. To them, quality and progress rest firmly on the forthright recognition and confrontation of uncertainty. In contrast, policy makers are usually under pressure to act quickly, and they must justify their actions on some sort of information and analysis, regardless of its completeness. Only when these quick fixes become obvious failures must new information be sought for new decisions chosen from new sets of alternatives.

Hazardous waste policy provides evidence of this type of behavior. Before passage of RCRA in 1976, policy makers had devoted little time to hazardous waste problems and policy options (Cohen 1984). EPA lacked both the resources and the mandate to explore the details of environmental problems in addition to the major issues of air and water, telling Congress in 1974: "The technology for hazardous waste management generally is adequate. A wide array of treatment and disposal options is available for management of most hazardous wastes. The technology is in use today, but the use is not widespread because of economic barriers in the absence of legislation" (Environmental Protection Agency 1974).

By the time of the policy revisions in 1984, however, what was known about hazardous wastes had grown enormously. There was convincing evidence that landfill technology was inadequate to provide security even for solid wastes, from which hazardous substances could leach into ground water as rain passed through. A large assortment of alternatives to landfills and injection wells had been studied by 1984 (see Table 8-1). Because the scope of the hazardous waste problem had so obviously been underestimated, and because the system of implementation had been politically exploited by EPA, lawmakers also were willing to pay more attention to technological solutions. Although a study on hazardous waste management by the Congressional Budget Office (1985) found large gaps in the HSWA revision (suggesting that Congress still resorted to satisficing behavior on some issues), by 1984 it took much more information for Congress to be satisfied.

Congress.   During the 97th and 98th Congresses (1981-1982, 1983-1984) more than sixty days of hearings were held on what would become the Hazardous and Solid Waste Amendments of 1984. A range of witnesses, including representatives of the Chemical Manufacturers Association, industrial interest groups, environmental groups, EPA, state agency officials, and academic researchers, testified before eight congressional committees and thirteen subcommittees (see Table 8-2). The hearings focused mainly on two topics: the dangers of landfills and the failures of EPA to implement RCRA aggressively, and a consistent theme of both questions and testimony was the topic's complexity. Members of Congress also confronted the difficulty of obtaining simple or straight answers from EPA officials.

Table 8-1 Primary Alternative Technologies for Hazardous Waste Treatment

Technology	Definition
Biological treatment	Placing wastes in contact with a mixture of microorganisms, thereby allowing organic compounds in the waste to be decomposed; can be controlled by altering the level of dissolved oxygen, by adding nutrients, and by changing the concentration of microorganisms and wastes
Carbon adsorption	Using physical and chemical forces to hold substances to the surface of specially treated carbon; commonly used to remove organic compounds from waste water
Dechlorination	Removing chlorine from wastes by the addition of a nontoxic substance, usually hydrogen or hydroxide ions
Incineration	Thermal destruction of wastes by open burning, liquid injection, rotary kilns, molten salt, or other processes
Neutralization	Decreasing either the acidity of acids or the alkalinity of alkaline wastes by combining acids with alkalines
Oxidation	Decreasing the valence (number of electrons) by chemical reaction, potentially producing only carbon dioxide and water for organic wastes; particularly useful for cyanides, phenols, and organic sulfur compounds
Precipitation	Transforming a portion of a liquid waste into a solid that can be separated by sedimentation; commonly used to remove inorganic metals from water
Recovery/Reuse/ Recycling	Removing a substance (usually solvents, acids, or metals) from a stream of wastes and returning it to a productive use
Solidification/ Stabilization	Removing water from waste materials, resulting in a solid mass containing wastes not easily transported by liquid

Source: Donald C. White, "EPA Program for Treatment Alternatives for Hazardous Waste," *Journal of the Air Pollution Control Association* 35 (April 1985): 370. Reprinted with permission.

As a result, congressional staff members contacted officials in states with ambitious policies for hazardous waste management, and Congress requested comprehensive studies of the hazardous waste problem from the National Academy of Sciences and the Office of Technology Assessment. OTA became especially active, in part because its staff was outspoken in its skepticism of EPA estimates of the scope of the hazardous waste problem and the dangers of landfill techniques. Its 1983 report to Congress, *Technologies and Management Strategies for Hazardous Waste Control,* systematically surveyed the risks and trade-offs of policy options and was cited by many members of Congress as a useful and reliable source of information.

Table 8-2   Congressional Committees and Subcommittees Holding Hearings on HSWA, 1981-1984

Committee	Subcommittee
Senate	
Environment and Public Works	Environmental Pollution
	Toxic Substances and Environmental Oversight
Governmental Affairs	Investigations
House of Representatives	
Energy and Commerce	Commerce, Transportation, and Tourism
	Health and the Environment
Government Operations	Environment, Energy, and Natural Resources
Merchant Marine	Fisheries and Wildlife Conservation
	Oceanography
Public Works and Transportation	Investigations and Oversight
	Water Resources
Science and Technology	Investigations and Oversight
	Natural Resources, Agriculture Research, and Environment
Small Business	Energy, Environment, and Safety Issues Affecting Small Business

Environmental Protection Agency.   Although Congress began to show more initiative in learning about hazardous wastes and policy choices, the major source of knowledge was EPA. During the Carter years the agency had failed to come to grips with the need for hazardous waste R & D: for example, of 1,280 new personnel authorized for EPA during 1976-1977, only 20 were assigned to its Office of Research and Development (ORD), which studied other environmental problems in addition to hazardous wastes. Considering the relatively small base of understanding with which EPA began under RCRA, even a concerted attempt to analyze the hazardous waste problem would have created confusion as the actual size of the task became apparent. Delays in gathering information and issuing regulations led to court cases, and missed judicial deadlines led to a growing recognition that EPA needed to upgrade its R & D efforts. By the end of the Carter administration the hazardous waste R & D budget at EPA had finally begun to show significant growth.

RCRA had called for EPA to conduct research on hazardous waste technologies, but low budgets were hampering the agency's Office of

Research and Development and research laboratories in Cincinnati, Research Triangle Park (North Carolina), and Las Vegas. The ORD budget for solid and hazardous wastes grew from $7.6 million in fiscal year 1978 to $16 million in fiscal year 1980, and in belated recognition of the need for more hazardous waste R & D, Carter's last budget for fiscal year 1981 provided $32 million. Much of this research was earmarked for supporting imminent regulatory deadlines, not long-range research into alternative hazardous waste technologies. The Reagan budget requests for hazardous waste research called for several years of funding cuts (in constant dollars) before a slight increase (to $34.8 million) in fiscal year 1985 (see Table 8-3). In general, spending for all R & D at EPA had dropped by 25 percent between 1974 and 1985.

Apart from criticisms of the low levels of funding for EPA research on hazardous waste technologies, there were more specific complaints. Internal proposals for ORD research work were taking an average of thirty months to be approved. EPA was also faulted for failing to establish a long-term data base and for focusing its efforts on tactical research aimed at justifying pending regulations rather than on innovative projects (Brown and Byerly 1981). EPA defended its research emphasis on land disposal, for example, by citing the large number of landfill applications on which it had to rule, but critics pointed out that minimal efforts on resource recovery research had virtually guaranteed continued reliance on landfills. The same problem with timing was revealed when an ORD official explained a 17-percent decrease in hazardous waste research for fiscal year 1984 by pointing to "completion of hazardous spills control technology development activities, completion of preliminary evaluation for advanced thermal destruction techniques, and completion of the first series of technical manuals for land disposal and

Table 8-3 EPA Budget for Hazardous Waste Research, Fiscal Year 1985 (Millions of Dollars)

Area of Research	Budget Allocation
Risk assessment	7.1
Waste identification and measurement	7.0
Land disposal	5.1
Incineration	3.2
Alternative technologies	3.1
Dioxin	2.7
Releases of hazardous materials	1.9
Quality assurance	1.9
Land treatment of wastes	1.6
Disposal of high-hazard wastes	1.1

Source: U.S. House of Representatives 1984a, 136.

storage wastes." Besides, he argued, "it is not EPA's responsibility to develop for the regulated community new technologies" (U.S. House of Representatives 1983b, 7, 5).

Many members of Congress disagreed with this interpretation of RCRA. In response to EPA research cutbacks, nineteen Democratic and eight Republican members of the House Science and Technology Committee sent a letter to President Reagan, asking him to revoke EPA's budget cuts in R & D; and Sen. Dave Durenberger (R-Minn.) recommended that Congress statutorily require that 25 percent of EPA's operating budget be designated as R & D funds. Although such efforts could not guarantee that hazardous waste R & D would be used in EPA policy making (former administrator Anne Gorsuch reportedly ignored technical reports on hazardous wastes), Congress subjected EPA research to unusually intense scrutiny and repeatedly expressed its unhappiness with the agency's efforts. Several sections of the 1984 HSWA require EPA to develop treatment standards and to identify alternative technologies for hazardous wastes. The proposed 1985 Superfund reauthorization bill called for three distinct hazardous waste R & D programs, costing nearly $225 million over five years, and even stipulated special liability standards to allow new technologies to be more easily tested.

The controversies about EPA's ability or willingness to develop and apply new information on hazardous wastes did not reflect concern simply about whether the agency was making "good" policy. It was one aspect of the question whether EPA was doing its mandated job. Without technical information the agency could not propose reliable and reasonable standards. Without those standards the states could not promulgate their implementation plans, nor could industry confidently anticipate what would be required. And without the cooperation of state and local governments and industry, the status quo would go unchallenged and would deteriorate.

It is impossible to separate and rank the importance of improved technological knowledge and other factors as causes of the 1984 HSWA policy revisions, but several changes from the 1976 policy process are clear. RCRA had allowed technological change by default, providing few incentives for it to occur and leaving it up to EPA to encourage or regulate R & D. In contrast, many of the provisions of HSWA were explicitly based on technological changes during the preceding eight years, and the law used this knowledge in setting new minimum technical requirements. Policy learning occurred, but it was not neat and easy.

Coordination of the Use of Technology in Hazardous Waste Policy

Different agencies or levels of government can produce contradictory policies or allow gaps in policies because of confusion or timidity. Yet centralized policy making also presents problems, such as rigidity or restrictions on public access to decisions. Hazardous waste policy has shown elements of both problems. Federal hazardous waste policy is centralized in EPA, but other agencies have had a hand in shaping policy. The states have also been active in developing and implementing hazardous waste programs. Coordination became a problem in hazardous waste policy after passage of RCRA because it contained "very broad, encompassing goals which demand extensive cooperation among the EPA, industry, state government, and the public. For this to occur, some consensus [had to] be reached on the severity of the problem, how best to resolve that problem, and what constitutes successful performance" (Riley 1983, 41). That consensus was not found quickly.

Coordination within the Environmental Protection Agency

The need to coordinate a particular policy within an agency is clear: though individuals or offices may disagree, ultimately the pieces must be put together before the policy is presented to the outside world. According to Jurgen Schmandt, environmental policy at EPA

> suffers from an internal contradiction. On the theoretical level it is widely agreed that policy must take into account interactions between different parts of the environment. But in practice, legislation and rule making are dominated by media-specific strategies [air, water, solid wastes] that give scant attention to the transfer of pollutants among media (Schmandt 1985, 309).

Schmandt concluded that the EPA hierarchy has contributed to the weakness in the programs for toxic substance control because the agency depends more on powerful specific program offices (air and radiation, pesticides and toxic substances, solid waste, water) rather than on functional organization (management, research, and so on). The problem goes further, however. Coordination sometimes evades even the program offices. During 1982 and 1983, for example, the Office of Radiation Protection proposed three regulations on the health effects of low doses of ionizing radiation, but the three groups within the office that prepared the rules relied on different sets of health studies. Some elements in their analyses were similar, such as the dose-response relationship used to assess the risk of cancer; others, however, contained wide differences, such as a range in standards for permissible whole-body radiation exposures from 2 to 25 millirem (mrem) (Hileman 1983).

There are other elements to the problem of internal coordination. Problems have arisen in the interpretation of data at EPA because of tensions across professional disciplines. Scientists and engineers have disagreed with lawyers and policy analysts about the use of data, such as carcinogen risks or estimates of ambient pollutant concentrations. In addition, though EPA's Office of Research and Development is designated as coordinator for policies on health threats, analytical measurement and monitoring techniques, and modeling methodologies, it is divided into six offices (among them, Environmental Processes and Effects Research, Health Research, Health and Environmental Assessment), which do not always see the same data or interpret them similarly.

EPA's Science Advisory Board (SAB) has been touted as a means for improving internal coordination at EPA because it has had the mandate of overseeing long-range research, reviewing in-house research programs at EPA laboratories, and reviewing the technical basis for proposed regulations. A 1981 analysis of SAB (conducted at the request of EPA) found, however, that it lacked the necessary credibility to live up to its potential as a source (or judge) of scientific and technical information. In response, Administrator Ruckelshaus took steps to increase SAB's diversity, visibility, staff, and scope (U.S. House of Representatives 1982, 1984a). Before EPA issued its proposed rule for implementing HSWA in January 1986, it submitted a fundamental component (its model of ground-water transport) to SAB and made revisions based on the board's comments.

Coordination with Other Agencies

EPA may have dominant domain over the implementation of hazardous waste policy, but among federal agencies it has neither exclusive jurisdiction nor the sole right to assess hazardous waste problems or carry out programs. Congressional agencies have played a significant role in the analysis of information and policy options. OTA has undertaken comprehensive reviews of EPA policies, GAO has issued many reports criticizing the agency's implementation of RCRA, and the Congressional Budget Office has analyzed the taxation tools that could discourage landfills and promote alternative treatment technologies. The provisions in HSWA on leaking underground storage tanks were based in part on information provided by the Congressional Research Service of the Library of Congress.

EPA has also had difficulty in working with the Departments of Energy and Defense. Section 6001 of RCRA requires all federal agencies to comply with federal and state hazardous waste requirements, but subsection 1006(a) exempts nuclear facilities if RCRA would be "inconsistent" with the requirements of the Atomic Energy Act. A federal court was required to settle a dispute over whether the Department of Energy was subject to RCRA. Environmental groups and the state of Tennessee persuaded the court to order the Energy Department to stop massive leaks of mercury, PCBs, and other wastes from a nuclear weapons plant in Oak Ridge (*Legal Environmental Assistance Foundation and Natural Resources Defense Council v. Hodel*, No. 3-83-562 [Eastern District of Tennessee, decided April 13, 1984]; U.S. House of Representatives 1983e). Controversies have also occurred over the regulation of the numerous hazardous waste sites operated by the Defense Department. Even the National Science Foundation has failed to cooperate as EPA would have liked: it rejected an EPA proposal to transfer responsibility for long-term exploratory research to the science agency.

EPA has had more success in coordinating with other federal mission agencies. For example, it has worked with the National Oceanic and Atmospheric Administration on assessments of ocean disposal technologies, and it adopted a memorandum of agreement with the U.S. Geological Survey for joint research on toxic material migration in ground water. As of April 1984 the agency had about 300 interagency agreements on research, including projects such as "Results of Controlled Air Incineration of Pentachlorophenol Treated Ammunition Boxes" with the Defense Logistics Agency.[3]

Coordination with State Governments

RCRA requires EPA to work with state and local governments on the development and implementation of hazardous waste policies, a task that included planning and research. Under Section 3006 states could propose regulatory programs that would be subject to EPA approval, interim authorizations would allow two-year periods of "substantially equivalent" state programs, and final authorizations would require "equivalent" and enforceable programs (Lieber 1983). This system was complex, and remains so. GAO studies have cited the ineffectiveness of state efforts, largely the result of EPA's failure to provide the technical assistance required for monitoring state programs. In addition, significant variations have been found among the efforts of state legislators to regulate hazardous wastes (Lester et al. 1983).

Part of the problem in coordination with the states has been EPA's tendency, especially under Administrator Gorsuch, to pass the buck for enforcement and standard setting to the states. Whether as part of a "new federalism" or for nefarious reasons, the outcome was predictable: if hazardous waste R & D is to be useful, it must be applied consistently; otherwise, hazardous waste producers will shift or ship their production to states that lag behind their neighbors. In addition, without stable federal guidelines, states that might consider innovation run the risk of EPA's undermining their investment in new storage or treatment methods. For example, Missouri declined to implement several innovative techniques for dioxin cleanup in favor of simply storing the wastes in the traditional way (Stanfield 1984, 1764-1765).

California, by contrast, responded to EPA inaction with a comprehensive study of alternatives to land disposal. It produced a detailed survey of the types and quantities of wastes in the state, identified the most hazardous landfill wastes, and examined more than 100 alternative waste management technologies. California then issues a phased ban on land disposal of cyanides, toxic metals, strong acids, PCBs, and halogenated organic compounds such as chloroform and polyvinyl; this list was later incorporated by Congress in the 1984 HSWA. Rhode Island, which has a large costume jewelry industry that produces hazardous wastes and does not have many "aways" in which to throw them, eliminated the federal exemption of 1,000 kilograms per month (reduced to 100 kilograms per month by HSWA) for small-quantity generators of hazardous wastes. Not all states took the initiative, however, and state environmental officials complained about EPA tardiness and obstruction of effective hazardous waste policies. The Environmental Defense Fund and the State of Illinois, for example, sued EPA in 1978 to force the agency to publish hazardous waste rules (*Illinois v. Castle,* 12 ERC 1597 [D.D.C. 1979]; *Illinois v. Gorsuch,* 580 F. Supp. 340 [D.D.C. 1981]).

What seemed to have emerged from the confusion over federal hazardous waste policy by the mid-1980s was a near-consensus among producers, "consumers," and regulators of hazardous wastes, if not on the substance of regulations, at least on the need for more research into hazardous waste technologies. Early in 1984 the representatives of several chemical industries and public interest groups combined their efforts to lobby Congress for increased funding for R & D at EPA (U.S. House of Representatives 1984a). There were also indications that EPA was working more closely with state governments on some aspects of hazardous waste policy. When responsibility for the hazardous waste management programs of Texas was shifted among agencies by the state legislature in 1985, EPA worked with state officials to authorize the new implementation system in less than two months (*Federal Register,* October 4, 1985, 40526-40527). These and other attempts to improve the coordination of hazardous waste policy were partially a result of improved understanding of the scope of the problem and the inadequacy of past hazardous waste methods. Scientific and technological progress cannot, however, account for all of the changes. As for most policies, the political context of hazardous waste policy has been a major factor in the degree to which science and technology were used as a tool of policy making.

Politics in Hazardous Waste Policy Making

Although political context is a major determinant of how scientific and technological knowledge affects policies, simple relationships between politics and the use of expertise are hard to find. On the one hand, if the political climate is intense, with a particular topic high on the public agenda, publicity and the mobilization of interest groups can force policy debate away from the scientific or technological merits and toward political or economic considerations. Under these circumstances policy makers may seek expertise as a way out of their political bind: they convert issues into scientific or technological disputes, delegate the evaluation of options to panels of obscure experts, and deflect the inevitable anguish of the losers. This opens the possibility that science and technology would be exploited.

On the other hand, if the political context is bland, with little public controversy and few organized interests, the experts could have a smoother path as they try to advise policy makers. Members of Congress would not be distracted by extraneous political appeals and could calmly consider the information provided by' scientists and technologists. Yet, once again the picture is not so simple. Unless an issue creates enough heat that its smoke becomes a problem, policy makers are not likely to seek new ways to put out the fire. They will not deliberately shun scientific and technological information, but they may view it as costly or irrelevant.

The case of hazardous wastes illustrates the infuence of the political climate on the use of science and technology in policy making. Before 1976 the hazardous waste issue was generally not recognized as significant, so members of Congress paid little attention to scientific and technical information about the scope of the problem or alternative disposal and treatment techniques. During consideration of RCRA in 1976, the issue became more salient, but there was still relatively little conflict about hazardous waste policies. As a result, legislators assumed that regulators at EPA would know what to find out, what to do, and how to do it.

By the early 1980s the hazardous waste issue had become very salient and very conflictual. The ·issue had become entangled with political wranglings about the mismanagement of EPA, and it was becoming obvious that many dollars (and, probably, lives) were at stake in hazardous waste policy making. In 1980 the surgeon general had reported to Congress that

> while at this time it is impossible to determine the precise dimensions of the toxic chemical problem, it is clear that it is a major and growing public health problem. We believe that toxic chemicals are adding to the disease burden of the United States in a significant although as yet ill-defined way. In addition, we believe that this problem will become more manifest in the years ahead (U.S. Senate 1980).

During the 1980 and 1982 reauthorizations members of Congress asked many questions about hazardous waste problems and alternatives, but they still avoided major changes. The scientific and technological information was sought and received, but not yet applied.

Finally, by 1984, the political climate for hazardous waste policy had evolved into high salience and less conflict. Many members of Congress of both parties had learned that their districts or states were not immune from hazardous waste dumps, and the failure of EPA to respond adequately to its legislative mandate had become unarguable. Substances such as PCBs and dioxin had become "political" wastes as they moved from the obscurity of industrial chemistry to the headlines and "60 Minutes." Under these circumstances, scientific and technological information was recognized as not only useful, but also essential. The emphasis in HSWA on alternative technologies was the result.

The Role of the Public and Groups

The 1976 RCRA included the following mandate:

Public participation in the development, revision, implementation and enforcement of any regulation, guidelines, information or program under this Act shall be provided for, encouraged and assisted by the Administrator [of EPA] and the States. The Administrator, in cooperation with the States, shall develop and publish minimum guidelines for public participation in such process. (Resource Conservation and Recovery Act, Section 7004[b]).

To this end, EPA allocated more than a half-million dollars yearly from 1978 to 1980 for citizen participation programs. The rationale for attempts at increasing public involvement was expressed by Walter Rosenbaum (1983, 181): "Given the inherent technical complexity of the hazardous substance problem it seems almost essential that a public involvement program contain generous resources for production and dissemination of such information together with opportunities for organized citizens education." There are, however, many problems with such assistance.

First is the perennial question "which citizens?" It is impossible to educate all Americans about the technical aspects of hazardous waste control. To most citizens, hazardous waste issues are irrelevant and uninteresting and take no priority over other technical questions; most people would resist attempts to convince them otherwise. Those who are interested and educable about the issue *and* its scientific and technological underpinnings must somehow be found and recruited. The most—perhaps the only—practical way to involve the public is through self-selection, which raises a second problem with public participation programs. Those who become involved must generally have intense reasons to become involved, such as fears about neighboring landfills or incinerators. Participation will generally become one-sided, and so any efforts to encourage or oppose it will be interpretable as politically motivated. Thus, the Reagan administration's elimination of EPA's citizen programs may have been a political move; but the effect, if not the intent, of creating those citizen programs could have received the same criticism.

There have been other mechanisms for public participation in hazardous waste policy. Members of the public have been invited to testify at congressional hearings, but they rarely have the training to offer new technological alternatives or scientific evidence of health hazards. A few persons have also taken the initiative in organizing the public. A homemaker from Love Canal, New York, Lois Gibbs, formed the Citizens Clearing House for Hazardous Wastes in 1981, in part to provide technical assistance for other groups that become involved in hazardous waste disputes. Individuals and groups, however, face the difficult obstacle of the division of responsibilities across federal, state, and local agencies.

The "not-in-my-backyard" syndrome and persistent suspicions about technological solutions to environmental problems combine to give public participation in hazardous waste policy the potential for mischief. Local officials have yielded to fearful opposition from residents and delayed the use of innovative technologies that can remove or destroy PCBs (Piasecki and Gravander 1985). If public education is not likely to overcome such resistance to waste management programs, regulatory negotiation might. Morrell and Magorian (1982) have suggested a two-stage process of public review and comment: information sessions to introduce local residents to the issues of hazardous waste siting, followed by adversarial hearings between facility developers and the community. The virtue of such a system would be its opportunities for motivated individuals to become at least partially familiar with technical questions about hazardous wastes before entering into negotiations (or more commonly, warfare) with the operators of hazardous waste sites. Negotiations may be jeopardized, however, by persistent suspicions of EPA's neutrality in the face of industry pressures. Another problem is the scope of the task: the 1984 HSWA extended EPA's jurisdiction over 800,000 hazardous waste producers that previously had not been subject to federal regulations. Under the circumstances, it requires extreme optimism to expect that a consistent and technologically justifiable system of hazardous waste management will emerge from negotiations among producers, waste management companies, state and federal regulators, and the general public.

The Role of Congress and the White House

Congressional and executive politics have shaped the nation's hazardous waste policies by establishing the general assumptions about hazardous wastes that have been reflected in laws and regulations. Elected officials have incorporated their understanding of scientific risks and technological alternatives into RCRA and HSWA, and they have defined the broad boundaries within which regulators can operate as they consider new information.

Two aspects of the evolution of hazardous waste policy are relevant to understanding the political constraints on applying R & D. First, Congress initially shortchanged its hazardous waste policies by not adequately assimilating the continuing need for progress in hazardous waste research. This failure was manifested in small budgets and weak legislative mandates for research; it was not a deliberate political choice made under pressure from interest groups, but a reflection of the state of knowledge at the time and the lack of incentives for members of Congress to take the lead in shaping an aggressive and innovative hazardous waste program.

Second, the involvement of the White House in this case may have been unusually intense and ideological, but it is informative. As hazardous waste policies slowly emerged from EPA during Carter's term, there was a gradual recognition of the need for more R & D to *prevent* hazardous waste problems, but it was given low priority because of the seemingly more pressing problems of air and water pollution and remedial hazardous waste cleanup. With a new president came radical changes that forced the hand of Congress.

The Office of Management and Budget (OMB) took an active role in slowing the pace of hazardous waste policy making and enforcement at EPA. It imposed sharp cutbacks on EPA's budget and personnel, reflecting David Stockman's statement in a 1980 planning memo that RCRA was a "monument to mindless excess" (Mosher 1981). OMB specifically exempted from the cost-benefit requirements of Executive Order 12291 any EPA actions to *remove* substances from hazardous waste lists, but not efforts to *add* them; and while it criticized proposed EPA rules for inadequate data, it denied the agency the R & D funds and staff it needed to gather that data. Congressional suspicions of OMB became undisguised; at a 1981 hearing Rep. Albert Gore (D-Tenn.) asked James Miller, who was then OMB administrator for information and regulatory affairs, about the role of OMB in hazardous waste regulation:

> Mr. Gore: You had a 20-minute meeting with the Chemical Manufacturers Association talking about regulatory relief a month before you asked [EPA] to pull back the regulations on hazardous waste disposal, and you are telling me under oath that you did not even mention hazardous waste with the Chemical Manufacturers Association?
> Mr. Miller: I am telling you, to the best of my recollection that topic did not come up, and I am under oath when I am saying that I do not recollect that (U.S. House of Representatives 1981b, 62).

EPA left little doubt that it was responding to the new Executive Office mandate. For example, the number of hazardous waste actions referred to EPA by regional offices dropped from 86 in 1980 to 9 in 1981, and enforcement actions referred to the Justice Department fell from 131 in 1980 to 27 in 1982.

Even more telling was the shift in political climate at EPA itself. It was Administrator Anne Gorsuch's refusal to furnish two House committees with documents pertaining to EPA's enforcement of hazardous waste laws that led the House to vote 259-105 to cite her for contempt of Congress, leading to her resignation in March 1983. It was on the subject of hazardous wastes that the assistant administrator for hazardous waste, Rita Lavelle, perjured herself to Congress and was sentenced to six months in prison.

Like any particular case, this one will not be repeated exactly, but these events have had a lasting effect on hazardous waste policy. They contributed to a revocation of much of EPA's delegated power in the 1984 HSWA, including sharper mandates to consider technological alternatives to traditional methods of hazardous waste disposal. In addition, it is possible that members of Congress will be more deliberate in the application of science and technology in other policy areas as a result of the experience with hazardous waste policy. This will depend on the conjunction of a variety of factors, including the salience of the issue, the amount of political conflict, the existing extent of scientific and technological knowledge, and the rate of progress.

Conclusion

There is no typical example of the use of science and technology in policy making. Other issues may never touch local communities, or become very politicized, or entail the same types of economic trade-offs. Nevertheless, the case of hazardous waste policy illustrates the importance of the general factors—laws, knowledge, coordination, and politics—that shape public policies. In addition, simple descriptions of the roles and importance of each type of constraint would be misleading; they differ over time and across issues, as do the relationships among them. Perhaps the closest appropriate analogue from the physical and biological sciences to the factors that shape science and technology policy is the virus, which is able to respond to threats and opportunities by strategically changing its own basic characteristics.

After nearly a decade of conflict, experimentation, confusion, and adjustments, were the science and technology components of federal hazardous waste policy resolved after the 1984 HSWA was passed? If the discussion above about the need for repeated reevaluations was correct, no final resolution will ever be possible. Early indications are that it is the scientific and technological component that is still causing the most trouble, since EPA was once again forced to interpret a trans-scientific term when it issued a proposed rule for implementing the land-disposal restrictions of HSWA in January 1986. HSWA appeared to some to ask for a total prohibition of land disposal, but EPA can allow it in cases in which the agency can prove that human health and the environment are fully protected. EPA's proposed rule had to incorporate a standard for evaluating risk to human health: water from a drinking well 500 feet from a dump would be considered a health hazard if a lifetime of drinking it would cause one person in a million to get cancer. Also, EPA would consider a site near a community of 100 persons less risky than one near a community of 1,000. The outcry from environmental groups and Congress over this distinction has revealed that the scientific and health questions are far from settled.

The experiences of the first decade of federal hazardous waste policy demonstrate a point made by economist Kenneth Arrow in 1962: the market system includes several features that "lead to the conclusion that for optimal allocation to invention it would be necessary for the government or some other agency not governed by profit-and-loss criteria to finance research and invention" (1962, 623). Or, as several asked during the hazardous waste debates in Congress, "If the EPA doesn't do the research, who will?" For the government to sponsor research and development, it must receive some impetus—perhaps from an entrepreneurial public official, but more likely from the realm of politics.

Rep. Claudine Schneider (R-R.I.) asked the basic question at a hazardous waste hearing: "Does policy determine what technology will come to the forefront, or does technology determine what policy we will develop?" (U.S. House of Representatives 1984a, 38). Because politics and policy often bear a relationship to science and technology similar to faintly heard foreign languages spoken in different dialects that occasionally undergo sudden changes, the answer to Representative Schneider's question can only be: both.

Notes

1. The D.C. Circuit Court of Appeals upheld EPA, stating that its projections fit the requirement of "reasonable" interpretation. *National Resources Defense Council, Inc. v. U.S. Environmental Protection Agency,* 655 F.2d 318 (1981). See Stanley (1983).
2. The Edgar amendment passed the House by a vote of 212-211. The United States was not alone in reacting strongly to uncertain evidence of dioxin's risk to humans; see Brickman, Jasanoff, and Ilgen (1985, 211-215).
3. See the list in U.S. House of Representatives (1984a, 72-101).

9

Policy for Science:
The Space Telescope

> . . . A presence that disturbs me with the joy
> Of elevated thoughts; a sense sublime
> Of something far more deeply interfused,
> Whose dwelling is the light of setting suns,
> And the round ocean and the living air,
> And the blue sky, and in the mind of man.
>
> "Lines Composed a Few Miles
> above Tintern Abbey"

His thoughts were probably more metaphysical than physical, but these few lines by William Wordsworth encompass both the inspiration and the frustration of astronomy. The sky appears blue when the sun is high because its red rays are absorbed in the atmosphere, and at sunrise or sunset the sky is orange or red because these wavelengths penetrate the obliquely viewed blanket of air better than scattered blue rays. Similarly, the "living air" consists of moving layers of air at widely ranging temperatures and densities, sometimes flowing at speeds of more than 350 miles per hour at jet stream altitudes (six or seven miles) and making the window through which we see space resemble a layer of rippling glass that bends and distorts the light of "twinkling" stars. The round ocean feeds a weather system that often renders the most sophisticated observatories useless. None of this may have concerned Wordsworth, but it matters greatly to scientists who want to see all of the light the heavens have to offer. So the minds of men developed elevated thoughts.

The Space Telescope is the most expensive astronomical project ever undertaken, a project intended to allow astronomers to be rid of the sky as they study objects seven times more distant and fifty times fainter than any object ever observed before. Until January 28, 1986, it had been scheduled for launch in October 1986, but after the loss of the space shuttle *Challenger* and the resulting moratorium on launches, the Space Telescope's deployment was postponed for at least two years. Nevertheless, the project has been a remarkable scientific undertaking not only because of its potential for revolutionizing much of what is known about the dimensions, composition, structure, and age of the universe, but also because it is the quintessence of "pure science." Congress and several presidents have been willing to allocate more than $1.1 billion to a scientific project with no promises of technological spinoffs, commercial breakthroughs, or military advantages—and this in spite of hundreds of millions of dollars in cost overruns and years of delays. Furthermore, the new Space Telescope Science Institute (STSI) will be an innovation in the management of a major scientific facility, since it will be operated by the scientist-users themselves.

In a sense, the Space Telescope program is an extreme example of many of the characteristics of science and technology policy discussed in this book. It has been *both* a science program (providing astronomers with a tool for research) and a technology program (requiring sophisticated techniques for the device's construction and deployment). Hazardous wastes are a pressing subterranean problem plagued by uncertain science and technology; the Space Telescope, by contrast, is a voluntary extraterrestrial public program, also of great complexity but involving no fundamental uncertainties about what was demanded of it. Although the two cases differ strongly in many ways, the factors of law, knowledge, coordination, and politics are still applicable. After a brief summary of the Space Telescope's history and basic features, the project's policy development will be examined.

Setting the Stage for the Space Telescope

In 1925 the German astronomer Hermann Oberth observed that one day a telescope above the atmosphere would be a great asset to science. Princeton's Lyman Spitzer raised the issue again in 1946, and in that same year the Naval Observatory began space-based science by launching a spectrometer on a small rocket that carried it above most of the earth's atmosphere.[1] During the 1950s balloons lifted instruments to altitudes of more than twenty miles, but though these experiments produced useful results, they were short-lived and unstable.

After the launch of *Sputnik* in 1957, scientists could begin thinking seriously about the ideas of Oberth and Spitzer. A satellite telescope in earth orbit could see space objects more clearly than ever possible on earth, so in 1962 the first of a series of Orbiting Solar Observatories was launched, focusing on the easiest star to observe—the sun. These were followed by two Orbiting Astronomical Observatories (1968-1973 and 1972-1981) that were used mainly for observations of stellar ultraviolet radiation, which is blocked by the atmosphere. The manned Skylab mission in 1973 included a special telescope mount for solar observations, and in 1978 the International Ultraviolet Explorer was launched by the National Aeronautics and Space

Administration (NASA) with contributions from the European Space Agency and the British Science Research Council.

Useful as these projects were, none fulfilled the potential of space science (a term generally referring to the study of space *from* space). Most of the rocket-launched and orbiting instruments had rather small mirrors to gather light from faint stars and galaxies; light-gathering power increases in proportion to the square of the radius of the mirror (a 36-inch mirror is four times better than an 18-inch mirror), and what scientists really wanted was a very large device capable of performing a variety of functions. Building larger telescopes on earth could produce images of fainter objects, but the atmosphere would always reduce the resolution, or clarity, of telescope images.[2]

In 1962 a panel at the National Academy of Sciences (NAS) recommended to NASA that the future of space science should include a large space telescope, 100 inches or more, though some scientists argued that the Orbiting Astronomical Observatory with its 30-inch mirror was sufficient for a while. After preliminary engineering studies, the Space Science Board (SSB) of NAS recommended in 1965 that NASA begin development of a space-based telescope. The expense of the Apollo moon-landing program, however, and a rapid series of ground-based breakthroughs in the late 1960s (the discovery of quasars and pulsars, for example) deflected the budget and the enthusiasm for a space telescope.

In 1972 another NAS committee surveyed the options for astronomy during the 1970s in an attempt to provide NASA and Congress with a consensus of the scientific community on priorities for research. Without being specific about its design, the report rated the Space Telescope project highly. At the same time, a team of astronomers assembled by NASA was working on preliminary designs with engineers at two of NASA's field centers, the Marshall Space Flight Center in Huntsville, Alabama, and the Goddard Space Flight Center in Greenbelt, Maryland. Late in 1972 NASA issued contracts for "definition and development" of Space Telescope components. In 1973 twelve academic astronomers were brought together by NASA to help with the basic design of the instrument, and by 1975 NASA was ready to go to Congress with a "new start" proposal.

Until this step, the Space Telescope was primarily a topic for astronomers and engineers. Although they were aware of outside constraints (especially budget limitations), their committees and working groups had exclusive jurisdiction over the project's scope and characteristics. Then, elected officials entered the process. NASA submitted a proposed budget for fiscal year 1975 with a separate line item for the Space Telescope. The House Appropriations Committee voted against it, but the Senate favored it, and a conference committee restored $3 million for the Space Telescope in fiscal year 1975 (half of what NASA had requested). In addition, Congress instructed NASA to study less expensive programs and the possibility of significant international cooperation (that is, joint funding).

Another working group was formed by NASA, including sixty scientists in a wide range of disciplines from thirty-eight institutions, to work with the space agency on the design of the instrument. Another NAS committee was asked to make recommendations about the Space Telescope and its management, and in 1977 Congress approved the program with funding beginning in fiscal year 1978. This sequence of events shaped not only the Space Telescope, but also later conflicts about its design and operation: the scientific community thought of the project as their own, a piece of scientific equipment of, for, and by those who would use it.

The Design of the Space Telescope

Because the Space Telescope project was shaped by its purpose, design, and functions, the policy cannot be understood unless the basic characteristics of the device are appreciated. The Space Telescope is approximately 43 feet long and 14 feet in diameter, shaped like a long cylinder with an opening at one end. Two solar panels supplied by the European Space Agency (in return for 15 percent of the viewing time) are attached parallel to the telescope, will supply at least 2,400 watts to the telescope, and will recharge its batteries for nightside operation. At launch the entire assembly will weigh about 25,500 pounds.

For purposes of design, production, and operation, the Space Telescope is divided into three major units (see Figure 9-1). The most critical is the optical telescope assembly (OTA) in which a primary mirror gathers and reflects light to a secondary mirror that focuses and intensifies the beam and sends it to the scientific instruments. The primary mirror is 2.4 meters (94.5 inches) in diameter, made of special fused-silica glass, and is capable of collecting a billion times more light than the human eye. It was ground and polished to such a smoothness that if it were the size of the United States, no distortion would exceed 2.5 inches (Bahcall and Spitzer 1982). In orbit the enormous temperature variations between sunlight and shadow would distort the mirror, so hundreds of small heaters will control the mirror's temperature to within 0.1° F. The mirror will achieve an angular resolution (a clear and detailed focus) ten times better than earth telescopes.

The second major system is the package of scientific instruments that receive the light from the OTA. Initially the Space Telescope will carry five instruments, each exchangeable in orbit by astronauts from the space shuttle. Two of the instruments are cameras: a faint object camera developed by the European Space Agency, and a wide field planetary camera developed by Cal Tech's Jet Propulsion Laboratory. The faint object camera will help astronomers test theories about the evolution of stars. The wide field planetary camera will produce detailed images (30 million bits of information per picture) of planets, galaxies, and extragalactic objects. It

Figure 9-1 The Space Telescope

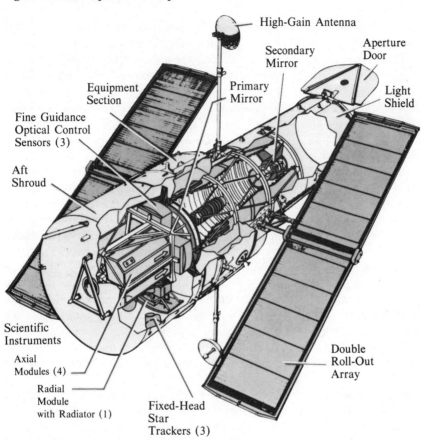

High-Gain Antenna

Secondary
Mirror

Aperture
Door

Equipment
Section

Primary
Mirror

Light
Shield

Fine Guidance
Optical Control
Sensors (3)

Aft
Shroud

Scientific
Instruments

Axial
Modules (4)

Double
Roll-Out
Array

Radial
Module
with Radiator (1)

Fixed-Head
Star
Trackers (3)

Source: National Aeronautics and Space Administration

will also watch for "wobbles" in the motion of stars—evidence of planetary systems other than our own. Photographic film would be impractical for the Space Telescope, so light will be gathered by electronic light detectors that are 3,000 to 10,000 times more sensitive than film and whose data can be transmitted more easily to researchers on the ground.

There is also a high resolution spectrometer made by Ball Aerospace that will study the chemical composition of interstellar gases and clouds, providing information about the evolution of galaxies. A faint object spectrometer made by Martin-Marietta will be able to reveal the chemical composition of the most distant objects in the universe: quasars more than 10 billion light-years from earth. The University of Wisconsin's high speed photometer will be used to search for black holes. Some of these instruments can work simultaneously.

The third major component of the Space Telescope is the support systems module (SSM) that provides electric power, communications, guidance and control, and other necessary functions. The SSM includes the shroud that encloses the entire telescope, radio antennas, and a light shield to protect the OTA from stray light or strong sunlight. The pointing system uses reaction wheels rather than control jets (whose exhaust would contaminate the mirrors) to turn the Space Telescope, locking onto guide stars programmed into its on-board computers and capable of keeping the Space Telescope precisely aimed for hours.

The Space Telescope was designed to be launched into a 320-mile-high orbit from the space shuttle, whose payload bay it will entirely fill. After maneuvering the Space Telescope out of the shuttle using the remote manipulator arm, the astronauts will wait nearby until the solar panels and radio antennas deploy and preliminary tests are completed. After the astronauts' departure the Space Telescope's systems will continue to be checked for several months (at intervals with the first research observations). The Space Telescope was designed so that shuttle astronauts can replace scientific instruments, should any problems develop, and perform other maintenance. (Initial plans to bring the entire unit back to the ground occasionally for maintenance were dropped.) Because of atmospheric drag even at 320 miles altitude, the Space Telescope will gradually decline to about 300 miles and need to be reboosted to its proper altitude by the shuttle about every two years.

The Space Telescope was designed as a complex integrated system of technologically sophisticated parts to work in a hostile environment with great precision for at least fifteen years. Its dependence on other parts of the NASA system was demonstrated by the launch delay caused by the loss of the *Challenger* and by the loss of a vital data-communications satellite being carried aloft by the shuttle; that satellite would have been one of the paths by which the Space Telescope information was relayed to researchers on the ground. Apart from these misfortunes, its development was a challenge requiring perseverance in overcoming the obstacles of complexity (coordinating the agencies and contractors that built and operate it) and hostility (from those who thought the project ill-conceived). Like other large-scale science projects, the Space Telescope had to contend with these constraints before getting off the ground.

Legal Constraints on the Space Telescope Project

Space science is subject to relatively few legal limitations. Although NASA coordinates many of its activities with other agencies and governments, the National Aeronautics and Space Act of 1958 put the nation's civilian space program firmly in the hands of NASA with an enormous amount of discretion over its general direction and specific projects. NASA was not required by law to consult with particular groups before ranking the Space Telescope as more important than other space science projects, and though the firms that received contracts to develop and construct the Space Telescope were bound by laws on accounting, employment, and other practices, none applied specifically to the Space Telescope. These legal requirements appear to have had no significant effect on the program.

Nevertheless, like most other basic science programs, the Space Telescope did produce externalities, that is, costs, such as environmental degradation or health risks, that are imposed on people who may not wish to contribute to the effort. As discussed in Chapter 7, laboratory researchers are bound by regulations intended, among other things, to protect human or animal subjects and to prevent dangerous biological or chemical substances from leaking out of the lab. The Space Telescope carried no hazardous substances and no living organisms involved in the research, yet two aspects of the project came under the control of statutory limitations.

Each time the space shuttle's engines have ignited on the pad at Cape Kennedy, the solid rocket boosters (the two smaller rockets that became so recognizable after the *Challenger* disaster) began converting one million kilograms of fuel (mostly aluminum powder) into energy and aluminum oxide, while the shuttle's main engines burned a cleaner mixture of liquid oxygen and liquid hydrogen. Because of concerns about the effect of frequent shuttle launches on the atmosphere, federal laws required NASA to assess the environmental impact, not only of the launch itself, but also of related activities, such as the production of the shuttle propellants and refurbishment of its tanks. It was estimated, for example, that an extra 72,500 automobile miles would be driven by contractors' employees as a result of the production of twenty-four "flight sets" of rocket engines (*Federal Register,* February 3, 1984, 4285-4287, and October 19, 1984, 41122-41124).

NASA also has had to worry about related aspects of space activities. The *Challenger* exploded only seventy-three seconds into its flight, and all of its debris fell into the Atlantic Ocean; but what if the shuttle, or the Space Telescope, crashed into Zimbabwe? The 1967 Treaty on Principles Governing the Activities of States in the Exploration and Use of Outer Space, Including the Moon and Other Celestial Bodies and the 1973 Convention on International Liability by Damage Caused by Space Objects provide that the U.S. government would be liable for damages. The *Challenger* accident raised additional safety questions about potential health risks from the small nuclear reactors that provide power to some spacecraft carried aloft by the shuttle.

Finally, there is always the potential for Congress to impose specific statutory constraints on a science project for pork-barrel reasons, to address research priorities, or to control the budget. Some members of Congress have tried unsuccessfully to require NASA to distribute its contractor's dollars on the basis of geographical (that is, political) criteria, but no such intervention was threatened on the Space Telescope project. Nevertheless, budget authorizations usually have included a statement that "it is the sense of the Congress that it is in the national interest that consideration be given to geographical distribution of Federal research funds whenever feasible" (P.L. 98-52, Fiscal Year 1984 Authorization Act, Section 105).

Several appropriations bills have included specific limits on Space Telescope funding, but NASA retained some flexibility, and Congress generally provided additional funds as needed. Congress did assert itself specifically on one occasion at the very beginning of the program. When it approved $3 million for definition of the Space Telescope project in fiscal year 1975, Congress stipulated that NASA investigate lower-cost designs and the possibilities for substantial international cooperation. As a result, NASA instructed the three companies working on the preliminary OTA design to recommend a cheaper but still scientifically acceptable system. Mirror sizes of 1.8, 2.4, and 3.0 meters were studied, and it was shown that a 2.4-meter mirror would be much cheaper than a 3.0-meter mirror with little sacrifice of scientific quality, but a 1.8-meter mirror would produce less savings and much less performance. NASA headquarters then chose the 2.4-meter mirror (National Aeronautics and Space Administration 1976).

Apart from this direct intervention, legal limitations had little influence on policy making for the Space Telescope. As a result of the discretion granted to NASA under the law, other factors had a relatively greater effect. Budgetary constraints *were* crucial, but instead of being directed at specific parts of the project by law, they usually affected the Space Telescope indirectly by setting limits on its scientific and technological characteristics. This reluctance to use statutory instructions to shape scientific projects has been typical in American science policy, though projects with larger potential effects (on national security, commerce and trade, or redistribution of health or economic costs) have faced more direct constraints than the Space Telescope.

The Constraints of Knowledge, Technology, and Funding

A common theme throughout this book is that policy makers must eventually yield to scientific and technological realities if public policies are to have the desired effects on the problems they address. There have been examples of gross disregard or ignorance of constraints imposed from outside the political system, but it is more common for scientific and technological knowledge to be deliberately included—though not always wisely—as just one of many factors in policy making for health, safety, defense, and so on.

It might be expected that when the purpose of policy is to *support*, rather than use, scientific or technological research, external constraints, such as the knowledge of experts, should play a more prominent role. In the case of the Space Telescope the scientific element was the sole public reason for the policy, so eventually all other considerations had to be reconciled with their contribution to scientific goals. Because the research goals could be achieved only if there was adequate technological ability and sufficient funding, these factors constantly shaped the definition of the scientific task, and therefore of the Space Telescope program.

The Scientific Task

The scientific limits of the Space Telescope project were established over a period of years by committees and working groups composed of astronomers and NASA personnel. Even in the early planning stages it was recognized that the project's definition would be constrained by budget and technical limitations. For example, the NAS committees that set overall priorities for space science explicitly acknowledged their self-restraint in calling for new and expensive research projects. Early in the project definition process, however, there was little hard information about such factors as the launch system (how large and heavy the Space Telescope could be), so uncertainty was a constant element in early proposals.

The planners wanted to maximize the scientific output of the Space Telescope, but trade-offs were unavoidable. A project of this scope and expense was certain to consume a large portion of the space science budget for many years, and some researchers worried that if their own particular projects were not aboard the Space Telescope, their work would suffer for the program's duration. Some astronomers wanted to use the Space Telescope to study nearby stars and the possible existence of other planetary systems; others were concerned with such topics as distant galaxies and quasars, star formation, stars that emit variable amounts of light, ultraviolet astronomy, infrared astronomy, and visible-light astronomy. The Space Telescope was also seen as a tool for studying objects within the solar system, such as comets, planets, and their moons. Each astronomical specialty would be affected by the final choices for the Space Telescope's mirror assembly and scientific packages.

What evolved over the years of meetings and discussions was a set of minimum criteria for scientific performance, such as a mirror of some minimum diameter and capability for observing ultraviolet radiation that cannot penetrate the atmosphere. Precision in mirror resolution was absolutely vital, and the entire unit had to be capable of extremely accurate aiming and tracking. At the same time, maximum technical limits were set: for example, the assembly could be only a certain size, and it could include only a limited number of scientific packages. Its design would allow it to point no closer than 50° from the sun, 15° from the moon, and 70° from the bright edge of the earth. The Space Telescope would be able to move only slowly, taking about fifteen minutes to turn 90° and requiring about three minutes to lock onto its guide stars (Waldrop 1983b, 250).

Because of such limitations and their implications for research, scientists were very interested in working with NASA engineers during the Space Telescope's development, though few astronomers wanted to work full-time on a project that would produce no research benefits for years. The involvement of scientists created some important coordination problems as NASA planned for post-launch operations. Apart from controversy over the science institute that would operate the Space Telescope, there were persistent concerns that NASA, being a first-rate builder of new things (and with political incentives to focus on development of new projects), might shortchange the scientific budget for operations and data analysis after the Space Telescope was successfully launched.[3]

Technical Limitations

The standards of scientific performance determined the technological challenges facing the Space Telescope's designers and builders. Conversely, technical problems in providing what the scientists wanted led not only to worries about the Space Telescope's capability to live up to its promise, but also to budget problems that caught the attention of Congress.

Because the Space Telescope was to be a totally new instrument, the difficulty of actually building it was not completely understood at the outset. NASA had initially granted preliminary definition contracts to three companies (Boeing, Martin-Marietta, and Lockheed) to resolve initial questions about overall design, and several advisory groups continued to help NASA staff over the years of development. It gradually became clear that some aspects of the project had been underestimated. To scientists the task was straightforward, if not simple, because there were "no major technical unknowns," meaning that the developers were "not required to find new laws of nature in order to carry out the project." Yet one NASA official commented that "virtually every aspect of the program with which Perkin-Elmer [the mirror assembly contractor] deals has been on the cutting edge of technology" (U.S. House of Representatives 1983d, 56, 43).

Contractors had forecast in 1974 that the major technical challenges would be in pointing and stabilizing the Space Telescope (*Aviation Week and Space Technology* 1974, 24). As it turned out, problems occurred in several areas—the guidance system, the wide field planetary camera, the latches that hold the scientific instruments to the OTA—but the most significant problem was the mirror assembly. Perkin-Elmer Corporation produced a mirror whose surface and reflectivity exceeded NASA's specifications, but during testing and assembly a thin layer of dust settled on a small portion of the mirror's surface. In June 1983, NASA officials told a congressional committee that "it is dust that covers two-tenths of 1 percent of the surface," or "roughly 25 percent of the allowable buildup of particulates before we could begin to affect science" (U.S. House of Representatives 1983d, 44-45). In May 1984, Congress was told that "the budget, or the allowable accumulation is a 5-percent aerial coverage of the mirror. We now believe we have 1.4 percent" (U.S. House of Representatives 1984c, 123).

The dust contamination was troubling because it could scatter enough light to reduce the precise resolution of images that scientists needed, and because getting rid of it was extremely difficult. The mirror could not be wiped clean without scratching its reflective coating, so a special cleaning device was developed to remove the dust specks using jets of nitrogen gas and vacuums. Just before the mirror was sealed into the telescope, Perkin-Elmer estimated the contamination to be only 0.6 percent. The problem had, however, caused delays that cascaded through the tight schedule and budget for the entire project. Between October 1980 and February 1983 Perkin-Elmer made sixty changes in the OTA program at the request of its engineers, NASA, and scientists. These related to hardware, testing, design improvements, and systems engineering and arose because of new information, such as the loads and vibration that the Space Telescope would undergo during launch in the shuttle (U.S. House of Representatives 1983d, 258).

Other delays were caused by tests of the computer software that would guide the telescope and by anomalies in the ground support system, and each problem added weeks or months to the Space Telescope's schedule. In the early spring of 1985 the head of NASA's Space Sciences and Applications office told Congress, "I will have to admit that we are hanging on by our fingernails. We are using the program reserves. . ." (U.S. Senate 1985, 279). The most crucial aspect of the program was not sacrificed, however; according to congressional investigators, "NASA has taken extraordinary measures to maintain adherence to the established design requirements and operational plans" (U.S. House of Representatives, 1984c, 41). When technical problems were overcome to protect the scientific goals, additional resources were needed, and something had to yield. In this case, it was time and money.

Schedule and Budgets

When NASA approved the Space Telescope design proposals and operating specifications in October 1977, it was estimated that the total development cost would be $435 million with a launch date in 1983. As shown in Table 9-1, the budget began to grow quickly after the project was "rebaselined" in 1980. The R & D costs grew to almost $800 million in 1984, and the launch date slipped by three years. In addition, it was necessary to add to the Space Telescope budget the costs of operations, maintenance, and refurbishment that had been omitted from the original cost estimate.

Table 9-1   Growth in the Total Space Telescope Budget, Fiscal Years 1978-1984 (Millions of Dollars)

Fiscal Year	Research and Development	Operations	Maintenance and Refurbishment	Total
1978	435			435
1979	464.1			464.1
1980	490.6	60.1		550.7
1981	511.6	51.6		563.2
1982	720.0	148.7[a]		868.7
1983	745.3	186.4[a]	153.1[a]	1,084.8
1984	797.7	241.5[a]	252.0[a]	1,291.2

Sources: U.S. House of Representatives 1983c, 19; U.S. House of Representatives 1984b, 921-985.

[a] NASA estimate.

The degree to which the Space Telescope delays and cost overruns were the result of poor decision making was the subject of considerable study and discussion at NASA and in Congress. NASA officials attributed the cost increases to technical and managerial problems ($224.3 million) and to inflation ($138.4 million). NASA and its contractors complained that the cost overruns were not as severe as the numbers suggested because the original budget was required to use unrealistic inflation factors provided by the Office of Management and Budget (OMB). Questions were also raised about the failure to include the total cost of the program, and not just R & D costs, in the initial estimates to Congress. Nevertheless, even as the yearly budget authorizations grew (Table 9-2), shutting the program down was never seriously considered.

Budget controversies plagued the program from its beginning. A report from the General Accounting Office (GAO) in 1977 claimed that NASA had underestimated the total cost of the Space Telescope project by one-half. To NASA's estimate of $435-470 million in development costs, GAO added $227.2 million in additional development costs and $709.4 million in operational costs for the Space Telescope's fifteen- to twenty-year life. NASA responded by citing technical errors in the GAO analysis and forecast only $10-15 million per year for operations (*Aviation Week and Space Technology* 1977, 47). In 1983, however, NASA was estimating yearly operating costs of $40 million; and in 1984, $50-60 million (including research support for astronomers using the Space Telescope). Much of this increase was a result of the expansion of the Space Telescope Science Institute, and the lumping together of research expenses with operating and maintenance costs was a cause of worry to some who feared that in a battle

Table 9-2   Space Telescope Budget Authority, Fiscal Years 1978-1986 (Millions of Dollars)

Fiscal Year	Budget
1978	36.0
1979	79.2
1980	112.7
1981	119.3
1982	121.5
1983	182.5
1984	195.6
1985	195.0
1986	127.8

Sources: Office of Technology Assessment 1982, 45; U.S. House of Representatives 1984b, 208; U.S. Senate 1985, 286.

over budget constraints between day-to-day operations and scientific support, the latter was likely to lose.

The Space Telescope was not alone in its budget troubles. Through much of the 1970s NASA had faced tight budgets and therefore had cut back on personnel and spare parts for other programs, including the *Landsat D* remote sensing satellite and other space science projects (*Physics Today* 1983b, 48). There were also concerns after the destruction of the shuttle *Challenger* that budget problems and schedule pressures might have caused NASA to try saving time and money by eliminating equipment tests that might have detected the problems with the joints and seals on the solid rocket boosters.

The Space Telescope's budget constraints had immediate and obvious effect. For example, Perkin-Elmer's subcontractor for the fine guidance sensor electronics, Harris Corporation, had been forced to eliminate personnel because of cost overruns, then had to hire new and inexperienced people to complete development and testing (Waldrop 1983a, 173). Another potential result of budget constraints was "molecular contamination," which could have resulted from a thin coating of hydrocarbons "outgassing" from the Space Telescope structure in the vacuum of space and depositing as a thin oil film on the mirror surface, with catastrophic effects for ultraviolet astronomy. Trying to cut costs, NASA officials first took the chance that this would not occur, but later decided "it was the better part of valor to follow standard aerospace practice and do a bake-out," a procedure in which telescope parts are heated in a vacuum to get rid of volatile substances that could contaminate the mirror (*Physics Today* 1984, 18).

The schedule and budget problems that arose from technical uncertainties during the Space Telescope's development were also suspected of having a major effect on other NASA space science programs. In fiscal year 1978 a House Appropriations subcommittee salvaged the Space Telescope program by killing the Galileo mission to Jupiter as part of what some scientists called "The Slaughter of the Innocents": the cancellation, postponement, or cutback of about seventeen R & D programs, including the elimination of the American mission to Halley's comet in 1986 (Waldrop 1983a, 174, and Van Allen 1986, 36). Relatively few new space science programs were begun during the Space Telescope's development. One exception, the Solar Maximum Mission, or "Solar Max" (which was spectacularly repaired by shuttle astronauts in 1985), was allowed to begin development in 1977, partially because the start of the Space Telescope had been delayed for a year and because Solar Max cost less than one-third of the Space Telescope estimate. Another important project, the Solar Optical Telescope, was repeatedly delayed because of the high cost of the Space Telescope.

On the one hand, it is risky to attribute the problems of funding specific programs to particular trade-offs. For example, when the Space Telescope development budget fell by $67.2 million in fiscal year 1986, $46.8 million of that was lost to NASA's space science program altogether, with most of the remainder going to the Solar Optical Telescope and Space Telescope operations and refurbishment (U.S. Senate 1985, 54, 335). On the other hand, the trade-offs are sometimes clear. In fiscal year 1986 there were no new starts on space science programs, according to NASA administrator James Beggs, because of increases in funding for development of an American space station.

It is necessary to ask whether NASA was able to accommodate the constraints imposed by scientific and technological knowledge by learning how to adjust to them. The evidence is mixed. First, NASA already had similar experience on which to draw. The history of the Orbiting Astronomical Observatory (OAO) program is remarkably similar to that of the Space Telescope:

> Snags were encountered in developing the guidance and control system that took inordinate amounts of time and money to solve. Moreover, the seven-year-long development time for the observatory adversely affected experimenters who had to mark time with their experimental programs while the spacecraft was being developed. In this connection it should be noted that a number of scientists had advised NASA to fly a less complicated observatory first (Newell 1980, 402).

Like the Space Telescope, the OAO required constant temperatures, a stable observation mount, and a guidance system that would lock onto guide stars. Its budget rose from $50 million to $200 million, its launch date slipped from 1963 to 1966, and its state-of-the-art design required unanticipated testing and subsystem integration procedures. A NASA management team studied OAO problems and recommended that future large-scale innovative projects include full-time technical representatives assigned to each prime contractor, centralized testing, and close supervision of all phases of development (Mark and Levine 1984, 127-129). Nevertheless, many of the OAO's problems reemerged to plague the Space Telescope's development.

A space science administrator at NASA wrote of the irony of the phrase "the real world of budget and finance," which to scientists in research programs was the epitome of tedium but which set the basic limits on what NASA could do (Newell 1980, 379). Cutbacks in space science programs occasionally led disgruntled researchers to organize letter-writing campaigns to petition NASA for increased funds. As a technology-development agency that is simultaneously in the business of doing science, it has been necessary for NASA constantly to find balances—between space science and space applications, between manned and unmanned programs, between short-range objectives and long-range goals. Thus, when Administrator Beggs testified about the Space Telescope program to Congress in 1984, saying, "After the space shuttle, this program is clearly the top priority program in NASA," he implicitly spoke of the trade-offs forced upon NASA's leaders by the external constraints of scientific goals, technological development, and financial limitations (U.S. House of Representatives 1984b, 263).

Coordination of the Space Telescope Program

It will never be possible to prove that hunger or unemployment has ended, that Americans have the fairest and most efficient tax system possible, or that the nation's armed forces have finally achieved the goal of peace throughout the world. An examination of how any of these policies has evolved must be open-ended and incomplete. Similarly, the coordination of an unbounded task will usually be difficult to achieve.

In contrast, some (but certainly not all) science and technology policies have clear demarcations, for example, a known completion date and a fixed list of agencies participating in the program. It is almost certain that health programs have completely eliminated smallpox, and it will be possible to declare that the development of the Space Telescope is complete when it starts returning information to earth from orbit. For this reason, "science and technology efforts, especially large-scale technological development projects, seem to bring out relevant policy management issues with particular clarity" (Lambright 1985, 183). In addition, because many science and technology programs fall into the exclusive (or at least predominant) domain of one federal mission agency, investigation of the coordination problem is somewhat more tractable. In astronomy, NASA has jurisdiction over space-based research, and NSF supports ground-based astronomy. (Although this is true of space science policy, it is not the case for space applications, where NASA's functions are shared with the armed services, the National Oceanic and Atmospheric Administration, the Federal Communications Commission, the Departments of Agriculture, Interior, and Health and Human Services, the Maritime Commission, and Comsat.)

Because science and technology programs are often novel and unique, coordination problems frequently are exacerbated by lack of applicable experience—or by a simplicity of agency organization and jurisdiction that makes it difficult to hide forever from responsibility when things go wrong. In the Space Telescope program the coordination problem was rooted in a complex division of labor and responsibility.

> Communications among the contractors, their subcontractors, NASA head-quarters and the two space-flight centers involved in the program, Marshall and Goddard, were sporadic and often guarded to avoid revealing any embarrassing technical glitches or, as the Pentagon would have it, any sensitive optical technologies. As a consequence, almost everything that could go wrong invariably went wrong (*Physics Today* 1983b, 47).

This is an exaggeration since many things actually went right, or at least not completely wrong; but the statement is a reminder that when coordination problems occur, someone is likely to notice, if only because by definition the failure of coordination involves more than one office or agency and so is hard to cover up permanently.

The coordination of a large-scale science project such as the Space Telescope entails four major types of organization. First, scientists must work together to choose the basic requirements for the project. Second, the technologists who develop the project (that is, design and build the telescope) must understand what the scientists want, and the scientists must understand and respect the technological limits within which the project must progress. Third, there must be communication between those responsible for R & D and the decision makers who authorize funding (in this case, NASA, Congress, and the executive branch). Finally, these decision makers must reach agreement on what is demanded of the project and what will not be allowed. Any project will suffer if it is guided by dissenting and competing forces among agencies, Congress, and the White House.

Coordination among Scientists and Technologists

The astronomers, astrophysicists, and cosmologists who participated in the development of the Space Telescope began with a common goal—to advance scientific knowledge—but they also had a common problem. Not only were they somewhat in competition with one another, but each subdiscipline of space science had its own agenda, and each wanted to advance its own interests under the constraints of limited time and money. A NASA space science administrator referred to scientists as "a contentious lot, habituated to open debate and free expression of views, and the tremendous opportunitites of the space program inspired them to more intense debate than usual" (Newell 1980, 221). After all, the advisory groups that helped shape the Space Telescope in its early definitional stage were not monolithic. Later, when the Space Sciences Board of NAS evaluated the proposal for a manned space station, it concluded that it could foresee no compelling scientific justification for its development for the next two decades, but some members of the board expressed a desire to participate with their own experiments if the space station were to be built.

As described earlier, there were problems with relations between astronomers and the Space Telescope development team. The formation of the Space Telescope Science Institute was a controversy dating back to a similar dispute in 1962, and once the 1976 NAS committee recommended that the scientists be trusted with operating the Space Telescope, it was hard to argue that they should not also have a direct hand in developing it. Some suspected that NASA's three-year delay in formally proposing a Space Telescope Science Institute following the NAS report may have reflected NASA's desire to have less confusion between scientists and those already involved in its development. As it turned out, the scientists were correct about the need for them to be involved, and NASA was correct about the re-sulting tension. The scientists discovered, for example, that the ground support system was being designed (by TRW) with "dumb" computer terminals that lacked sufficient memory for interactive imaging (which allows images to be manipulated by an astronomer at a terminal), so contracts and equipment were reluctantly changed at some expense and delay (U.S. House of Representatives 1983d, 73).

NASA used an eighteen-member Science Working Group not only to advise it on development matters, but also to satisfy those outside scientists who distrusted the "machine-builders" at the agency. Some administrators at NASA saw general advisory committees as compromises with outsiders who would limit the agency's freedom of action and slow things down (Newell 1980, 217). Nevertheless, because those scientists who were in-volved in the Space Telescope's development were generally in agreement on vital changes in the program, NASA had little choice but to respond.

Coordination between Scientists and Policy Makers

At the outset of the Space Telescope program, many at NASA assumed that scientists would participate in its development and operation but that they would not manage it. Other similar scientific projects had been administered by NASA and its field centers, especially the Goddard Space Flight Center. Space scientists had different ideas. Ground-based astronomy is the domain of the National Science Foundation, which funds the national observatories but generally leaves their management and operation to scientists and universities, so there was early and persistent pressure on NASA to allow the Space Telescope to be managed in the same way.

The issue of who would operate the Space Telescope became inflamed in the mid-1970s when the overall space science budget was falling and many

scientists felt that NASA was spurning them. Some lobbied their representatives and senators, and five members of the Science Working Group formally
asked NASA's administrator to listen to their complaints about the Space
Telescope program (Walsh 1976, 544). The advisory committee members
may have felt manipulated, as well. Some committees had been asked to
rank mission proposals on a scale of one to four, on the basis of originality,
validity, importance, capability, and other qualities. Usually only category 1
projects were chosen, but "with an eye to the future, NASA often funded the
research and development needed to raise a category 3 experiment to
category 1" (Newell 1980, 216).

The Space Telescope Science Institute

The most contentious issue in the Space Telescope program was the
formation and operation of STSI. NASA officials preferred to let the
Goddard Space Flight Center manage the post-launch operations of the
Space Telescope, viewing the long-term operation of a major research
institution by scientists as a risky experiment (though it was not unknown in
scientific research, as in high-energy physics).

Once the decision was finally made to establish a separate scientific
Space Telescope institute, other choices had to be made quickly: location,
director, scale, and budget. NASA avoided the inevitable political dangers in
choosing a site by issuing a request for proposals. It received bids from
Princeton University, the Universities of Chicago, Maryland, and Colorado,
and several university consortia that ran other national laboratories. The
contenders contacted Space Telescope contractors and in one case assembled
a mock NASA evaluation team to review its draft proposals. The winner was
the seventeen-member Association of Universities for Research in Astronomy (AURA), operator of Kitt Peak and two other national observatories.[4]
Recognizing the value of locating its proposed institute in suburban Washington near Goddard (which would be handling most of the nonscientific
aspects of Space Telescope operation), AURA considered proposing the
University of Maryland and Johns Hopkins University, near Baltimore, as
possible sites for STSI. When Johns Hopkins and the state of Maryland
offered a location, low-interest state bonds, and $2 million of the $10-million
cost of the building, AURA recommended Johns Hopkins, which NASA
then selected in January 1981 (Waldrop 1983c, 535).

The next step was to choose a director. After four months, a list of sixty
candidates was narrowed to Riccardo Giacconi of the Harvard-Smithsonian
Center for Astrophysics, who had not only the appropriate scientific
credentials but also experience in managing the scientific use of NASA's
Uhuru and *Einstein* orbiting X-ray observatories. Some officials at NASA
worried about his aggressiveness, and as the STSI began to take shape
questions were raised about Giacconi and the scope of STSI's operation. One

account suggested Giacconi was guilty of "not-too-subtle empire building, hoping to position the institute to assume scientific responsibility for future satellite observatories," such as the proposed advanced X-Ray Astrophysics Facility (AXAF), since the Space Telescope's life span was only fifteen to twenty years (Beardsley 1985, 613).

Other concerns were raised at NASA and in Congress about STSI's growth. The NAS committee that had recommended formation of STSI in 1976 had estimated a full-time staff of 90 at launch and 120 within a year or two. Yet by 1984 the staff numbered about 140, and estimates for STSI's eventual size ranged up to 310 (U.S. House of Representatives 1984b, 981). Part of the growth in staff was attributable to initial underestimates for STSI, which had not included plans for staff on a twenty-four hour, seven-day basis. Also, it had been assumed that STSI would host about 200 guest observers per year; by 1985 the estimate was 400 to 600.

Two other scientific aspects of the Space Telescope project explain much of the increase in STSI's size and some of the ill feelings among and about the scientists who were running it. First, during the delays while the engineers were worrying about mirror contamination and faulty latches, the astronomers at STSI were preparing for launch by reviewing their ability to operate the system. Among other details, this preparation entailed the experience of the catalog of precisely-located stars for the Space Telescope's guidance system, which would aim the device by locking onto known objects in the same field of view. Old star charts sometimes turned out to be inaccurate, and the Space Telescope's faint-object capabilities required the addition of millions of fainter stars to the catalog, for a total of twenty million stars.

Preparations also involved the Science Operations Ground System (SOGS), an enormous assembly of computer software that would be used for planning, managing, and operating the Space Telescope and for analysis of data. The prelaunch SOGS staff had grown by 30 percent over early estimates, largely because its contractor, TRW, had failed to work closely with the system's scientist-users. NASA and members of Congress expressed concerns about the added expense and time needed to have SOGS ready for launch, to which astronomers at STSI responded that without the fortunate hardware-related delays in the Space Telescope's launch, the SOGS system would have been unable to follow planets and comets or to perform the required "astrometrics," that is, the precise measurements of the positions of stars.

The second major problem for STSI was the development of procedures for the allocation of observing time. A questionnaire sent to 7,500 astronomers led to estimates of 1,500 to 2,300 proposals for viewing time each year, but only about 300 requests could be granted. Working groups of specialists within five subdisciplines (solar system studies, stars and star clusters, interstellar/intergalactic medium and supernovas, galaxies and clusters of galaxies, quasars and active nuclei) would rank the appropriate proposals, then a Time Allocation Committee would make recommendations to STSI's director. (The teams that developed the scientific instruments would get all of the viewing time for the first two months of the Space Telescope's operation.) All data would be stored in STSI's library, where after one year it would become available to other researchers. The STSI staff also had to prepare for the education and assistance of guest observers who were not familiar with the Space Telescope system.

For these and other reasons the task for STSI became much larger than was originally anticipated, and given the value to each researcher of a piece of the Space Telescope's time, STSI's procedures were a sensitive matter. Scientists took pains to demonstrate to NASA and Congress that it was a fair and efficient system. Astronomer Sandra Faber explained the system in a committee hearing:

> I think there is a natural tension between two groups of people which to some extent share different goals. The ideal of the Institute is, of course, to [maximize] its service to the community and the benefit from space telescope. . . . Of course that costs money. The motivation of NASA and Goddard, as I understand it, is to deliver an . . . exceptional product of high quality, but to allow room in the budget to pursue other projects as well (U.S. House of Representatives 1984c, 147).

Trade-offs had to be made, and eventually the responsibility for them would have to be accepted by the decision makers at NASA and in Congress.

Coordination among Decison Makers

NASA is divided into five major offices: Space Science and Applications (OSSA), Aeronautics and Space Technology, Space Flight, Space Tracking and Data Systems, and Management. The Space Telescope was primarily an OSSA project, but coordination problems arose from NASA's complicated management structure. OSSA, which should have overseen the project, was plagued by high turnover, having five directors in six years; and there was no single office at NASA dedicated to the Space Telescope. Responsibility for the program was split between the Goddard Space Flight Center (under OSSA), which would develop scientific instruments and manage post-launch operations, and the Marshall Space Flight Center (under a different NASA division), which would engineer the spacecraft. The two field centers had been known to act as rivals, with distinct "personalities" shaped by their origins and missions, and each had a *project* orientation rather than the broader *program* perspective of NASA head-quarters (Newell 1980, 245, 247). Tensions between the centers and with headquarters had become exacerbated when projects ended and the centers faced personnel cutbacks or redeployments, and there were suspicions that the Space Telescope had been divided between Marshall and Goddard partly to keep both centers busy (Mark and Levine 1984, 181). Similar coordination problems had tragic consequences for the space shuttle program; the Rogers Commission on the *Challenger* accident placed much of the blame for the solid rocket booster problem on poor management and communication among NASA headquarters, field centers, and contractors.

When NASA administrator James Beggs was told in January 1983 (only weeks before defending his budget requests to Congress) that the Space Telescope schedule was slipping very badly, he ordered that a "Tiger Team" from NASA headquarters be assembled to independently review the entire project. Based on this internal review, he explained to Congress that NASA had seriously underestimated the technical challenge of the Space Telescope. In addition, he admitted that the management structure had been too success-oriented, leaving no room for flexibility in time, design, or budget (U.S. House of Representatives 1983d, 263-266). To repeat, very similar problems emerged from the investigation of the shuttle *Challenger* disaster.

Two committees of the House of Representatives were moved to investigate the Space Telescope program after Beggs's confession to Congress in 1983 that the budget and schedule were in more trouble than he had been told. Rep. Edward Boland (D-Mass.), chair of the Subcommittee on HUD-Independent Agencies of the Appropriations Committee, had his staff analyze NASA's management problems and visited the contractors' facilities himself. The staff investigation identified three major failures of coordination in the Space Telescope program. First, the number of personnel initially assigned to the Space Telescope was capped until 1979 at the request of the Defense Department, which wanted to limit the "penetration" of defense contractors by NASA personnel. Second, the Marshall Space Flight Center failed to oversee its contractors and to coordinate its work internally, with scientists, and with headquarters. Third, Perkin-Elmer's work on the mirror and the optical telescope assembly had been poorly managed (which Marshall claimed was responsible for half its $225 million cost overruns).[5] The agreement between NASA's internal investigation and Boland's staff inquiry on the major flaws in the Space Telescope program quieted many of the legislators' grumblings.

The House Science and Technology Committee also studied the Space Telescope's problems, agreeing with its Appropriations counterpart on most of the major coordination problems within NASA. Its recommendations to NASA were intended to serve as a warning of future scrutiny. For example, the committee asked NASA and its advisory groups to review the Space Telescope's development and the STSI's initial operations as guides to future large science programs, and it asked NASA to be explicit in future budget requests about Space Telescope operations and maintenance (especially reboost to higher orbit and instrument refurbishment). Congress reminded NASA that it was watching, yet it never forced NASA to change the direction or pace of the program.

Politics and the Space Telescope

One crucial aspect of the relationship between NASA and policy makers is unmistakable and, given the program's difficulties, remarkable: at no point did Congress or the White House threaten to cut Space Telescope funds or to stop the project entirely, even after the schedule delays and cost overruns were made public. The lawmakers had decided that the Space Telescope was a reasonable goal for NASA, then allowed the agency to pursue the program in relative autonomy. Congress and the executive branch allowed the budget and schedule problems to remain inside NASA by granting it the discretion to reprogram funds within budget categories. Perhaps because there were no headlines about the Space Telescope's promise or problems, there were few political demands for elected officials to fund the Space Telescope program, and there were few complaints about the program's execution.

The White House and the Office of Management and Budget

The most active participant in the Space Telescope program in the executive branch was the Office of Management and Budget. OMB's effects were felt only at the beginning of the program, and at first only indirectly. Because the Space Telescope would be carried into orbit by the space shuttle, the fates of the two projects were intertwined. When President Nixon overrode OMB's objections to the shuttle program, OMB managed to delay the program for more than a year by cutting NASA's requests for shuttle funds; at the same time it was able to cut early Space Telescope funding (for fiscal year 1975, from $11.2 million to $6.2 million) because its delivery system was being delayed. For fiscal year 1977 OMB negotiated with NASA on the start of Space Telescope design and construction, and it exchanged the Solar Max mission for the Space Telescope.

After the Space Telescope program was firmly under way, OMB was very supportive. It was "one of the few programs in NASA that OMB has never stinted; the agency has always gotten pretty much what it asked for" (Waldrop 1983a, 174). A former OMB official told Congress in 1981 that "when it comes to protecting space research . . . you will find that the values among [OMB] people are probably as good as there are in the country, because they sort of fear political interference from the White House and from the Hill as not understanding science" (U.S. House of Representatives 1981e, 259).

Congress

The role of Congress in the Space Telescope program is better described as a political shadow than as a political force. It has always been generally supportive of the space program, with members occasionally bragging that their institution responded to the launch of *Sputnik* before President Eisenhower did. Congress usually has been willing to allocate lump amounts for space science and then let NASA and the scientists decide how to spend the funds. In cases of controversy the legislators have frequently turned to an expert, outside, disinterested forum—the Space Sciences Board of NAS— for guidance on research priorities.

Nevertheless, Congress has not been completely absent as a political force, if only because of its potential for involvement. Apart from the yearly budget cycles, NASA's acute awareness of congressional attitudes is suggested by its unwillingness to become involved in possible pork-barrel wranglings over the location of STSI, its strong reaction to the 1977 GAO report on underestimates of total Space Telescope costs, and the speed with which Administrator Beggs informed Congress of the schedule problems in 1983. When Beggs referred to the Space Telescope as "the eighth wonder of the world" at a House hearing, Representative Boland interrupted him with, "It ought to be at that cost," to which Beggs responded, "You bet" (U.S. House of Representatives 1984b, 25).

Of course, not only does Congress help NASA, but members of Congress see no harm in letting NASA help them. Political pressures generally arise from individual voters or from interest groups, and though little of this pressure came to bear on the Space Telescope program, it was still a consideration. Rep. George E. Brown Jr. (D-Calif.), generally a strong supporter of science programs, once remarked, "Of course one of our concerns in the Congress and in this committee is to maintain an adequate base of public understanding of major scientific areas, so that when we go home at least one or two constituents will say, 'My, I'm glad you funded that space telescope,' or something like that," to which scientists on the Space Telescope team were astute enough to respond that public information programs would require an increase over the original budget (U.S. House of Representatives 1984c, 22).

The Public

With the exception of several organizations of very space-attentive citizens, the public plays a minor and indirect role in shaping policy for space science. Americans are generally supportive of the space program; about two-thirds of survey respondents, for example, favor the space shuttle (a percentage that actually increased slightly after the loss of the *Challenger*). Space science, however, attracts less attention than manned programs. Advocates of NASA programs sometimes cite sales figures from the Government Printing Office—half of its best sellers are space books—but the public is significant in space policy more by its abstention than by demonstrations of its support.

Scientists and NASA

As the major participants and beneficiaries of the Space Telescope program, NASA and the community of space scientists are the major political actors in policy decisions. If "political" forces include those based on self-interest, negotiation and compromise, and strategic manipulation of choices and trade-offs, then the political role of scientists and NASA becomes a rich explanatory concept. Astronomers who zealously promote their own research projects to the exclusion of other projects may also be acting in the best interest of "science," and hence, presumably, the public; but their influence on a science policy can also be interpreted as rational self-interest without condemning such motives as base greed.

For years there has been a "tacit understanding between the research community and NASA that the scientists would restrain their criticism [of expensive manned space flight programs] so long as NASA devoted a reasonable minimum of its budget to sustaining important research projects in the space science program" (Walsh 1976, 544). The truce is occasionally strained when massive new programs are proposed that have the potential of upsetting old compromises. The space science community has made it clear, for example, that it is keeping a jaundiced eye on NASA's space station program; pioneer astrophysicist James Van Allen complained about the "quasi-religious belief that space is a natural habitat of human beings," and pointed out that "the overwhelming majority of scientific and utilitarian achievements in space have come from unmanned, automated and commandable spacecraft" (Van Allen 1986, 32). Suspicious of "new starts" by NASA engineers, the scientific community has revealed an insistence on being included in policy decisions and a willingness to tell Congress what it thinks, if not in blunt terms then at least by discreet indiscretion.

Three NASA programs illustrate tensions between scientists and NASA, which have affected policy support by Congress. First, the space shuttle was sold to Congress and to skeptical space scientists in large part as a tool for conducting scientific research. NASA argued that projects such as the Space Telescope would be smaller, less flexible, and shorter in duration without in-orbit servicing by astronauts. Second, NASA officials told Congress that servicing and repairing the Space Telescope was one of the most important scientific justifications for building a permanent manned space station. Third, there is a connection, NASA officials explained, between a space telescope and a possible return to the moon. For a variety of physical and astronomical reasons a space telescope in lunar orbit would have several major scientific advantages over a counterpart in low earth orbit. It was pointed out at the NASA Symposium on Lunar Bases in 1984 that a space telescope in lunar orbit could provide assistance in finding useful materials on the moon's surface to be used in constructing a lunar base, and in return the lunar presence would be necessary for maintaining the lunar space telescope.

This example illustrates what Mark and Levine called *defensive research,* what Kingdon discussed as adding ideas to the "policy primeval soup," and what Weinberg described as justifying basic science as an overhead charge on the more easily justifiable applied science (Mark and Levine 1984, 111; Kingdon 1984; Weinberg 1967, 97). Especially for an agency whose scientific and technological projects are expensive and require long lead times, it is vital not only for the agency to have a ready list of proposals that can slide through a short-lived policy window, but also for the proposals to have connections with other projects. A shuttle-launched space telescope became a scientific justification for the shuttle program, and a space telescope too delicate to bring back to earth for refurbishment is becoming a similar rationale for the space station. NASA's argument is, "Since we have already sunk the costs in one, we can afford—in fact, we would be silly not to have—the other." The considerations Arthur Levine (1975, 155) described in the mid-1970s were still pertinent a decade later: "With fiscal constraints, military competition, and public apathy looming as large factors in NASA's future, the support of scientists will be increasingly important in insuring a vigorous civilian space effort." Connections between scientific projects and technological projects have been one way to elicit the scientists' political support.

Conclusion

Research and development for technology or for science that will inform policy making can be justified by direct economic payoffs: production techniques, new products, energy supplies, better methods for improving health, and so on. Funding for "pure science" or basic research, however, must find a different rationale, so the policy process for the Space Telescope faced a combination of constraints different from those that affected hazardous waste policy.

Because of the absence of large external environmental, economic, or health and safety costs, legal constraints counted for very little in the Space Telescope program, unlike the enormous implications of law for policies affecting hazardous waste technology. The Space Telescope was a straightforward science and technology program, not an environmental program with strong scientific and technological underpinnings, so it was more directly shaped by external constraints in the form of the laws of physics and the limitations of engineers. Similarly, because it was a program with definable boundaries and a clear beginning and end, budgetary and time constraints were more important in Space Telescope policy than in hazardous waste policy. Few public programs require adjustments as explicit as those forced upon the Space Telescope project by the loss of the *Challenger* and the vital data-relay satellite that was on board. It is not common for teams of highly trained and motivated scientists to be forced to wait nearly two years to continue their work.

There were also differences in the types of coordination and political problems that arose in the two cases. Although coordination was an issue, the Space Telescope program was not plagued by conflicts from state or local agencies or from competing federal agencies that undermined the administering agency's authority, as was the hazardous waste program. Politics did influence the Space Telescope program (albeit with a more scholarly group of activists), but the demands to inform the public about stellar formation and intergalactic materials were much quieter than the demands to do something about leaking landfills.

Neither hazardous waste policy nor a space science program is typical of science and technology policy, nor are they (or, probably, any examples) ideal cases of the use of R & D for policy making or of policy making for R & D. They simply suggest and illustrate some of the characteristics of science and technology policy.

Alvin Weinberg (1967) wrote of "Big Science"—massive and expensive research projects, far beyond both the garage tinkerer and the largest industrial laboratories; the Space Telescope certainly fits his label. (Hazardous wastes are better described as a Big Problem.) Big Science demands hard choices, especially among projects for which limited resources are available. Because Big Science cannot be done halfway, compromises are difficult. Decisions must be made on what Weinberg called (1) internal criteria (is the field ready for exploitation and are the scientists competent?) and (2) external criteria, such as technological, scientific, and social merit. These are political choices, and always will be. People will lose or gain because of such decisions, and regardless of their status as scientists or laypersons they will act on the basis of their expected loss or gain.

Notes

1. Spectrometry is the study of the chemical composition of stars and other objects by analyzing light spectra.
2. The largest ground-based telescope is a device with a 260-inch mirror in the Soviet Union. The largest American instrument has been the 200-inch telescope at Palomar Mountain, California, but a new device nearly 400 inches in diameter (the "Keck telescope"), is being built atop Mauna Kea in Hawaii using newly designed optical and computer systems.
3. These concerns came from a variety of sources. See National Academy of Sciences (1982a), General Accounting Office (1977), and Office of Technology Assessment (1982).
4. The members of the Association of Universities for Research in Astronomy are: the University of Arizona, California Institute of Technology ("Cal Tech"), the

University of California, the University of Chicago, the University of Colorado, Harvard University, the University of Hawaii, the University of Illinois, Indiana University, Johns Hopkins University, the University of Michigan, Massachusetts Institute of Technology, Ohio State University, Princeton University, the University of Texas, the University of Wisconsin, and Yale University.

5. See the memoranda prepared by the staff of the House Appropriations Committee, dated March 16 and June 24, 1983, and February 1, 1984, reprinted in U.S. House of Representatives (1984b, 921-985).

10

Science, Technology, and Public Choices

Some readers of the preceding chapters may have been disappointed by the absence of sweeping recommendations for improving the science and technology policy process. These chapters have made no calls for educating judges, legislators, and presidents in science and technology. They have said nothing about the inherent benefits of having scientists and technologists play a larger or smaller part in policy making. They have presented wider public participation in government decisions as an improbability and, therefore, as irrelevant to much of the policy process.

The perspective of this book has been analytical rather than prescriptive, except insofar as analysis prescribes caution in recommending reforms. On the one hand, analysts want to know more about the policy process before advocating changes; apart from the evident risk of failure, there is the antecedent risk that no one will—nor should—take uninformed prescriptions seriously. On the other hand, they cannot wait for complete enlightenment before proposing improvements. Things will change, with or without conscious guidance. The question is not whether the relationships between science, technology, and government should remain the same, but whether anyone is capable of knowing how they should be changed. Thus, three aspects of science and technology policy in general must be addressed: what is wrong with it, what could make it better, and what is possible?

What Is Wrong with Science and Technology Policy Making?

Most criticisms of the current science and technology policy process fall into three broad categories. First is the coordination problem discussed in each chapter of this book. It affects, among other things, the assessment of risk, allocations of responsibility, the integrity of problem solving, and patterns of participation. Science and technology policies are made by executives, legislators, bureaucrats, and judges in federal, state, and local governments, under pressure from public groups, industry, universities, the military, and foreign governments. It is argued, therefore, that the American government is too fragmented, uncoordinated, or undisciplined to make coherent and consistent decisions on science and technology issues (Price 1983, 53; President's Commission on a National Agenda for the Eighties, 1980). Duplication, inattention, confusion, and inefficiency are the result of poor coordination.

A second theme in criticisms of science and technology policy making is that it fails too often to properly reflect what is known about science and technology. Policy makers and the public are untrained and often uncomprehending. They must rely on experts who carry their own biases. Laws lock current limitations into place by ignoring the uncertainty and self-improvement inherent in scientific and technological knowledge. Again, in this book each participant in the policy process has been shown to contribute to the tension between scientific understanding and policy making.

The third category of criticism is the most common, largely because it is the most difficult to disprove and because it leads to the most expansive deductive conclusions. Much has been written about the lack of responsibility and accountability in science and technology policy making. The public is removed from policy making by the emphasis on the autonomy of scientists and by the delegation of authority to experts. Democratic principles of widespread participation are subjugated to unelected and anonymous technocrats who hide behind advisory committees and peer review, and who need not answer to the public for the consequences of scientific research or technological developments. The public and various communities of experts play roles in the science and technology policy process that are not in perfect accord with democratic theory.

It is inappropriate to ask simply whether each of these criticisms is fair, because there is at least an element of truth in each complaint. In addition, because the range of issues, institutions, and procedures that fall under the rubric "science and technology policy" are so complex and varied, policy analysts should be very careful in judging whether the policy process genuinely needs drastic improvement if parts of it are found to be faulty. Certainly a line can be drawn between the political roles and social obligations of cosmologists and genetic researchers, but it is impossible to find a steady, distinct demarcation between freedoms, levels of risk acceptability, and other norms. Criticisms are credible, moreover, only in a comparative sense: ultimately they must be accompanied by explanations of what feasible alternatives might exist.

What Will Make Science and Technology Policy Better?

This question presupposes that the nature and causes of the flaws in the policy process can be identified or at least suggested. Mechanics and doctors may occasionally make things better by accidental tinkering, but advocates of changes in the policy process must admit that if the stakes are high enough to make change necessary, then they are too high for policy changes to be based on poorly understood causes of undesired effects. Conjectures about improving the science and technology policy process must take into account the range of factors that shape such policies; but, as discussed throughout this book, even when the factors that affect science and technology policy are placed in the four general categories of law, knowledge, coordination, and politics, they are not easily reconciled. Making one dimension of the policy process "better" (by increasing political responsiveness, for example) may make another aspect (the use of scientific knowledge) worse.

Prescriptions for improving coordination of science and technology policy have often prompted the goals of consistency and simplicity. Legally and logically it is desirable to have policies that are consistent between issues and over time. The risk of death from exposure to hazardous wastes should be managed proportionately with the risk of death from motor vehicle accidents. As discussed in Chapters 4 and 5, agencies have been constrained by legal requirements for procedural consistency, and interagency task forces have tried to devise consistent formulas for evaluating risks.

The principal problem that confronts consistency is complexity. It is hardly clear what constitutes consistency for all policies. Different science and technology policies can have vastly different goals, ranging from the protection of ground water from selenium contamination to the discovery of what lies at the core of the Milky Way. Even narrow policy areas often lack the concepts and measures that are necessary for consistency: how does a small acute health risk compare with a large chronic health risk, or how can the aesthetic, economic, health, and political benefits of reducing acid rain be consistently evaluated?

When Alexander the Great was faced with the complex and unyielding Gordian knot, his response was to slice through the rope with his sword, leaving as a legacy a faith in simple solutions to convoluted problems. Congress tried to simplify and coordinate the problem of carcinogens in food with the Delaney Amendment, but the saccharin episode revealed that there was more to the problem than a neutral and objective measure of health risks from food additives. Similarly, proposals for a federal Department of Science have failed because of the lack of consensus on how much or what type of coordination is desirable. The future holds little hope for simplicity. As we learn more about science and technology, the world becomes more complex. Similarly, as we learn more about the policy process, it becomes more difficult to define what "better" coordination would be.

Those who propose to reform the policy process by increasing and improving the utilization of scientific and technological knowledge have confronted similar problems. Chapter 6 examined the forlorn hope that a world comprising better-informed citizens and public officials is possible and therefore desirable. After all, policy-making institutions already have adequate access to expert assistance when they need and request it. The faults lie not in the amount or quality of information, but in the incentives for decision makers to ignore uncertainty by imposing simplicity where it does not exist. Those incentives lie in the political realm, so making the use of knowledge significantly "better" must hinge upon fundamental political changes, not mere adjustments to the policy process.

Finally, calls for more responsibility and accountability in the science and technology policy process are often based on easy democratic principles. A common argument is that because the American political system is a democracy, more public participation is automatically better. In truth, however, much of the demand for increased participation results from the elevation of false principles: the United States actually was to be a democratic republic, not a pure democracy, and many of the Founders were clear in their skepticism about the ability of the general public to participate not just in direct policy making, but even in the selection of representatives. Reforms in the policy process must be based on firmer ground than this.

Apart from the belief that widespread participation (however defined) of the public (however defined) is inherently good, or at least inherently American, arguments for such reforms might derive from the ability of the public to help formulate or implement science and technology policies more effectively. It has not been demonstrated (nor is it being argued here) that broader participation is inherently bad or damaging, but neither is there compelling evidence that an expanded policy role for the lay public would have much of a beneficial effect other than legitimizing the decisions of public officials. That is not an insignificant goal, but reformers should be frank about it if that is all that can be expected. The gains that are commonly attributed to public participation should be attributed to the participation of the *attentive* public, a group to which any citizen can apply for membership. It must be left to the reader to decide whether American society provides the opportunities for each person to have an equal chance to become an attentive and active citizen.

Along with greater public participation there have been proposals to improve science and technology policy making by increasing the accountability of scientists. Because of the potential effects of research and development on society, a preventive step in the right direction would be to urge or require scientists to think socially rather than selfishly before undertaking risky experiments in "inopportune" science. There are several paths, not mutually exclusive, by which this could be accomplished. First, scientists could be encouraged or educated to recognize their obligations to society; the self-policing that was demonstrated by the genetic researchers at Asilomar would then become more common. Courses on ethics could be required in science and engineering curricula, or professional societies could be persuaded to adopt stricter guidelines of behavior. Second, legal mechanisms could be established by which researchers would be held liable for the results of their actions. Both approaches would be analogous to extending technology assessment back one step to "science assessment." Just as technology assessors find it difficult to predict the cascading social, economic, and environmental effects of technological change, science assessors (whether public officials or the scientists themselves) would face an even greater obstacle since scientific research is usually more removed from application than is technological development. Like calls for broader public participation, simple prescriptions for increased accountability of scientists imply an understanding of causes and effects which is still inadequate.

What Improvements Are Feasible?

One common word in this book has been *complex*. That is hardly reassuring to a student of the policy process who is searching for a device to aid comprehension, but recognizing complexity is a vital first step. Inappropriate simplifications are worse than wrong: they are misleading. They cause us to ask the wrong questions, for which "correct" answers are tantalizingly convenient.

The complexity of the science and technology policy process is manifested in three ways: fragmentation of decision making, the inseparability of facts and values, and the balancing of considerations. Each of these is a fundamental characteristic that underlies nearly every stage of the process by which all policies are made, and each must be accommodated by proposed reforms.

Fragmentation

Harvey Averch (1985, 1) has described the science and technology enterprise as "a 'messy,' adaptive system whose interconnections are constantly changing. It uses the information it produces reflexively, on itself to change itself. No persuasive theory of its operations has been advanced or may be advanceable." Among the many requirements such a theory must satisfy are several that follow from the fragmentation discussed in the preceding chapters. A theory of science and technology policy must allow for the interaction of participants and for their disunity (since policy actors do not follow the same roles or rules). It must also allow for dynamic change without making the unnecessary, inappropriate, but commonly implicit assumption that whatever takes place is part of a natural progression toward some ideal equilibrium.

A theory of science and technology policy must also explain why, in contradiction to dominant political and economic theories of policy making, billions of dollars are appropriated to an activity that lacks an organized constituency capable of providing political benefits or sanctions comparable to those offered by competing interest groups from other policy areas. Why should Congress spend more than a billion dollars on the Space Telescope rather than on weapons, hospitals, or highways? The lobbyists for the National Aeronautics and Space Administration, Perkin-Elmer, and the American Astronomical Society cannot offer the same magnitude of incentives as lobbyists from other sectors. If legislators anticipate future contributions or votes from the grateful beneficiaries of funding for antiviral research or superconducting supercolliders, then the common assumptions about self-interested politicians' time frames must change (Clark 1985, 230).

The editor of *Science,* Daniel Koshland (1985, 589), recently addressed the question of fragmentation:

> One argument for a Department of Science is administrative tidiness. The present sprawling giant with fingers reaching into numerous departments and agencies does not produce aesthetic organization charts or clear lines for policy implementation. The consequent pluralism in funding and in administrative mechanisms could be vastly simplified in a single department. An accountant's nightmare, however, may be a scientist's sweet dream of happiness. Science is basically untidy—a mixture of big science and little science; programs that need expensive hardware, like astronomy; and programs that need only time for thinking, like some mathematics; programs that can be planned in advance, like a space station, and programs that rise unexpectedly, like the response to the AIDS epidemic. A single department could succumb to the hobgoblin of internal consistency and thus eliminate the individualistic administrative practices on which science has thrived.

"Curing" the science and technology policy process of fragmentation and uncoordination must depend on how intentional and desirable those traits are. To Don Price, fragmentation was tolerated—and sometimes deliberately created—to prevent centralization under a science establishment, congressional appropriators, the military, or the champions of either pure science or applied research. Coherence of policy was engineered out of the system by an "unwritten constitution" of fixed political customs, political parties, congressional division of labor, the executive structure, the media, and freedom of information (Price 1983). The American Constitution also plays a role insofar as it embodied the Madisonian principle of fragmentation of power by means of fragmentation of interests. Science and technology themselves contribute; as John Dewey (1927, 137) wrote sixty years ago, "The ramification of the issues before the public is so wide and intricate, the technical matters involved are so specialized, the details are so many and so shifting, that the public cannot for any length of time identify and hold itself." Perhaps fragmentation can be better managed; it is hard to imagine how it can be greatly reduced.

Inseparability

Concepts are used not only by students of the policy process, but also by policy makers themselves, and confusion about concepts leads to problems for all. In the first chapter several concepts were discussed, none of which is easily defined. Basic science and applied science, science and technology, scientific method and scientific knowledge, science policy and technology policy—all have been used in the policy process, but as demonstrated by nuclear fusion policy, genetic research, and many other examples in this book, the ambiguity of these terms has had very real policy implications. A study by the National Science Foundation concluded that nonscientific criteria can be as important as scientific criteria in determining priorities for research funding, because the public is unable to separate problems with "innovation" from problems with "science" (National Science Foundation 1985a, 9).

An even more intrinsic problem is the confusion and tension that result from incorporating both scientific facts and political values in public policy, particularly in those policy issues that explicitly derive from the application of scientific or technological knowledge. An argument made throughout this book is that in the practice of law, politics, or policy analysis it is extremely difficult, if not impossible, to be assured that values have not affected the compilation, selection, or presentation of scientific facts. Separability of facts and values is best treated as a Holy Grail to be only spiritually discerned but whose pursuit is still worthwhile. If analysts and reformers cannot find a boundary between science and politics, then they can at least be honest about where confusions lie.

The inseparability of science and politics in public policy has implications for questions of fragmentation and coordination. Decentralization may exist within an agency or a legislature where different experts have jurisdiction over different subsets of policy options (Hammond and Miller 1985). Each policy option has several dimensions—economic, redistributive, political, *and* scientific/technological—that cannot be perfectly separated; so no matter how the policy process is organized, overlaps will still exist. For example, the hazardous waste experts in the Office of Solid Waste of the Environmental Protection Agency (EPA) can consider all of the technological policy options that are permitted under law, but they are not allowed to make formal political decisions. Yet it is as certain that nonscientific considerations will become a part of the EPA experts' calculations as it is certain that technological questions influenced the selection of options allowed under law. Multidimensionality and inseparability allow the enormous variety of policy actors to communicate and compromise. If these policies were not inseparable, it would be impossible to balance interests.

Balancing of Considerations

Science is not built upon balance. Political decisions are. Science and technology policy making is part of the political process, so balancing is unavoidable. In some cases balancing is expressly mandated by law, as in the Federal Advisory Committees Act. More fundamentally, it is implied by the constitutional structure of government, by the combination of rule by the majority and protection of minorities, and by strategies for collective decision making. Not only do political pressures compel policy makers to find balances, but balancing should be expected when values are, or appear to be, mutually contradictory and when that which is undesirable is also inevitable. We desire national security and individual responsibility, but we also want freedom of inquiry and freedom to take risks. We accept the idea that it is impossible to totally eliminate insect and chemical contaminants from foods, so we search for ways to balance health and aesthetic benefits with the marginal costs of stronger standards.

William Blanpied of NSF has said that the American science policy has been not to have a science policy. Political and social values conflict and change, legal and organizational constraints bend and adjust in response, and the many different sciences and technologies grow smoothly or fitfully, depending on factors beyond any person's control. The flexibility implied by balancing is what prevents the science and technology policy process from failing under the stresses created by uncertainty and change.

Conclusion

This discussion of balancing might be interpreted as a justification for a laissez-faire approach: let the political system work its will; whatever is, is right. One could say, for example, that if science and technology can flourish only under free inquiry, then the tensions between open scientific communication and national security will eventually produce an equilibrium of secrecy and openness. Such an attitude would be an abdication of responsibility and is not intended here. Nevertheless, insofar as the whole sometimes is different from the sum of the parts, there is something of an invisible hand at work in the policy process. The Industrial Revolution did not occur because someone intended it or designed it, nor did anyone decide to reshape women's role in American society by inventing an electric starter for automobiles, which made it possible for women to be much more independently mobile. Changes occur without intentions, intentions themselves sometimes change, and actions usually have unintended consequences. In this sense, the policy process is not completely determinate.

Another fundamental tenet of this book, stated in the first chapter, is that policy entails going from what *is* to what *should be*. As a result, the process requires both empirical knowledge about the current world and our abilities to alter it, and the application of our political values to that knowledge. Both aspects—scientific knowledge and political values—are imperfectly known and imperfectly separable. It would be inconsistent, then, to apply any different perspective to policy reform. Just as science and technology inform us of our current situation and how we might change it, and political philosophy clarifies the value choices we can make, the study of public policy should guide our attempts to relate the two.

Such study is an enormous undertaking because of the many factors that can be relevant, because our understanding of both where we are and where we want to go is so uncertain, and because the chasm between the realms of science and of values has been so vast. Frameworks of factors, like the one used in this book, are most useful for pointing to the size of the task and the obstacles to be overcome. Once we have a better appreciation of where we are, we should be more successful in reaching our goals.

References

Abraham, Kenneth S., and Richard A. Merrill. 1986. "Scientific Uncertainty in the Courts." *Issues in Science and Technology* 2 (Winter): 93-107.

Abrams, Nancy E., and R. Stephen Berry. 1977. "Mediation: A Better Alternative to Science Courts." *Bulletin of the Atomic Scientists* 33 (April): 50-53.

Almond, Gabriel. 1950. *The American People and Foreign Policy.* New York: Harcourt, Brace, and Co.

————. 1960. "Introduction." In *The Politics of the Developing Areas,* edited by Gabriel A. Almond and James S. Coleman. Princeton: Princeton University Press.

Altimore, Michael. 1982. "The Social Construction of a Scientific Controversy: Comments on Press Coverage of the Recombinant DNA Debate." *Science, Technology, and Human Values* 7 (Fall): 24-31.

American Association for the Advancement of Science. 1975. *Scientific Freedom and Responsibility.* Washington, D.C.: American Association for the Advancement of Science.

Anderson, James E. 1975. *Public Policy-Making.* New York: Praeger.

Anderson, Paul A. 1981. "Justification and Precedents as Constraints in Foreign Policy Decision-Making." *American Journal of Political Science* 25 (November): 738-761.

Arrow, Kenneth A. 1962. "Economic Welfare and the Allocation of Resources for Invention." In Universities-National Bureau Committee for Economic Research, *The Rate and Direction of Inventive Activity.* Princeton: Princeton University Press.

Ashford, Nicholas A. 1984. "Advisory Committees in OSHA and EPA: Their Use in Regulatory Decisionmaking." *Science, Technology, and Human Values* 9 (Winter): 72-82.

Association of American Universities. 1980. *The Scientific Instrumentation Needs of Research Universities: A Report to the National Science Foundation.* Washington, D.C.: Association of American Universities.

Averch, Harvey A. 1985. *A Strategic Analysis of Science and Technology Policy.* Baltimore: Johns Hopkins University Press.

Aviation Week and Space Technology. 1974. "NASA Awards Space Telescope Studies." 101 (November 25): 24-25.

————. 1977. "GAO Space Telescope Study Disputed." 106 (May 23): 47.

Bahcall, John N., and Lyman Spitzer, Jr. 1982. "The Space Telescope." *Scientific American* 247 (July): 40-51.

Baltimore, David. 1978. "Limiting Science: A Biologist's Perspective." *Daedalus* 107 (Spring): 37-45.

Barfield, Claude E. 1982. *Science Policy from Ford to Reagan: Change and Continuity.* Washington, D.C.: American Enterprise Institute.

Barke, Richard P. 1984. "Regulatory Delay as Political Strategy." In *Federal Administrative Agencies,* edited by Howard Ball. Englewood Cliffs, N.J.:

Prentice-Hall.

———. 1985a. "Policy Learning and the Evolution of Federal Hazardous Waste Policy." *Policy Studies Journal* 14 (September): 123-131.

———. 1985b. "Regulation and Cooperation among Firms in Technical Standard-Setting." *Journal of Behavioral Economics* 14 (Winter): 141-154.

Beardsley, Tim. 1985. "Space Telescope: Hubble's Terrestrial Tail Threatens to Wag Dog." *Nature* 313 (February 21): 613.

Beazley, J. Ernest, and Leon E. Wynter. 1984. "Pentagon Proposal for a Software Institute Spurs School Rivalry and Industry Concern." *Wall Street Journal* (October 18): 35.

Beckler, David Z. 1974. "The Precarious Life of Science in the White House." *Daedalus* 103 (Summer): 115-134.

Biden, Joseph R., Jr. 1985. "The Role of Advice and Consent in Constitutional Interpretation." Speech delivered at Georgetown University Law Center, Washington, D.C., November 6. Reprinted in *Congressional Record,* December 17, S 17821-17824.

Blank, Robert H. 1981. *The Political Implications of Human Genetic Technology.* Boulder, Colo.: Westview Press.

Boehm, George A. W. 1958. "The Pentagon and the Research Crisis." *Fortune* 57 (February): 137-160.

Boffey, Phillip. 1975. *The Brain Bank of America.* New York: McGraw-Hill.

Boffey, Phillip M., and Bryce Nelson. 1969. "NSF Director: Nixon Admits He Was Wrong." *Science* 164 (May 2): 532-534.

Brewer, Garry D. 1973. *Politicians, Bureaucrats, and the Consultant.* New York: Basic Books.

Breyer, Stephen. 1982. *Regulation and Its Reform.* Cambridge: Harvard University Press.

Brickman, Ronald, Sheila Jasanoff, and Thomas Ilgen. 1985. *Controlling Chemicals: The Politics of Regulation in Europe and the United States.* Ithaca, N.Y.: Cornell University Press.

Bromberg, Joan Lisa. 1982. *Fusion: Science, Politics, and the Invention of a New Energy Source.* Cambridge: MIT Press.

Brooks, Harvey. 1968. *The Government of Science.* Cambridge: MIT Press.

———. 1982. "Science Indicators and Science Priorities." *Science, Technology, and Human Values* 7 (Winter): 14-31.

———. 1984. "The Resolution of Technically Intensive Public Policy Disputes." *Science, Technology, and Human Values* 9 (Winter): 39-50.

Brown, George E., Jr., and Radford Byerly, Jr. 1981. "Research in EPA: A Congressional Point of View." *Science* 211 (March 27): 1385-1390.

Bruff, Harold H. 1984. "Legislative Formality, Administrative Rationality." *Texas Law Review* 63 (October): 207-250.

Bulkeley, William M. 1985. "Manufacturers Seek to Create More Safety-Conscious Robots." *Wall Street Journal* (October 4): 23.

Burger, Edward J., Jr. 1980. *Science at the White House: A Political Liability.* Baltimore: Johns Hopkins University Press.

Burke, John G. 1966. "Bursting Boilers and the Federal Power." *Technology and Culture* 7 (Winter): 1-23.

Cahn, Anne Hessing. 1974. "American Scientists and the ABM: A Case Study in Controversy." In *Scientists and Public Affairs,* edited by Albert H. Teich, Cambridge: MIT Press.

Caldwell, Lynton, 1982. *Science and the National Environmental Protection Act.* University, Ala.: University of Alabama Press.

Cardozo, Michael H. 1981. "The Federal Advisory Committee Act in Operation." *Administrative Law Review* 33 (Winter): 1-62.

Carey, William D. 1982. "Scientific Exchanges and U.S. National Security." *Science* 215 (January 8): 139-141.

Carroll, James D. 1971. "Participatory Democracy." *Science* 171 (February 19): 647-652.

Carter, Luther J. 1974. "EPA Study: National Academy Set to Serve Two Masters." *Science* 185 (August 23): 678-680.

———. 1975a. "Energy: Nuclear Critics Say Academy Names a 'Stacked' Panel." *Science* 190 (December 5): 961-964.

———. 1975b. "Somber Reflections on Congress by a Retiring Member." *Science* 190 (December 26): 1276.

Casper, Barry M. 1976. "Technology Policy and Democracy: Is the Proposed Science Court What We Need?" *Science* 194 (October 1): 29-35.

———. 1977. "Scientists on the Hill." *Bulletin of Atomic Scientists* 33 (November).

Casper, Barry M., and Paul David Wellstone. 1981. *Powerline: The First Battle of America's Energy War*. Amherst: University of Massachusetts Press.

Central Intelligence Agency. 1982. *Soviet Acquisition of Western Technology*. Washington, D.C.: Government Printing Office.

Chalk, Rosemary. 1980. "Scientists as Whistleblowers." In *Science and Ethical Responsibility*, edited by Sanford A. Lakoff. Reading, Mass.: Addison-Wesley.

Chubin, Daryl, and Sheila Jasanoff. 1985. "Peer Review and Public Policy." *Science, Technology, and Human Values* 10 (Summer): 3-5.

Clark, Evert, and Alan Hall. 1984. "The Administration vs. the Scientists: A Dangerous Rift over Locking Up 'Sensitive' Data." *Business Week* (June 4): 80.

Clark, Ian D. 1974. "Expert Advice in the Controversy about Supersonic Transport in the United States." *Minerva* 12 (October): 416-432.

Clark, Norman. 1985. *The Political Economy of Science and Technology*. Oxford: Basil Blackwell.

Coates, Joseph F. 1981. "Technology Assessment." In *Technology and Man's Future*. 3d ed., edited by Albert H. Teich. New York: St. Martin's.

Coates, Vary T. 1982. "Technology Assessment in the National Government." In *The Politics of Technology Assessment*, edited by David M. O'Brien and Donald A. Marchand. Lexington, Mass.: Lexington Books.

Cohen, Michael, James March, and Johan Olsen. 1972. "A Garbage Can Model of Organizational Choice." *Administrative Science Quarterly* 17 (March): 1-25.

Cohen, Steven, 1984. "Defusing the Toxic Time Bomb: Federal Hazardous Waste Programs." In *Environmental Policy in the 1980s: Reagan's New Agenda*, edited by Norman J. Vig and Michael E. Kraft. Washington, D.C.: CQ Press.

Cole, Leonard A. 1983. *Politics and the Restraint of Science*. Totowa, N.J.: Rowman and Allanheld.

Cole, Stephen, Leonard Rubin, and Jonathan R. Cole. 1977. "Peer Review and the Support of Science." *Scientific American* 237 (October): 34-41.

Congressional Budget Office. 1985. *Hazardous Waste Management: Recent Changes and Policy Alternatives*. Washington, D.C.: Government Printing Office.

Congressional Quarterly Inc. 1977. *CQ Almanac 1977*. Washington, D.C.: Congressional Quarterly Inc.

Conservation Foundation. 1984. *State of the Environment: An Assessment at Mid-Decade*. Washington, D.C.: Conservation Foundation. (Figure reproduced in Edward V. Lawless, Martin V. Jones, and Richard M. Jones, "Comparative Risk Assessment: Toward an Analytical Framework," draft final report to National Science Foundation, Grant no. PRA- 8018868, no date, 85.)

Crandall, Robert W., and Lester B. Lave, eds. 1981. *The Scientific Basis of Health and Safety Regulation.* Washington, D.C.: Brookings Institution.

Crawford, Mark. 1985. "Static Budgets Undercut NBS's Competence." *Science* 230 (October 18): 300-301.

Culliton, Barbara J. 1976. "Handler Defends Academy Elitism." *Science* 191 (February 13): 543.

——. 1978. "Science's Restive Public." *Daedalus* 107 (Spring): 147-156.

——. 1982. "The Academic-Industrial Complex." *Science* 216 (May 28): 960-962.

——. 1985. "NIH to Award 2200 New Grants." *Science* 229 (September 6): 947.

Curlin, James W. 1975. "Mutatis Mutandis: Congress, Science, and the Law." *Science* 190 (November 28): 839.

Cyert, Richard, and James G. March. 1963. *A Behavioral Theory of the Firm.* Englewood Cliffs, N.J.: Prentice-Hall.

David, Edward E., Jr. 1975. "One-Armed Scientists?" *Science* 189 (August 29): 679.

——. 1980. "Current State of White House Science Advising." In *Science Advice to the President,* edited by William T. Golden. New York: Pergamon Press.

——. 1985. "The Federal Support of Mathematics." *Scientific American* 252 (May): 45-51.

Delgado, Richard. 1977. "Organically Induced Behavioral Change in Correctional Institutions: Release Decisions and the 'New Man' Phenomenon." *Southern California Law Review* 50 (January): 215-270.

del Sesto, Steven L. 1979. *Science, Politics, and Controversy: Civilian Nuclear Power in the United States 1946-1974.* Boulder, Colo.: Westview Press.

——. 1983. "Uses of Knowledge and Values in Technical Controversies: The Case of Nuclear Reactor Safety in the U.S." *Social Studies of Science* 13 (August): 395-416.

de Solla Price, Derek. 1973. "The Relations between Science and Technology and Their Implications for Policy Formation." In *Science and Technology Policies,* edited by Gabor Strasser and Eugene M. Simons. Cambridge, Mass.: Ballinger.

Dewey, John. 1927. *The Public and Its Problems.* Athens, Ohio: Swallow Press.

Dickinson, John P. 1984. *Science and Scientific Researchers.* Paris: United Nations Educational, Scientific, and Cultural Organization.

Dickson, David. 1984. *The New Politics of Science.* New York: Pantheon.

Doniger, David D. 1978. *The Law and Policy of Toxic Substances Control: A Case Study of Vinyl Chloride.* Baltimore: Johns Hopkins University Press.

Dunwoody, Sharon. 1980. "The Science Writing Inner Club: A Communication Link between Science and the Lay Public." *Science, Technology, and Human Values* 5 (Winter): 14-22.

Dupree, A. Hunter. 1957. *Science in the Federal Government.* Cambridge: Harvard University Press.

Dyer, James S., and Ralph E. Miles, Jr. 1976. "An Actual Application of Collective Choice Theory to the Selection of Trajectories for the Mariner Jupiter/Saturn 1977 Project." *Operations Research* 24 (March): 220-244.

Easton, David. 1965. *The Political System.* New York: Knopf.

Ebbin, Steven, and Raphael Kasper. 1974. *Citizen Groups and the Nuclear Power Controversy: Uses of Scientific and Technological Information.* Cambridge: MIT Press.

Emerson, Thomas I. 1979. "The Constitution and Regulation of Research." In *Regulation of Scientific Inquiry: Societal Concerns with Research,* edited by Keith M. Wulff. Boulder, Colo.: Westview Press.

England, J. Merton. 1982. *A Patron for Pure Science: The National Science Foundation's Formative Years, 1945-57.* Washington, D.C.: National Science

Foundation.

Environmental Protection Agency. 1974."Report to Congress: Disposal of Hazardous Wastes." (SW-115). Washington, D.C.: Government Printing Office.

Environmental Science and Technology. 1984. "Groundwater and the Law." (September): 287A-289A.

Epstein, Samuel S., Lester O. Brown, and Carl Pope. 1982. *Hazardous Waste in America.* San Francisco: Sierra Club Books.

Fenno, Richard F. 1973. *Congressmen in Committees.* Boston: Little, Brown.

Ferguson, James R. 1985. "National Security Controls on Technological Knowledge: A Constitutional Perspective." *Science, Technology, and Human Values* 10 (Spring): 87-98.

Friedman, Robert S. 1978. "Representation in Regulatory Decision-Making: Scientific, Industrial, and Consumer Inputs to the FDA." *Public Administration Review* 38 (May/June): 205-214.

Garwin, Richard L. 1980. "Presidential Science Advising." In *Science Advice to the President,* edited by William T. Golden. New York: Pergamon Press.

General Accounting Office. 1977. *More Emphasis Needed on Data Analysis Phase of Space Science Programs.* Report PSAD-77-114 (June 27).

_____. 1978. *Federal Attempts to Influence the Outcome of the June 1976 California Nuclear Referendum.* Report E M D 78-31 (January 27).

Gerth, H. H., and C. Wright Mills. 1946. *From Max Weber: Essays in Sociology.* New York: Oxford University Press.

Gilpin, Robert. 1962. *American Scientists and Nuclear Weapons Policy.* Princeton: Princeton University Press.

Gilpin, Robert, and Christopher Wright, eds. 1964. *Scientists and National Policy-Making.* New York: Columbia University Press.

Glen, Maxwell. 1985. " 'Star Wars' Future Remains Uncertain Despite Its Early Successes in Congress." *National Journal* (August 10): 1832-1836.

Goggin, Malcolm L. 1984. "The Life Sciences and the Public: Is Science Too Important to Be Left to the Scientists?" *Politics and the Life Sciences* 3 (August): 28-40.

Goodell, Rae S. 1977. "Public Involvement in the DNA Controversy: The Case of Cambridge, Massachusetts." *Science, Technology and Human Values* 4 (Spring): 36-43.

Goodfield, June. 1981. *Reflections on Science and the Media.* Washington, D.C.: American Association for the Advancement of Science.

Goodwin, Irwin. 1985. "Funding Academic Research Facilities: A Duel over Tactics." *Physics Today* 38 (October): 59-61.

Gould, Stephen Jay. 1977. *Ever Since Darwin.* New York: Norton.

Grad, Frank P. 1985. "Compensating Toxic-Waste Victims." *Technology Review* 88 (October): 48-50.

Green, Harold P. 1979. "The Boundaries of Scientific Freedom." In *Regulation of Scientific Inquiry: Societal Concerns with Research,* edited by Keith M. Wulff. Boulder, Colo.: Westview Press.

Greenberg, Daniel S. 1967. *The Politics of Pure Science.* New York: New American Library.

Greenwood, Ted. 1984. *Knowledge and Discretion in Government Regulation.* New York: Praeger.

Grove, J. W. 1980. "Science as Technology: Aspects of a Potent Myth." *Minerva* 18 (Summer): 293-312.

Hadden, Susan G. 1984. "DES and the Assessment of Risk." In *Controversy: Politics of Technical Decisions,* 2d ed., edited by Dorothy Nelkin. Beverly Hills,

Calif.: Sage Publications.

———. 1986. *Read the Label: Providing Information to Control Risk.* Boulder, Colo.: Westview Press for the American Association for the Advancement of Science.

Haimann, Theo, and William G. Scott. 1974. *Management in the Modern Organization,* 2d ed. Boston: Little, Brown.

Hammond, Thomas H., and Gary J. Miller. 1985. "A Social Choice Perspective on Expertise and Authority in Bureaucracy." *American Journal of Political Science* 29 (February): 1-28.

Havender, William R. 1983. "The Science and Politics of Cyclamate." *Public Interest,* no 71 (Spring): 17-32.

Hechler, Kenneth. 1980. *Toward the Endless Frontier: History of the Committee on Science and Technology, 1959-79.* Washington, D.C.: Government Printing Office.

Heppenheimer, T. A. 1984. *The Man-Made Sun: The Quest for Fusion Power.* Boston: Little, Brown.

Hileman, Bette. 1983. "EPA's Rules on Radiation." *Environmental Science and Technology* 17 (December): 564A-567A.

Holden, Constance. 1980. "Republican Candidate Picks Fight with Darwin." *Science* 209 (September 12): 1214.

———. 1981. "Selling the Public on Nuclear Power." *Science* 214 (October 30): 527.

———. 1984. "Reagan versus the Social Sciences." *Science* 226 (November 30): 1052-1054.

Hollander, Rachelle. 1984. "Institutionalizing Public Service Science: Its Perils and Promise." In *Citizen Participation in Science Policy,* edited by James C. Petersen. Amherst: University of Massachusetts Press.

Hornig, Donald F. 1980. "The President's Need for Science Advice: Past and Future." In *Science Advice to the President,* edited by William T. Golden. New York: Pergamon Press.

Horwitz, Paul. 1976. "Congressional Interactions at Very Small Impact Parameter." *Physics Today* 29 (December): 28-32.

Houston Chronicle. 1986. "Court Decides Weather Service Not Liable for Erroneous Forecast," May 14: 6.

Humphrey, Hubert H. 1960. "The Need for a Department of Science." *Annals of the American Academy of Political and Social Science* 327 (January): 27-35.

Jachim, Anton G. 1971. *Science Policy Making in the United States and the Batavia Accelerator.* Carbondale: Southern Illinois University Press.

Jasanoff, Sheila, and Dorothy Nelkin. 1981. "Science, Technology, and the Limits of Judicial Competence." *Science* 214 (December 11): 1211-1215.

Jenkins-Smith, Hank. 1982. "Professional Roles for Policy Analysts: A Critical Assessment." *Journal of Policy Analysis and Management* 2 (Fall): 88-100.

Jones, Charles O. 1984. *An Introduction to the Study of Public Policy,* 3d ed. North Scituate, Mass.: Duxbury Press.

Jones, Daniel P. 1980. "American Chemists and the Geneva Protocol." *Isis* 71 (September): 426-440.

Jones, James H. 1981. *Bad Blood.* New York: The Free Press.

Kalberer, John T., Jr. 1985. "Peer Review and the Consensus Development Process." *Science, Technology, and Human Values* 10 (Summer): 63-72.

Katz, James E. 1978. *Presidential Politics and Science Policy.* New York: Praeger.

———. 1980. "Organizational Structure and Advisory Effectiveness: The Office of Science and Technology Policy." In *Science Advice to the President,* edited by William T. Golden. New York: Pergamon Press.

_____. 1984. "The Uses of Scientific Evidence in Congressional Policymaking: The Clinch River Breeder Reactor." *Science, Technology, and Human Values* 9 (Winter): 51-62.

Katz, Jay. 1972. *Experimentation with Human Beings.* New York: Russell Sage Foundation.

Kevles, Daniel J. 1971. "Federal Legislation for Engineering Experiment Stations: The Episode of World War I." *Technology and Culture* 12 (April): 182-189.

_____. 1978. *The Physicists: The History of a Scientific Community in Modern America.* New York: Knopf.

_____. 1985. *In the Name of Eugenics: Genetics and the Uses of Human Heredity.* New York: Knopf.

Keyworth, George A., II. 1983. "APS Steps into a Political Vortex." *Physics Today* 36 (May): 8.

Killian, James R., Jr. 1977. *Sputnik, Scientists, and Eisenhower.* Cambridge: MIT Press.

Kimura, Shigeru. 1985. *Japan's Science Edge.* Lanham, Md.: University Press of America.

Kingdon, John W. 1984. *Agendas, Alternatives, and Public Policies.* Boston: Little, Brown.

Koshland, Daniel E., Jr. 1985. "A Department of Science?" *Science* 227 (February 8): 589.

Krimsky, Sheldon. 1984. "Pure Science and Impure Scientists: Dilemmas for Public Policy." *Politics and the Life Sciences* 3 (August): 49-51.

_____. 1986. "Local Control of Research Involving Chemical Warfare Agents." In *Science, Technology, and Their Governance,* edited by Malcolm L. Goggin. Knoxville: University of Tennessee Press.

Kuehn, Thomas J., and Alan L. Porter, eds. 1981. *Science, Technology, and National Policy.* Ithaca: Cornell University Press.

Kuhn, Thomas S. 1970. *The Structure of Scientific Revolutions.* 2d ed. Chicago: University of Chicago Press.

Kuklinski, James H., Daniel S. Metlay, and W. D. Kay. 1982. "Citizen Knowledge and Choices on the Complex Issue of Nuclear Energy." *American Journal of Political Science* 26 (November): 615-642.

Ladd, Everett Carll, Jr., and Seymour Martin Lipset. 1972. "Politics of Academic Natural Scientists and Engineers." *Science* 176 (June 9): 1091-1100.

Lakoff, Sanford A. 1974. "Congress and National Science Policy." *Political Science Quarterly* 89 (Fall): 589-611.

Lambright, W. Henry. 1976. *Governing Science and Technology.* New York: Oxford University Press.

_____. 1985. *Presidential Management of Science and Technology: The Johnson Presidency.* Austin: University of Texas Press.

Lapp, Ralph. 1965. *The New Priesthood: The Scientific Elite and the Uses of Power.* New York: Harper and Row.

Lappe, Marc, and Patricia Archibold Martin. 1978. "The Place of the Public in the Conduct of Science." *Southern California Law Review* 52 (September): 1535-1554.

Large, Arlen J. 1985. "NRC, Other Agencies Try to Keep Public in Dark on Some Decisions by Sidestepping Sunshine Law." *Wall Street Journal* (September 24): 64.

Lederman, Leon M. 1984. "The Value of Fundamental Science." *Scientific American* 251 (November): 40-47.

Lepkowski, Wil. 1984. "The Making of a Conservative Science Policy." *Technology*

Review 87 (January): 39-46.

Lester, James P., et al. 1983. "A Comparative Perspective on State Hazardous Waste Regulation." In *The Politics of Hazardous Waste Management,* edited by James P. Lester and Ann O'M. Bowman. Durham, N.C.: Duke University Press.

Leventhal, Harold. 1974. "Environmental Decisionmaking and the Role of the Courts." *University of Pennsylvania Law Review* 122 (January): 509-555.

Levine, Arthur L. 1975. *The Future of the U.S. Space Program.* New York: Praeger.

Lieber, Harvey. 1983. "Federalism and Hazardous Waste Policy." In *The Politics of Hazardous Waste Management,* edited by James P. Lester and Ann O'M. Bowman. Durham, N.C.: Duke University Press.

Lindblom, Charles E. 1959. "The Science of Muddling Through." *Public Administration Review* 14 (Spring): 79-88.

Liroff, Richard A. 1981. "NEPA Litigation in the 1970s: A Deluge or a Dribble?" *Natural Resources Journal* 21 (April): 315-330.

Lloyd, Marilyn. 1985. "Fusion Program," Letter to *Science* 229 (September 13): 1036.

Logsdon, John. 1970. *The Decision to Go to the Moon.* Cambridge: MIT Press.

Lowi, Theodore J. 1979. *The End of Liberalism,* 2d ed. New York: Norton.

Lowi, Theodore J., and Benjamin Ginsberg. 1976. *Poliscide.* New York: Macmillan.

Lowrance, William W. 1976. *Of Acceptable Risk: Science and the Determination of Safety.* Los Altos, Calif.: William Kaufmann.

Machalaba, Daniel. 1983. "High-Technology Age Causes New Problems in Coverage by Media." *Wall Street Journal* (August 24): 1.

Malakoff, David. 1985. "Biotech Gadfly Engineers Counterrevolution in Courts." *National Journal* 29 (July 29): 1699.

Mark, Hans, and Arnold Levine. 1984. *The Management of Research Institutions.* National Aeronautics and Space Administration Scientific and Technical Information Branch, SP-481. Washington, D.C.: Government Printing Office.

Marshall, Eliot. 1982. "USDA Official Defends Loyalty Checks." *Science* 216 (June 25): 1391.

Matheny, Albert R., and Bruce A. Williams. 1984. "Regulation, Risk Assessment, and the Supreme Court: The Case of OSHA's Cancer Policy." *Law and Policy* 6 (October): 425-449.

Mazur, Allan. 1973. "Disputes between Experts." *Minerva* 11 (April): 243-262.

McGarity, Thomas O. 1979. "Substantive and Procedural Discretion in Administrative Resolution of Science Policy Questions: Regulating Carcinogens in EPA and OSHA." *Georgetown Law Journal* 67 (February): 729-810.

———. 1984. "Judicial Review of Scientific Rulemaking." *Science, Technology, and Human Values* 9 (Winter): 97-106.

Meehan, Richard L. 1984. *The Atom and the Fault: Experts, Earthquakes, and Nuclear Power.* Cambridge: MIT Press.

Meier, Hugo. 1957. "Technology and Democracy, 1800-1860." *Mississippi Valley Historical Review* 43 (March): 618-640.

Melnick, R. Shep. 1983. *Regulation and the Courts: The Case of the Clean Air Act.* Washington, D.C.: Brookings Institution.

Meltsner, Arnold. 1976. *Policy Analysts in the Bureaucracy.* Berkeley: University of California Press.

Mendeloff, John. 1979. *Regulating Safety: An Economic and Political Analysis of Occupational Safety and Health Policy.* Cambridge: MIT Press.

Mensch, Gerhard. 1979. *Stalemate in Technology: Innovations Overcome the Depression.* Cambridge, Mass.: Ballinger.

Miller, Jon D. 1983. "Scientific Literacy: A Conceptual and Empirical Review."

Daedalus 112 (Spring): 29-48.

_____ . 1985. "The Politics of Emerging Issues: An Analysis of the Attitudes of Leaders and Larger Publics Toward Biotechnology." Paper presented at the annual meeting of the American Political Science Association, New Orleans, August 29-September 1.

Miller, Jon D., Kenneth Prewitt, and Robert Pearson. 1980. "The Attitudes of the U.S. Public toward Science and Technology." Chicago: National Opinion Research Center, University of Chicago.

Miller, Stanton. 1984. "Whither Environmental Progress?" *Environmental Science and Technology* 18 (January): 10A.

Mitchell, Robert Cameron. 1982. "Public Response to a Major Failure of a Controversial Technology." In *Accident at Three Mile Island: The Human Dimensions,* edited by David L. Sills, C. P. Wolf, and Vivien B. Shelanski. Boulder, Colo.: Westview Press.

Moe, Terry M. 1984. "The New Economics of Organization." *American Journal of Political Science* 28 (November): 739-777.

Morrell, David, and Christopher Magorian. 1982. *Siting Hazardous Waste Facilities: Local Opposition and the Myth of Preemption.* Cambridge, Mass.: Ballinger.

Mosher, L. 1981. "Reaganites, with OMB's List in Hand, Take Dead Aim at EPA's Regulations." *National Journal* (February 14): 256-259.

Naismith, Nancy Carson, and Mary E. Procter. 1985. "Policy Analysis for Congress: Producing Useful Knowledge." Paper presented at the annual meeting of the American Political Science Association, New Orleans, August 29-September 1.

National Academy of Sciences. 1982a. Space Science Board. *Data Management and Computation, Volume I: Issues and Recommendations.* Washington, D.C.: National Academy Press.

_____ . 1982b. *Scientific Communication and National Security.* Washington, D.C.: National Academy Press.

National Aeronautics and Space Administration. 1976. *The Space Telescope.* Washington, D.C.: Government Printing Office.

National Commission on Excellence in Education. 1983. *A Nation at Risk: The Imperative for Educational Reform.* Washington, D.C.: Government Printing Office.

National Journal. 1985. "OSTP." 17 (May 18): 1104.

National Research Council. 1983. Committee on the Institutional Means for Assessment of Risks to Public Health, Commission on Life Sciences. *Risk Assessment in the Federal Government: Managing the Process.* Washington, D.C.: National Academy Press.

National Science Board. 1978. *Basic Research in the Mission Agencies: Agency Perspectives on the Conduct and Support of Basic Research,* part 2, chap. 8. Washington, D.C.: Government Printing Office.

_____ . 1985. *Science Indicators: The 1985 Report.* Washington, D.C.: Government Printing Office.

National Science Foundation. 1983. *Federal Funds for Research and Development, Fiscal Years 1981, 1982, and 1983,* vol. 31. Washington, D.C.: Government Printing Office.

_____ . 1984. *Federal Funds for Research and Development, Fiscal Years 1983, 1984, and 1985,* vol. 33. Washington, D.C.: Government Printing Office.

_____ . 1985a. *National Science Foundation Advisory Council Report on Science and the Public.* NSB-85-269. Washington, D.C.: Government Printing Office.

_____ . 1985b. *Science Indicators: The 1985 Report.* Washington, D.C.: Government

Printing Office.

————. 1985c. *Federal Funds for Research and Development, Fiscal Years 1984, 1985, and 1986.* Washington, D.C.: Government Printing Office.

Nelkin, Dorothy. 1981. "Anti-nuclear Connections: Power and Weapons." *Bulletin of the Atomic Scientists* 37 (April): 36-40.

————. 1982. *The Creation Controversy: Science or Scripture in the Schools.* Boston: Beacon Press.

Nelkin, Dorothy, ed. 1984. *Controversy: Politics of Technical Decisions,* 2d ed. Beverly Hills, Calif.: Sage.

Nelkin, Dorothy, and Susan Fallows. 1978. "The Evolution of the Nuclear Debate: The Role of Public Participation." *Annual Review of Energy* 3: 275-312.

Neustadt, Richard E., and Harvey V. Fineberg. 1978. *The Swine Flu Affair: Decision-Making on a Slippery Disease.* Washington, D.C.: Government Printing Office.

Newell, Homer E. 1980. *Beyond the Atmosphere: Early Years of Space Science.* National Aeronautics and Space Administration Scientific and Technical Information Branch, SP-4211. Washington, D.C.: Government Printing Office.

Nichols, Guild K. 1979. *Technology on Trial: Public Participation in Decision-Making Related to Science and Technology.* Paris: Organization for Economic Cooperation and Development.

Norman, Colin. 1984. "President Vetoes NIH Bill." *Science* 226 (November 16): 811-812.

O'Brien, David M. 1982. "The Courts, Technology Assessment, and Science-Policy Disputes." In *The Politics of Technology Assessment,* edited by David M. O'Brien and Donald A. Marchand. Lexington, Mass.: D. C. Heath.

Office of Management and Budget. 1986a. "Special Analysis K." *Budget of the U.S. Government, 1987.* Washington, D.C.: Government Printing Office.

————. 1986b. *Budget of the U.S. Government, Fiscal Year 1987, Appendix.* Washington, D.C.: Government Printing Office.

Office of Technology Assessment. 1982. *Space Science Research in the United States: A Technical Memorandum* (September). Washington, D.C.: Government Printing Office.

————. 1983. *Technologies and Management Strategies for Hazardous Waste Control.* Washington, D.C.: Government Printing Office.

————. 1984. *Human Gene Therapy: Background Paper.* OTA-BP-BA-32. Washington, D.C.: Government Printing Office.

Olson, Mancur, Jr. 1965. *The Logic of Collective Action: Public Goods and the Theory of Groups.* Cambridge: Harvard University Press.

Oppenheimer, Robert. 1948. "Physics in the Contemporary World." *Bulletin of the Atomic Scientists* 4 (March).

Orlans, Harold. 1980. "On the Responsibility of Scientists," *Minerva* 18 (Fall): 521-528.

Orren, Karen. 1976. "Standing to Sue: Interest Group Conflict in the Federal Courts." *American Political Science Review* 70 (September): 723-741.

Pattie, Kenton H. 1984. "DOD's Softwave Engineering Institute." *Computer Graphics World* (August).

Penick, James L., et al. 1972. *The Politics of American Science: 1939 to the Present.* Cambridge: MIT Press.

Petersen, James C., ed. 1984. *Citizen Participation in Science Policy.* Amherst: University of Massachusetts Press.

Physics Today. 1983a. "News: APS Council Adopts Nuclear-War Resolution." 36 (March): 63-64.

_____. 1983b. "Washington Reports: Space Telescope: 2 Years Late, $1.2 Billion and Still Counting." 36 (November): 47-49.

_____. 1984. "News: Perkin-Elmer Ships 2.3-m Optical Space-Telescope Assembly." 37 (November): 17-19.

Piasecki, Bruce, and Jerry Gravander. 1985. "The Missing Links: Restructuring Hazardous-Waste Controls in America." *Technology Review* 88 (October): 43-52.

Pool, Ithiel de Sola. 1983. "Human Subjects Regulations on the Social Sciences." *Annals of the New York Academy of Sciences* 403 (May 26): 101-110.

President's Commission for a National Agenda for the Eighties. 1980. *Science and Technology: Promises and Dangers in the Eighties.* Washington, D.C.: Government Printing Office.

Prewitt, Kenneth. 1982. "The Public and Science Policy." *Science, Technology, and Human Values* 7 (Spring): 5-14.

_____. 1983. "Scientific Illiteracy and Democratic Theory." *Daedalus* 112 (Spring): 49-64.

Price, Don K. 1965. *The Scientific Estate.* New York: Oxford University Press.

_____. 1978. "Endless Frontier or Bureaucratic Morass?" *Daedalus* 107 (Spring): 75-92.

_____. 1983. *America's Unwritten Constitution: Science, Religion, and Political Responsibility.* Baton Rouge: Louisiana State University Press.

Priebe, Paul M., and George B. Kauffman. 1980. "Making Governmental Policy under Conditions of Scientific Uncertainty: A Century of Controversy about Saccharin in Congress and the Laboratory." *Minerva* 18 (Winter): 556-574.

Primack, Joel, and Frank von Hippel. 1974. *Advice and Dissent: Scientists in the Political Arena.* New York: Basic Books.

Public Papers of the Presidents of the United States, Dwight D. Eisenhower, 1960-1961. Washington, D.C.: Government Printing Office.

Rabi, I. I. 1980. "The President and His Scientific Advisers." In *Science Advice to the President,* edited by William T. Golden. New York: Pergamon Press.

Racker, Efraim. 1979. *Science and the Cure of Diseases: Letters to Members of Congress.* Princeton: Princeton University Press.

Raven-Hansen, Peter. 1983. "Quid Pro Quo for Public Dough." *Annals of the New York Academy of Sciences* 403 (May 26): 83-100.

Reagan, Michael D. 1969. *Science and the Federal Patron.* New York: Oxford University Press.

Regens, James L., Thomas M. Dietz, and Robert W. Rycroft. 1983. "Risk Assessment in the Policy-Making Process: Environmental Health and Safety Protection." *Public Administration Review* 43 (March/April): 137-145.

Reiser, Stanley Joel. 1966. "Smoking and Health: The Congress and Causality." In *Knowledge and Power,* edited by Sanford A. Lakoff. New York: Free Press.

Rich, Robert F. 1980. "The Political Implications of Laetrile: Who Gets What, When and How." In *Politics, Science, and Cancer: The Laetrile Phenomenon,* edited by Gerald E. Markle and James C. Petersen. Boulder, Colo.: Westview Press.

Riker, William H. 1982. *Liberalism against Populism.* San Francisco: W. H. Freeman.

Riley, Richard. 1983. "Toxic Substances, Hazardous Wastes, and Public Policy: Problems in Implementation." In *The Politics of Hazardous Waste Management,* edited by James P. Lester and Ann O'M. Bowman. Durham, N.C.: Duke University Press.

Ripley, Randall B., and Grace A. Franklin. 1976. *Congress, the Bureaucracy, and*

Public Policy, rev. ed. Homewood, Ill.: Dorsey Press.

Roback, Herbert. 1968. "Congress and the Science Budget." *Science* 160 (May 31): 964-971.

Rodgers, William H. 1981. "Judicial Review of Risk Assessments: The Role of Decision Theory in Unscrambling the *Benzene* Decision." *Environmental Law* 11 (Winter): 301-320.

Rogers, Michael. 1977. *Biohazard.* New York: Knopf.

Rosenbaum, Walter Á. 1983. "The Politics of Public Participation in Hazardous Waste Management." In *The Politics of Hazardous Waste Management,* edited by James P. Lester and Ann O'M. Bowman. Durham, N.C.: Duke University Press.

Rosenberg, Nathan. 1982. *Inside the Black Box: Technology and Economics.* New York: Cambridge University Press.

Rothman, Stanley. 1983. "Contorting Scientific Controversies." *Society* (July/August): 25-32.

Ruckelshaus, William D. 1983. "Science, Risk, and Public Policy." *Environmental International* 9: 245-247.

Rushefsky, Mark E. 1985. "Assuming the Conclusions: Risk Assessment in the Development of Cancer Policy." *Politics and the Life Sciences* 4 (August): 31-44.

Schmandt, Jurgen. 1984. "Regulation and Science." *Science, Technology, and Human Values* 9 (Winter): 23-38.

———. 1985. "Managing Comprehensive Rule Making: EPA's Plan for Integrated Environmental Management." *Public Administration Review* 45 (March/April): 309-318.

Science. 1974. "Point of View: Kissinger on Intellectuals." 186 (November 15): 617.

Shapiro, Michael H., ed. 1982. *Biological and Behavioral Technologies and the Law.* New York: Praeger.

Shapley, Deborah. 1973. "White House Foes: Wiesner Target of Proposal to Cut M.I.T. Funds." *Science* 181 (July 20): 244-246.

———. 1974. "Science Board Gets a Nod from Congress." *Science* 186 (October 4): 35.

Shapley, Willis H., et al. 1982. *Research and Development: AAAS Report VII, Federal Budget—FY 1983.* Washington, D.C.: American Association for the Advancement of Science.

Simon, Herbert A. 1947. *Administrative Behavior.* New York: Macmillan.

———. 1964. "On the Concept of Organizational Goals." *Administrative Science Quarterly* 9 (June): 1-22.

———. 1985. "Human Nature in Politics: The Dialogue of Psychology with Political Science." *American Political Science Review* 79 (June): 293-304.

Smith, Alice Kimball. 1970. *A Peril and a Hope: The Scientists' Movement in America 1945-47,* rev. ed. Cambridge: MIT Press.

Smith, R. Jeffrey. 1984. "The Knives Are Out for OSTP." *Science* 226 (December 21): 1399-1400.

Smith, V. Kerry. 1984. *Environmental Policy under Reagan's Executive Order: The Role of Benefit-Cost Analysis.* Chapel Hill: University of North Carolina Press.

Solnick, Steven L. 1983. "The Politics of Apathy." *Technology Review* 86 (July): 9, 11.

Staats, Elmer B. 1980. "Reconciling the Science Advisory Role with Tensions Inherent in the Presidency." In *Science Advice to the President,* edited by William T. Golden. New York: Pergamon Press.

Stanfield, Rochelle L. 1984. "Superfund Backers Push Big Expansion of Program to

Clean Up Toxic Waste." *National Journal* (September 22): 1764.
———. 1985. "Causing Cancer." *National Journal* (June 22): 1495.
Stanley, John A. 1983. "Reasonable EPA Projection Techniques for Estimating Technological Advances Upheld." *Natural Resources Journal* 23 (January): 219-224.
Stewart, Richard B. 1975. "The Reformation of American Administrative Law." *Harvard Law Review* 88 (June): 1667-1814.
———. 1981. "Regulation, Innovation, and Administrative Law: A Conceptual Framework." *California Law Review* 69 (September): 1256-1376.
Sun, Marjorie. 1981. "EPA May Be Redefining Toxic Substances." *Science* 214 (October 30): 525-526.
———. 1984. "FDA Spars with HHS on Advisory Posts." *Science* 224 (May 18): 698.
———. 1985a. "A Science Primer for Freshman Legislators." *Science* 227 (February 8): 615.
———. 1985b. "EPA Approves Field Test of Altered Microbes." *Science* 230 (November 29): 1015-1016.
Task Force of the Presidential Advisory Group on Anticipated Advances in Science and Technology. 1976. "The Science Court Experiment: An Interim Report." *Science* 193 (August 20): 653-656.
Taylor, Robert E. 1985. "Bill to Broaden Clean-Air Mandate of EPA Attacked." *Wall Street Journal* (June 12): 10.
Teich, Albert H., and W. Henry Lambright. 1976. "The Redirection of a Large National Laboratory." *Minerva* 14 (Winter): 447-474.
Templer, Otis W. 1976. *Institutional Constraints and Conjunctive Management of Water Resources in West Texas.* Lubbock: Texas Tech University, Water Resources Center.
Thompson, E. P. 1963. *The Making of the English Working Class.* New York: Knopf.
Tribe, Laurence H. 1971. "Towards a New Technological Ethic: The Role of Legal Liability." *Impact of Science on Society* 21 (July/September): 215-222.
Tschirley, Fred. H. 1986. "Dioxin." *Scientific American* 254 (February): 29-35.
U.S. House of Representatives. 1977. *Clean Air Act Amendments of 1977.* House Report 95-294.
———. 1979. Subcommittee on Science, Research, and Technology, Committee on Science and Technology; and Subcommittee on Science, Technology, and Space, Committee on Commerce, Science, and Transportation, U.S. Senate. *Risk/Benefit Analysis in the Legislative Process.* Joint hearings, 96th Cong., 1st sess. (July 24, 25).
———. 1980. Subcommittee on Science, Research, and Technology, Committee on Science and Technology. *Long-Term Planning for National Science Policy.* Hearings, 96th Cong., 2d sess. (July 28-31).
———. 1981a. Subcommittee on Science, Research, and Technology, Committee on Science and Technology. *Analysis of Hearings on H.R. 6910, The National Technology Foundation Act of 1980.* Committee Print, Serial E (May).
———. 1981b. Subcommittee on Oversight and Investigations, Committee on Energy and Commerce. *Role of OMB in Regulation.* Hearing, 97th Cong., 1st sess. (June 18).
———. 1981c. Committee on Science and Technology. *Societal Risks of Energy Systems.* Hearing, 97th Cong., 1st sess. (June 18).
———. 1981d. Subcommittee on Natural Resources, Agricultural Research and Environment, and Subcommittee on Investigations and Oversight, Committee on Science and Technology. *Carbon Dioxide and Climate: The Greenhouse Effect.*

Hearing, 97th Cong., 1st sess. (July 31).

———. 1981e. Subcommittee on Space Science and Applications, Committee on Science and Technology. *Future Space Programs: 1981*. Hearings, 97th Cong., 1st sess. (September 21-23).

———. 1981f. Committee on Science and Technology. *The Risk Analysis Research and Demonstration Act of 1981*. Hearing, 97th Cong., 1st sess. (September 24).

———. 1981g. Subcommittee on Science, Research, and Technology, Committee on Science and Technology. *Risk: Assessment, Acceptability, and Management*. Report of Congressional Research Service. (November), Serial R.

———. 1982. Subcommittee on Natural Resources, Agriculture Research and Environment, Committee on Science and Technology. *Fiscal Years 1983 and 1984 Environmental Protection Agency Research and Development Authorization*. Hearings, 97th Cong., 2d sess. (February 24, March 2, 19).

———. 1983a. Committee on Science and Technology. *1983 Science and Technology Posture Hearing with the Director of the Office of Science and Technology Policy*. Hearing, 98th Cong., 1st sess. (February 3).

———. 1983b. Subcommittee on Natural Resources, Agriculture Research and Environment, Committee on Science and Technology. *Fiscal Year 1984 EPA Research and Development Authorization*. Hearings, 98th Cong., 1st sess. (March 10, April 19, 27).

———. 1983c. Committee on Appropriations. "The NASA Space Telescope Program." Memorandum. 98th Cong., 1st sess. (March 16).

———. 1983d. Subcommittee on Space Science and Applications, Committee on Science and Technology. *Space Telescope Cost, Schedule, and Performance*. Hearings, 98th Cong., 1st sess. (June 14, 16).

———. 1983e. Subcommittee on Investigations and Oversight, Committee on Science and Technology. *Impact of Mercury Releases at the Oak Ridge Complex*. Hearing, 98th Cong., 1st sess. (July 11).

———. 1984a. Committee on Science and Technology. *EPA's Office of Research and Development and Related Issues*. Hearing, 98th Cong., 2d sess. (March 14).

———. 1984b. Subcommittee on HUD-Independent Agencies, Committee on Appropriations. *Department of Housing and Urban Development—Independent Agencies Appropriations for 1985*. Hearing, 98th Cong., 2d sess. (March 27).

———. 1984c. Subcommittee on Space Science and Applications, Committee on Science and Technology. *Space Telescope: 1984*. Hearings, 98th Cong., 2d sess. (May 22, 24).

———. 1984d. Subcommittee on Oversight and Investigations, Committee on Energy and Commerce. *Biotechnology Regulation*. Hearing, 98th Cong., 2d sess. (December 11).

———. 1985. Committee on Science and Technology. *1985 Science and Technology Posture Hearing with the Director of the Office of Science and Technology Policy*. Hearing, 99th Cong., 1st sess. (February 5).

U.S. Senate. 1976. Temporary Select Committee to Study the Senate Committee System. *The Senate Committee System*. Committee print (July).

———. 1980. Committee on Environment and Public Works. *Health Effects on Toxic Pollutants: A Report from the Surgeon General and a Brief Review of Selected Environmental Contamination Incidents with a Potential for Health Effects*. Committee Print, vol. III.

———. 1981. Subcommittee on Toxic Substances and Environmental Oversight, Committee on Environment and Public Works. *The Effect of Chlorofluorocarbons on the Ozone Layer*. Hearings, 97th Cong., 1st sess. (July 23).

———. 1982. Committee on Environment and Public works. *Injuries and Damages from Hazardous Wastes—Analysis and Improvement of Legal Remedies.* Committee print (September).

———. 1985. Subcommittee on Science, Technology, and Space, Committee on Commerce, Science, and Transportation. *NASA Authorization for Fiscal Year 1986.* Hearings, 99th Cong., 1st sess. (February 26, March 27, 28, April 3, 4).

Uyehara, Cecil H. 1966. "Scientific Advice and the Nuclear Test Ban Treaty." In *Knowledge and Power: Essays on Science and Government,* edited by Sanford A. Lakoff. New York: Free Press.

Van Allen, James A. 1986. "Space Science, Space Technology and the Space Station." *Scientific American* 254 (January): 32-39.

Vig, Norman J. 1984. "The Courts: Judicial Review and Risk Assessment." In *Risk Analysis, Institutions, and Public Policy,* edited by Susan G. Hadden. Port Washington, N.Y.: Associated Faculty Press.

Vig, Norman J., and Patrick J. Bruer. 1982. "The Courts and Risk Assessment." *Policy Studies Review* 1 (May): 716-727.

Viscusi, W. Kip. 1985. "Cotton Dust Regulation: An OSHA Success Story?" *Journal of Policy Analysis and Management* 4 (Spring): 325-343.

von Neumann, John. 1955. "Can We Survive Technology?" *Fortune* 51 (June): 106-152.

Wade, Nicholas. 1972. "DES: A Case Study of Regulatory Abdication." *Science* 177 (July 28): 335-337.

———. 1977. *The Ultimate Experiment: Man-Made Evolution,* rev. ed. New York: Walker.

Waldrop, M. Mitchell. 1983a. "Space Telescope in Trouble." *Science* 220 (April 8): 172-174.

———. 1983b. "Space Telescope (I): Implications for Astronomy." *Science* 221 (July 15): 249-251.

———. 1983c. "Space Telescope (II): A Science Institute," *Science* 221 (August 5): 534-536.

———. 1985. "Astronomy and the Realities of the Budget." *Science* 227 (January 18): 283-285.

Walsh, John. 1976. "Large Space Telescope: Astronomers Go into Orbit." *Science* 191 (February 13): 544-545.

———. 1982. "Frank Press Takes Exception to NAS Panel Recommendations on Marijuana." *Science* 217 (July 16): 228-229.

Weinberg, Alvin M. *Reflections on Big Science.* Cambridge, MIT Press.

———. 1972. "Science and Trans-Science." *Minerva* 10 (April): 209-222.

Wengert, Norman. 1976. "Citizen Participation: Practice in Search of a Theory." *Natural Resources Journal* 16 (January): 23-40.

White, Donald C. 1985. "EPA Program for Treatment Alternatives for Hazardous Waste." *Journal of the Air Pollution Control Association* 35 (April).

Whiteman, David. 1982. "The Role of Support Agencies in Congressional Policy Making: Types, Areas, and Determinants of O.T.A. Use." Paper delivered at the annual meeting of the American Political Science Association, Denver, September 2-5.

Whittington, Dale, and W. Norton Grubb. 1984. "Economic Analysis in Regulatory Decisions: The Implications of Executive Order 12291." *Science, Technology, and Human Values* 9 (Winter): 63-71.

Wiesner, Jerome B. 1980. "Science and Technology: Government and Politics." In *Science Advice to the President,* edited by William T. Golden. New York: Pergamon Press.

Wigner, Eugene P. 1950. "The Limits of Science." *Proceedings of the American*

Philosophical Society 94 (October): 422-427.

Wilson, Woodrow. 1956. *Congressional Government.* New York: Meridian Books. Reprint. Boston: Houghton Mifflin, 1885.

Winner, Langdon. 1977. *Autonomous Technology.* Cambridge: MIT Press.

Woodhouse, Edward J. 1983. "The Politics of Nuclear Waste Management." In *Too Hot to Handle?: Social and Policy Issues in the Management of Radioactive Wastes,* edited by Charles A. Walker, et al. New Haven: Yale University Press.

Wright, Susan. 1985. "The Military and the New Biology." *Bulletin of the Atomic Scientists* 42 (May): 10-16.

Yankelovich, Daniel. 1982. "Changing Public Attitudes to Science and the Quality of Life." *Science, Technology, and Human Values* 7 (Spring): 23-29.

Yellin, Joel. 1981. "High Technology and the Courts: Nuclear Power and the Need for Institutional Reform." *Harvard Law Review* 94 (January): 489-560.

———. 1983. "Science, Technology, and Administrative Government: Institutional Designs for Environmental Decisionmaking." *Yale Law Review* 92: 1300-1341.

———. 1984. "Commentary." *Science, Technology, and Human Values* 9 (Winter): 126-129.

Zuckerman, Harriet. 1977. *Scientific Elite: Nobel Laureates in the United States.* New York: Free Press.

Name Index

Abraham, Kenneth S., 103
Abrams, Nancy E., 106
Almond, Gabriel A., 115, 145
Altimore, Michael, 131
Ancker-Johnson, Betsy, 69
Anderson, James E., 8
Anderson, Paul A., 14
Andrews, Michael A., 33
Arrow, Kenneth A., 179
Ashford, Nicholas A., 81
Austin, John, 103
Averch, Harvey A., 50, 213

Bacon, Francis, 113
Bahcall, John N., 184
Baltimore, David, 7
Baram, Michael S., 93
Bardeen, John, 53
Barfield, Claude E., 53
Barke, Richard P., 24, 79, 81, 137, 160
Barton, Joe, 28
Bauman, Robert, 26
Bazelon, David L., 102, 107
Beardsley, Tim, 199
Beazley, J. Ernest, 38
Beckler, David Z., 52
Beggs, James, 194, 195, 201, 203
Bellamy, Edward, 113
Berry, R. Stephen, 106
Biden, Joseph R., Jr., 103
Bingaman, Jeff, 29
Blank, Robert H., 35, 40, 105
Blanpied, William, 216
Boehm, George A. W., 7
Boffey, Phillip M., 58, 74
Bok, Derek, 140
Boland, Edward, 201, 203
Breslin, Jimmy, 123
Brewer, Garry D., 152
Breyer, Stephen, 11, 111
Brickman, Ronald, 180
Bromberg, Joan Lisa, 5, 26
Brooks, Harvey, 4, 10, 36, 78, 90, 130, 135, 154
Brown, George E., Jr., 28, 169, 203
Brown, Lester O., 157

Bruer, Patrick J., 96
Bruff, Harold H., 37
Bulkeley, William M., 121
Burger, Edward J., Jr., 55
Burke, John G., 22
Bush, Vannevar, 7, 49, 70
Byerly, Radford, Jr., 169

Cahn, Anne Hessing, 146
Caldwell, Lynton, 77, 119
Capek, Karel, 121
Cardozo, Michael H., 78
Carey, William D., 45
Carroll, James D., 130
Carson, Rachel, 50
Carter, Jimmy, 43-46, 48, 52, 53, 56, 110
Carter, Luther J., 28, 74, 93
Casper, Barry M., 29, 106, 130
Chalk, Rosemary, 141
Chubin, Daryl, 82
Clark, Evert, 138
Clark, Ian D., 154
Clark, Norman, 214
Coates, Joseph F., 30
Coates, Vary T., 22
Cobey, William, Jr., 28
Cohen, Michael, 10
Cohen, Stephen, 166
Cole, Jonathan R., 83
Cole, Leonard A., 40, 136, 141
Cole, Stephen, 83
Crandall, Robert W., 93
Crawford, Mark, 69
Culliton, Barbara J., 47, 74, 115, 140
Curlin, James W., 32
Cyert, Richard, 14

David, Edward E., Jr., 7, 52, 54, 55, 58, 134
Delgado, Richard, 137
DelSesto, Stephen L., 9, 130
DeSolla Price, Derek, 7
Dewey, John, 115, 214
Dickinson, John P., 137
Dickson, David, 23, 45, 140
Dietz, Thomas M., 76
Dingell, John, 28, 58

Doniger, David D., 88
Dunwoody, Sharon, 131
Dupree, A. Hunter, 37, 75, 91
Durenburger, David, 170
Dyer, James S., 145

Easton, David, 3
Ebbin, Steven, 111, 120
Edgar, Robert, 162
Edison, Thomas, 146
Ehrlich, Paul, 145
Ehrlichman, John, 51
Einstein, Albert, 113, 139, 148
Eisenhower, Dwight D., 2, 43, 48-50, 54, 203
Ellul, Jacques, 113
Emerson, Thomas I., 139
England, J. Merton, 75
Epstein, Samuel S., 157

Faber, Sandra, 200
Fallows, Susan, 131
Fenno, Richard F., 14
Ferguson, James R., 45, 138
Field, George, 145
Fineberg, Harvey V., 143
Fischhoff, Baron, 122
Ford, Gerald, 45, 52
Franklin, Grace, 42
Friedman, Robert S., 80
Fuqua, Don, 24

Galileo, 136
Garwin, Richard L., 52
Gerth, H. H., 63
Giacconi, Riccardo, 198
Gibbs, Lois, 176
Gilpin, Robert, 142, 147, 152
Ginsberg, Benjamin, 38
Glen, Maxwell, 146
Glenn, John, 28
Goggin, Malcolm L., 128
Goodell, Rae, 9, 114, 145
Goodfield, June, 131
Goodwin, Irwin, 81
Gore, Albert E., Jr., 36, 56, 89, 178
Gorsuch, Anne Burford, 91, 156, 170, 173, 178
Gould, Stephen Jay, 123, 142
Grad, Frank P., 161
Graham, William R., 53
Gramm, Phil, 82
Gravender, Jerry, 177
Green, Harold P., 139
Greenberg, Daniel S., 38, 56, 74
Greenwood, Ted, 15, 79, 81
Grove, J. W., 8
Grubb, W. Norton, 86, 120

Hadden, Susan G., 85, 86, 121
Haimann, Theo, 15
Hall, Alan, 138
Hammond, Thomas P., 87, 215
Handler, Phillip, 42, 74
Harris, Fred, 24
Havender, William R., 79
Hechler, Kenneth, 52
Helms, Jesse, 40
Heppenheimer, T. A., 5, 44, 46, 55, 58, 148
Hileman, Bette, 171
Holden, Constance, 48, 56, 124
Hollander, Rachelle, 124
Hoover, Herbert, 48, 70
Hornig, Donald F., 51
Horwitz, Paul, 143
Humphrey, Hubert H., 90

Ilgen, Thomas, 180

Jachim, Anton G., 37, 38
James, Henry, 11
Jasanoff, Sheila, 82, 105, 180
Jefferson, Thomas, 48, 49, 58
Jenkins-Smith, Hank, 85
Johnson, Lyndon B., 38, 135
Jones, Charles O., 9
Jones, Daniel P., 135, 150
Jones, James H., 19, 137

Kalberer, John T., Jr., 83
Kasper, Raphael, 111, 120
Katz, James E., 39, 49, 51, 58
Katz, Jay, 137
Kauffman, George B., 21, 48, 127
Kay, W. D., 129
Kennedy, Edward M., 31
Kennedy, John F., 43, 50, 51
Kevles, Daniel J., 27, 48, 69, 81, 130, 136, 148, 149
Keyworth, George W., II, 53, 58, 89, 135
Kilgore, Harley, 70
Killian, James R., 49, 54
Kimura, Shigeru, 130
Kingdon, John W., 10, 14, 15, 205
Kissinger, Henry, 152
Koshland, Daniel E., Jr., 214
Kranzberg, Melvin, 58
Krimsky, Sheldon, 119, 129
Kuehn, Thomas J., 7
Kuhn, Thomas S., 6, 10, 147
Kuklinski, James H., 129

Ladd, Everett Carll, Jr., 150
Lakoff, Sanford A., 10, 22, 42
Lambright, W. Henry, 12, 24, 56, 73, 75, 76, 88, 92, 195
Lapp, Ralph, 134

Lappe, Marc, 128
Large, Arlen J., 119
Lave, Lester B., 93
Lavelle, Rita, 156, 178
Lederman, Leon M., 7
Lepkowski, Wil, 58
Lester, James P., 173
Leventhal, Harold, 102, 105, 107
Levine, Arnold, 195, 201, 205
Levine, Arthur L., 205
Lichtenstein, Sarah, 122
Lieber, Harvey, 173
Lindblom, Charles E., 9
Lipset, Seymour Martin, 150
Liroff, Richard A., 119
Lloyd, Marilyn, 36
Logsdon, John, 40
Lowi, Theodore J., 38, 130
Lowrance, William W., 83
Lysenko, Trofim, 136

Machalaba, Daniel, 131
Magorian, Christopher, 177
Malakoff, David, 96
Mansfield, Mike, 25
March, James G., 10, 14
Mark, Hans, 195, 201, 205
Marshall, Eliot, 58
Martin, Patricia A., 128
Matheny, Albert R., 108
Mazur, Allan, 154
McCormack, Mike, 28
McDonald, Larry, 28
McGarity, Thomas O., 74, 77, 99, 112
Meehan, Richard L., 85
Meier, Hugo, 128
Melnick, R. Shep, 79, 81, 107, 117
Meltsner, Arnold, 17
Mendeloff, John, 80
Mensch, Gerhard, 11
Merrill, Richard A., 103
Metlay, Daniel S., 129
Miles, Ralph E., Jr., 145
Miller, Gary J., 87, 215
Miller, James, III, 178
Miller, Jon D., 115, 116, 121, 125, 128, 135
Miller, Stanton, 165
Mills, C. Wright, 63
Mitchell, Robert C., 121, 125
Moe, Terry M., 148
Morrell, David, 177
Mosher, Charles, 28
Mosher, Lawrence, 178
Moynihan, Daniel P., 134

Naismith, Nancy C., 29
Nelkin, Dorothy, 116, 120, 121, 127, 131
Nelson, Bryce, 58
Neustadt, Richard E., 143

Newell, Homer E., 194-198, 200
Nichols, Guild K., 12, 117
Nixon, Richard, 43, 47, 50-52, 56, 57, 202
Norman, Colin, 46

Oberth, Hermann, 182
O'Brien, David M., 111
Olsen, Johan, 10
Olson, Mancur, Jr., 125
Oppenheimer, J. Robert, 150
Orlans, Harold, 32, 143
Orren, Karen, 111, 117
Overton, William, 142

Parnas, David, 145
Pattie, Kenton H., 38
Pauling, Linus, 57, 147
Pearson, Robert, 125
Penick, James L., 7, 46, 48
Percy, Charles, 32
Petersen, James C., 119
Piasecki, Bruce, 177
Pool, Ithiel de Sola, 138
Pope, Carl, 157
Porter, Alan L., 7
Posner, Richard, 110
Powell, John Wesley, 91
Press, Frank, 38, 53, 149
Prewitt, Kenneth, 123, 125, 126, 128, 134
Price, Don K., 13, 16, 24, 32, 35, 88, 91, 143, 144, 151, 154, 210, 214
Priebe, Paul M., 21, 48, 127
Primack, Joel, 135, 144, 146, 152
Procter, Mary E., 29
Proxmire, William, 25

Rabi, I. I., 50
Racker, Efraim, 75
Raven-Hansen, Peter, 120
Reagan, Michael D., 154
Reagan, Ronald, 43, 45-48, 53, 110, 147, 158, 170
Regens, James L., 76
Reiser, Stanley Joel, 143
Rich, Robert F., 78, 121
Rifkin, Jeremy, 95, 97, 111
Riker, William H., 154
Riley, Richard, 171
Ripley, Randall B., 42
Ritter, Don, 28
Roback, Herbert, 25
Rockefeller, Nelson, 52
Rodgers, William H., 110
Rogers, Michael, 133
Roosevelt, Franklin D., 49, 54, 66, 148
Roosevelt, Theodore, 21, 48, 149
Rosenbaum, Walter A., 176
Rosenberg, Nathan, 7, 8
Roszak, Theodore, 113

Rothman, Stanley, 123
Ruckelshaus, William D., 162, 165, 172
Rushefsky, Mark E., 85
Rutherford, Ernest, 147
Rycroft, Robert W., 76

Sagan, Carl, 123, 145
Schlesinger, James, 148
Schmandt, Jurgen, 6, 171
Schmitt, Harrison, 28
Schneider, Claudine, 88, 180
Scott, William G., 15
Shapiro, Michael H., 19
Shapley, Deborah, 26, 58
Shapley, Willis H., 79
Simon, Herbert A., 14, 165
Slovic, Paul, 122
Smith, Alice K., 147
Smith, R. Jeffrey, 53
Smith, V. Kerry, 93
Smithson, James, 37
Solnick, Steven L., 154
Spitzer, Lyman, Jr., 182, 184
Staats, Elmer B., 54
Stanfield, Rochelle L., 84, 173
Stanley, John A., 180
Stewart, Richard B., 28, 111, 117, 130, 161
Stockman, David, 178
Sun, Marjorie, 28, 80, 89, 106

Taylor, Robert E., 28
Teich, Albert H., 24, 76
Teller, Edward, 147
Templer, Otis W., 104, 105
Tesla, Nikolai, 146
Thales, 2
Thompson, E. P., 113
Tribe, Laurence H., 111
Truman, Harry S, 43, 45, 46, 49, 54, 70
Tschirley, Fred H., 163
Tsongas, Paul, 32, 136

Uyehara, Cecil H., 32

Van Allen, James A., 194, 204
Veblen, Thorsten, 113
Vig, Norman J., 96, 97
Viscusi, W. Kip, 93
VonHippel, Frank, 135, 144, 146, 152
VonNeumann, John, 3

Wade, Nicholas, 86, 133
Waldrop, M. Mitchell, 145, 190, 193, 198,
  202
Walsh, John, 149, 198, 204
Washington, George, 48
Weber, Max, 63
Weinberg, Alvin M., 106, 205, 206
Wellstone, Paul David, 130
Wengert, Norman, 117
White, Donald C., 167
Whiteman, David, 31
Whittington, Dale, 86, 120
Wiesner, Jerome B., 31, 50, 58
Wigner, Eugene P., 143
Wildavsky, Aaron, 42
Williams, Bruce A., 108
Wilson, Woodrow, 33, 135
Winner, Langdon, 2
Woodhouse, Edward J., 35, 74
Wordsworth, William, 181
Wright, Christopher, 154
Wright, J. Skelly, 112
Wright, Susan, 68
Wynter, Leon E., 38

Yankelovich, Daniel, 129
Yellin, Joel, 10, 27, 105, 106

Zschau, Ed, 28
Zuckerman, Harriet, 135, 144

Subject Index

Administrative behavior patterns, 92
Administrative Conference of the United
States, 106
Administrative law, 99, 111
Administrative Procedure Act (APA), 77, 99
Advanced X-Ray Astrophysics Faculty
(AXAF), 199
Advisory Committee on Technical Standards,
81
Advisory committees, 80-82
Agriculture Department, 64
Air pollution. *See* Hazardous wastes
Air quality standards, 87
Allison Commission, 24, 91
American Association for the Advancement
of Science (AAAS), 145-146, 154n
American Chemical Society, 29, 135, 146,
150
American Physical Society, 29, 146
American Society of Mechanical Engineers,
154n
*American Textile Manufacturers Institute,
Inc. v. Donovan,* 109
Antarctic Treaty, 45
Applied science, 7
Applied Science and Research Applications
program, 72
Appropriations, as Congressional policy tool,
25-26
Arms Export Control Act, 138
Artificial sweeteners, 16, 21-22
Asilomar meeting, 133, 136
Association of Universities for Research in
Astronomy (AURA), 198, 206n-207n
Atomic Energy Act of 1954, 117, 138
Atomic Energy, Joint Committee on, (JCAE),
35
Atoms for Peace program, 35

Ballistic missile defense program, 81-82
*Baltimore Gas and Electric Co. v. National
Resources Defense Council, Inc.,* 13, 100
Basic science, 7
Benzene, 96-97, 101, 108-109
Biomedical Ethics Board, 31
Biotechnology Science Coordinating Commit-
tee (BSCC), 89

Bounded rationality, 13-14
Budget and Impoundment Control Act, 47
Bureaucracy, 63. *See also* Federal
bureaucracy
  general theories of, 92
Bureaucratic coordination problems, 87-88
  approaches to, 88-89

California v. Zook, 108
*Calvert Cliffs Coordinating Committee, Inc.
v. AEC,* 111
Challenger disaster, 186, 187, 193, 201, 205-
206
Chemical weapons, 135, 146, 150
Chlorofluorocarbons (CFCs), 61
Citizens Clearing House for Hazardous
Wastes, 176-177
*Citizens to Preserve Overton Park, Inc. v.
Volpe,* 101
Clean Air Act, 23, 109, 157, 161
Clear Water Act, 111
Clinch River Breeder Reactor program, 39,
58
Coalition-building, 39-40
Collective action, 125-126
Colliding Beam Accelerator, 37
Commerce Department, 64
Commerce, Science and Transportation Com-
mittee, Senate, 33
  subcommittees, 34
Commission for a National Agenda for the
Eighties, 55
Commission on Industrial Competitiveness,
89
Committees. *See* Congressional committees;
individual committees
Common law, 98-99
Compound 1080, 109
Comprehensive Environmental Response
Compensation and Liability Act, 162-163
Comprehensive Test Ban Treaty, 142
Confirmation process, as Congressional policy
tool, 26
Congress, 21-23
  coalition-building in, 39-40
  entrepreneurs and ad hoc groups in, 36

hazardous wastes issue in, 166-168, 177-179
knowledge and expertise in, 27-33
outside advisers to, 32-33
politics and science in, 36-40
support agencies of, 30-31
Congress, members of
entrepreneurial skills of, 36
training in science and technology of, 28,
42n
Congressional appropriations, presidential
power over, 47
Congressional Budget Office (CBO), 30
Congressional Caucus for Science and Technology, 36
Congressional Committees. See also individual committees
function of, 24-25
science and technology, 33-35
scientists and technologists on, 29-30
Congressional policy making, law and, 26-27
Congressional policy tools
appropriation as, 25-26
confirmation as, 26
legislation as, 23-24
publicity and investigations as, 24-25
Congressional Research Service, 30
Congressional Science Fellows, 29
Congressional Space Caucus, 36
Congressional staff, training in science and
technology of, 29-30, 42n
Constitution
Fifth Amendment, 98
First Amendment, 139
Fourteenth Amendment, 77
Fourth Amendment, 98
protection of experimental subjects and,
137
and rights of scientists, 139, 140
science and technology policy and, 44
as source of law, 98
supremacy clause, 108
Constitutional law, 26, 98
Constitutional powers, of president, 44-45
Consumer Product Safety Commission
(CPSC), 69, 76, 88
Convention on International Liability by
Damage Caused by Space Objects, 187
Coordination constraints, on policy process,
15-17
Coordination problems. See Bureaucratic coordination problems
Cost-benefit analysis, 85-87, 120
Council on Environmental Quality, 47
Courts
coordination among, 108-109
effects of incoordination within, 109-110
expanding role in science and technology
policy, 96-97

getting scientific and technical knowledge
into courts, 104-107
legal constraints on, 98-101
politics in, 110-111
relationship with agencies, 107-108
responsibility of, 111-112
scientific and technological knowledge in,
102-107
Cyclamates, 78, 79

Defense Advanced Research Projects Agency
(DARPA), 66-67
Defense Department (DOD), 64, 66-68
Defense programs, increase in research dol-
lars devoted to, 66, 67
Delaney Amendment, 16, 21, 22, 46, 79, 104.
See also Food, Drug, and Cosmetic Act
DES, 86
Design standards, 161
Diamond v. Chakrabarty, 140
Direct Broadcast Satellite (DBS) Service, 81
Disability benefits, 81
Domestic policy, presidency and, 45-46
Due-process clause, of Fourteenth Amend-
ment, 77

Earthquakes, study, 141-142
Economic policies, 10-11
Education Department, 64
Energy and Commerce Committee, House, 34
Energy and Natural Resource Committee,
Senate, 35
Energy Department, 64, 66, 124
Energy Security Act of 1980, 47
Engineered Organisms in the Environment,
36
Environment and Public Works Committee,
Senate, 35
Environmental groups, 126
Environmental issues, public participation in,
117
Environmental Protection Agency (EPA), 14,
23, 61, 68, 76
advisory committees of, 81
hazardous wastes and, 155-162, 166-180,
215
National Academy of Sciences' study of
programs and procedures of, 74
Reagan administration and, 91
Resource Conservation and Recovery Act
and, 157-158
Toxic Substances Control Act and, 84
Ethical codes of scientists, 136-137
Ethical questions, 79, 97
Ethics and Values in Science and Technology
program, 124
Ethyl Corp. v. Environmental Protection
Agency, 102, 108

European Space Agency, 184
Evolutionary theory, 142
Executive agencies, 68
Executive branch. *See also* Presidency
    coordination of the science and technology
        establishment within, 54-57
    science and technology knowledge within,
        48-54
Executive departments affecting science and
    technology policy, 63-68
Executive Order 12291, 85-86
Executive Orders, policy control through use
    of, 48
Experimental subjects, protection of, 137-138
Expert opinion, 105
Export Administration Act, 138
Export control legislation, 45
Extended Duration Orbiter, 30

*Fashion Originator's Guild v. Federal Trade
    Commission,* 80
Federal Advisory Committee Act (FACA),
    78, 80, 100, 216
Federal bureaucracy, 61-63
    coordination of science and technology pol-
        icy within, 87-90
    expertise within, 79-87
    legal constraints on, 75-79
    politics and science and technology policy
        within, 90-93
Federal Communication Commission (FCC),
    15, 69
Federal Council on Science and Technology,
    54
Federal courts, judicial review and, 100
Federal Drug Administration (FDA), 80
Federal laboratories, 69-70
Federal Tort Claims Act, 77
Federal Trade Commission (FTC), 69
Federally Funded Research and Development
    Centers (FFRDCs), 69-71
Federation of American Scientists (FAS), 146
Fermilab particle accelerator, 38
Financial assistance, for education, 12
Food and Drug Administration (FDA)
    and approval of use of experimental me-
        chanical heart, 76
    saccharin and, 21-22.
Food, Drug, and Cosmetic Act, 16. *See also*
    Delaney Amendment
Foreign Relations Authorization Act of 1979,
    47
Fragmentation of science and technology pol-
    icy, 213-214
Free speech
    conflict with national security, 45
Freedom of Information Act, (FOIA), 77, 97,
    110, 120

Fusion, 4
Fusion research, 4-6
Future of Space Science, 36

Garbage can model, 10
General Accounting Office (GAO), 30
General Services Administration (GSA), 68
Genetic engineering, 27, 95
Genetic screening, of potential employees, 98,
    148
Geological Survey, 91
Goddard Space Flight Center, 200
"Golden Fleece" awards, 25
Government in the Sunshine Act, 77, 110,
    118, 119
Government information programs, 123-125
Government regulation, 12
Governmental Affairs Committee, Senate, 35
Grace Commission, 55
*Gulf South Insulation v. Consumer Product
    Safety Commission,* 101

Hazardous and Solid Waste Amendments
    (HSWA), 14, 23, 158-160, 166
    Congressional committees and subcommit-
        tees holding hearings on, 168
Hazardous wastes, 155-156
    acquiring knowledge on, 165-170
    compensating victims of, 161-162
    coordinating use of technology in dealing
        with, 170-174
    defined, 164-165
    EPA's attempt to redefine, 160
    laws affecting, 156-160
    legal aspects of, 156-164
    obtaining and using knowledge regarding,
        164-170
    and politics regarding policy making, 174-
        179
    treatment of, 167
Health and Human Services Department, 63,
    64, 66, 80
Housing and Urban Development Depart-
    ment, 64
Human subjects, experimentation on, 134,
    138

Impoundments of expenditures, 47
Incremental policy model, 9-10
Independent regulatory commissions, 68-69
*Industrial Union Department, AFL-CIO v.
    American Petroleum Institute,* 97, 101, 108-
    109
Information sources for public, 122-123
    government information programs, 123-125
    mass media, 123
Institute of Electrical and Electronics Engi-
    neers, 29

Interagency coordination, 87-88
    approaches to, 88-89
    through a Department of Science, 89-90
Interagency Regulatory Liaison Group, 89
Interdepartmental Committee on Science Research and Development, 54
Interior Committee, House, 34
Interior Department, 64-65
International Harvester Co. v. Ruckelshaus, 107
International relations, presidency and, 45
International Ultraviolet Explorer, 182-183
Investigations, as Congressional policy tool, 24-25

Johnson administration, blacklisting of researchers by, 150
Joint Committee on Atomic Energy (JCAE), 35
Judges, science and technology policy and expertise of, 96
Judicial appointments, 110
Judicial expertise, 102-103
Judicial review, 100-101
Justice Department, 65

Knowledge constraints, on policy process, 15, 17

Labor Department, 65
Laboratory animals, experimentation on, 137
Landsat D remote sensing satellite, 193
Law
    changing scientific and technological bases for law, 103-104
    and scientists, 136-141
    sources of, 98-100
    technology and, 162-164
Legal constraints
    on bureaucracy, 75-79
    on hazardous waste policy, 160-162
    on policy process, 14, 17-19
    on scientists, 136-138, 141
Legal Environmental Assistance Foundation and Natural Resources Defense Council v. Hodel, 172
Legal formalism, 103
Legal protections of scientists, 139
    and freedom of inquiry, 139-140
    patents, 140
    and "whistle blowers" within field, 140-141
Legal realism, 103
Legislation, as Congressional policy tool, 23-24
Legislation clearance, 55
Legislative veto, 27
L-5 Society, 126
Lobbying efforts, 37-38
    by professional associations, 146

Logical positivism, 103

Magnetic Fusion Energy Engineering Act, 25
Man: A Course of Study, 25-26, 40
Marshall Space Flight Center, 200
Mass media, as provider of information to public, 123, 131*n*
Mohole project, 56
Moral issues, 79, 97

National Academy of Engineering, 74
National Academy of Sciences (NAS), 74
National Advisory Committee on Aeronautics, 68
National Aeronautics and Space Act of 1958, 8, 186-187
National Aeronautics and Space Administration (NASA), 13, 15, 16, 50
    failure to release information to Congress by, 24-25
    offices of, 200
    overview of, 68
    scientists and, 204-205
    Space Telescope project and, 183-184, 186-195
    Viking Fund and, 126
National Aeronautics and Space Council, 24
National Bureau of Standards (NBS), 69
National Defense Research Committee (NDRC), 66
National Environmental Policy Act (NEPA) of 1970, 77, 97, 110, 119
National Highway Traffic Safety Administration, 76
National Institutes of Health (NIH), 46, 47, 75, 81
    peer review process of, 83
    regulatory guidelines for research supported by, 133-134
National Medal of Science awards, 57
National Oceanic and Atmospheric Administration, 97
National Research Act of 1974, 137
National Research Council, 74
    study on marijuana use by, 149
National Research Fund, 70
National Science and Technology Policy, Organization, and Priorities Act, 52
National Science Board, 26, 70
National Science Foundation (NSF), 7, 13
    attempt to improve public knowledge of issues by, 124
    creation of, 22, 46, 70
    divisions and budget of, 72, 73
    fund allocation within, 82-83
    overview of, 70, 72-73
    statutory mandates and, 76
National security interests, conflict between speech and, 45

National security issues, presidency and, 44-45
National security limitations, restrictions on scientific activity and, 138
National Technical Information Service, 123
National Technology Foundation (NTF), 7
National Toxicology Program, 89
National Wildlife Foundation, 126
Natural Resources Defense Council (NRDC), 126
New Technology Opportunities (NTO) program, 51
Nixon administration
    attempts to politicize institutions of science and technology policy by, 57
    blacklisting of researchers by, 150
    solid waste programs and, 157
Nomination process, as Congressional policy tool, 26
Nuclear energy policy, 34-35
Nuclear fission, 4
Nuclear fusion policy, 4-6
Nuclear power, public policies on, 87
Nuclear Regulatory Commission (NRC), 13, 66, 69, 87
Nuclear Test Ban Treaty of 1963, 32

Oak Ridge National Laboratory, 24, 76
Objective rationality, 13
Occupational Safety and Health Act, 14, 23
Occupational Safety and Health Administration (OSHA), 76
    advisory committees of, 80, 81
    use of formaldehyde and, 88
    and worker exposure to benzene, 96-97, 101, 108
Office of Management and Budget (OMB), 47, 55-57
    and hazardous waste policy, 178
Office of Science and Technology (OST), 50-52
Office of Science and Technology Policy (OSTP), 52-54, 85
Office of Scientific Research and Development (OSRD), 66
Office of Technology Assessment (OTA), 30-31
Orbiting Astronomical Observatory (OAO), 182, 183, 194-195
Orbiting Solar Observatory, 182
Over-regulation, 91

Pain evaluation, 81
Participation, 116-117
Patents, 140
Patents and Trademarks Act of 1980, 140
Peer review, 82-83
Performance standards, 161
Physicists, as politically active scientists, 150
Planetary Society, 126

Policy for science, 4, 7, 39
Policy process, 8-9. *See also* Science and technology policy process
    models of, 9-10
    scientific approach and politics of, 10-11
    stages of, 9
Political constraints, on policy process, 16-17, 19
Political ideology of scientists, 149-151
Political pressures, 36-40
Political values, role of, in policy process, 11
Politics
    bureaucratic science and technology policy and, 90-92
    in courts, 110-111
    presidential science and technology policy and, 57-59
    and scientists, 143-144, 148-152
"Pork-barrel" politics, 37-38
Presidency. *See also* Executive branch
    Congressional appropriations and power of, 47
    Executive Orders used by, to control policy, 48
    impact on science and technology policy of, 46
    international relatives and, 45
    national security issues and, 44-45
    shaping science and technology policy by, 43-44, 59
    sources of science and technology knowledge to, 48-54
    statutory constraints on, 47-48
    veto power of, 45-46
President, politics and science and technology policy of, 57-59
Presidential veto, 45-46
President's Science Advisory Committee (PSAC), 49-50
Procedural constraints, 77-79
Procedural review, 100, 101
Public citizens
    coordination of, 125-129
    participation in science and technology policy by, 115-116
    perceptions of risks and benefits of science and technology by, 128
    politics and, 127-129
Public controversy, scientific disputes and, 114-115
Public knowledge, 120-122
    government information programs and, 123-125
    mass media and, 123
    of science by general public, 134
Public participation, 114-115
    and attentiveness to issues, 116
    coordination of, 125-129
    defined, 117

effects of incoordination on, 126-127
in hazardous waste issue, 176-177
law and, 117-120
need for increase in, 212
structure of, 115-116
types of controversies motivating, 116
virtues and vices of, 129-130
Public policy
defined, 4
formation, 10, 12
scientific facts and political values in, 215
Publicity, as Congressional policy tool, 24-25
Pure Food and Drug Act, 21

Rational model, 9
Reagan administration
attempt to eliminate EVIST by, 124
boundary-setting between R&D roles of
public and private sectors, 53
citizen participation programs and, 119
increase in research dollars devoted to
DOD during, 66, 67
science and technology policy of, 53, 58
Recombinant DNA Advisory Committee
(RAC), 95
Recombinant DNA research, 95, 114, 133-
134, 139
Regulatory commissions, 68-69
Research and Development (R&D), 2
centers receiving federal funds for, 69-71
federal offices conducting, 63-68
national expenditures as percentage of
GNP, 3
Research and development expenditures
for classified programs, 44
federal, 25
in universities and colleges, 151
Research and development funding, 12, 39
distribution of federal, 80
resulting from peer review system, 82
steps preceding expenditure of, 79
Research Applied to National Needs, 72
Reserve Mining Co. v. Environmental Protec-
tion Agency, 101
Resource Conservation and Recovery Act
(RCRA), 109, 157-158, 163, 176
Right-to-know laws, 119
Risk analysis, 85-86
meaning of, 83-84
Risk assessment, 42n, 84-85
Risk Assessment Research and Development
Act, 85
Risk management, 84-85
Risk-benefit analysis, 42n

Saccharin, 16, 21-22, 46, 79, 127
Safe Drinking Water Act, 109
Safety regulations, 76
Science

basic vs. applied, 7
defined, 6-7
importance of, 2
role of, in politics and policy, 3-4
Science advisers
as part of policy process, 144, 154n
to President, 49-54
Science Advisory Board (SAB), 54, 80-81,
172
Science and technology
educating the public about, 122-125
public perceptions of risks and benefits of,
128
Science and Technology: Promises and Dangers, 55
Science and Technology Committee, House,
24, 33
space project and, 201
subcommittees of, 34
Science and Technology Department, 89-90
Science and technology policy. See also Science policy; Technology policy
advisory committees and, 80-82
Congressional examination of, 24
coordination of bureaucratic, 87-90
defined, 10-11
executive agencies dealing with, 68, 78-79
Executive Branch and knowledge regarding, 48-54
factors that distinguish from other policy
issues, 12-13
federal laboratories and, 69-70
federal offices affecting, 63-68
federally funded research and development
centers and, 69-71
fragmentation of, 213-214
improving coordination of, 211
independent regulatory commissions and,
68-69
politics and bureaucratic, 90-93
presidential veto power and, 46-47
role of peer review in, 82-83
support of, 12
Science and technology policy process
Congress in, 21-42
constraints on, 13-14
coordination, 15-17
knowledge, 15, 17
law, 14, 17
politics, 16-17
courts and legal system in, 95-112
federal bureaucracy in, 61-93
legal constraints on, 75-79
President in, 43-59
problems regarding, 209-210
the public in, 113-130
scientists in, 133-153
Science clerks within court system, 105
Science court, 106

Science education in public schools, 122
Science for Citizens, 124
Science in policy, 4, 7
Science Operations Ground System (SOGS), 199
Science policy. *See also* Science and technology policy; Technology policy
  vs. technology policy, 6, 10-11
  tensions associated with, 10
Science Policy Research Division (SPRD), 30
Science-oriented administration, 92
Scientific advances, consequence of, 2-3
Scientific associations, 145-146
Scientific disputes, public controversy, 114-115
Scientific inquiry, freedom of, 139-140
Scientific knowledge, 6
  constraints of scientists regarding, 141-143
  constraints on bureaucratic use of, 87
  the public and, 120-125
Scientific process, 6
Scientific uncertainty, judicial system and, 103
Scientist-judges, 106
Scientists
  accountability of, 148-149, 212-213
  changes in legal constraints on, 141
  conflicts among, 146-148
  coordination of, in policy process, 144-148
  ideology of, 149-152
  legal limitations on, 136-138
  legal protections of, 139-141
  as part of policy process, 134-136
  politics and, 148-152
Scientists and Engineers for Johnson, 150
Self-regulatory guidelines of scientists, 136-137
Senior Interagency Group on Space, 89
Sierra Club, 126
Skylab mission, 182-183
Society-oriented administration, 92
Software Engineering Institute, 38
Solar Maximum Mission, 194
Solar Optical Telescope, 194
Solid Waste Act of 1970, 157
Solid Waste Disposal Act of 1965, 156
Space exploration policy, public groups interested in, 126
Space Policy Working Group, 146
Space science, 183
Space Telescope design, 184-186
Space Telescope project, 181-182
  background of, 182-184
  constraints of knowledge, technology, and funding on, 188-195
  coordination of, 195-202
  design of, 184-186
  legal constraints on, 186-188
  politics and, 202-205

schedule and budgetary limits on, 191-195
  scientific limits on, 189-190
  technical limitations on, 190-191
Space Telescope Science Institute (STSI), 182, 197, 198-200
Spectrometry, 206n
State Department, 65
Statutory law, 26-27, 99
Strategic Defense Initiative (SDI), 31, 43, 45, 145, 146
Subsidies, 12
Substantive constraints, 76-77
Substantive judicial review, 101
Superconducting Supercollider (SSC), 38
Superfund, 162, 163
Supersonic transport aircraft (SST), 51-52
Supreme Court, 99
  on advisory committees, 80
  on patents, 140
  procedural review by, 100
  substantive judicial review by, 101
Swine flu innoculation program, 77
Symposium on Lunar Bases, 204-205
Synthetic Fuels Corporation (Synfuels), 58, 66

Task Force on Science Policy, 24
Technological advances, consequences of, 2-3
Technology
  defined, 7-8
  importance of, 2
  law and, 162-164
  role of, in politics and policy, 3-4
Technology assessment, 30
Technology Assessment Board (TAB), 30, 31
Technology policy. *See also* Science and technology policy
  vs. science policy, 6, 10-11
  tensions associated with, 10
Toxic Substances Control Act (TSCA) of 1976, 14, 84
Trans-legal questions, 106
Transportation Department, 65
Trans-scientific questions, 79-80, 106
Treasury Department, 63, 65
Treaty on Principles Governing the Activities of States in the Exploration and Use of Outer Space, Including the Moon and Other Celestial Bodies, 187
Tuskegee study, 137

Union of Concerned Scientists (UCS), 146

Vermont Yankee Nuclear Power Corp. v. Natural Resources Defense Council, 99, 109
Veterans Administration (VA), 68
Viking Fund, 126

Water policies, 104-105
Water pollution. *See* Hazardous wastes
Water Quality Act of 1966, 165